JANUA LINGUARUM

STUDIA MEMORIAE
NICOLAI VAN WIJK DEDICATA

edenda curat

C. H. VAN SCHOONEVELD

Indiana University

Series Minor, 200

CONVERSATION ANALYSIS
The Sociology of Talk

by

DONALD E. ALLEN
Oklahoma State University

and

REBECCA F. GUY
Memphis State University

MOUTON

THE HAGUE · PARIS

ISBN 90 279 3002 3
© Copyright 1974 in The Netherlands
Mouton & Co. N.V., Publishers, The Hague

First printing 1974
Second printing 1978

LIBRARY OF CONGRESS CATALOG CARD NUMBER: 74-84243

Printed in Belgium by NICI, Ghent

PREFACE

The social sciences, and especially sociology, have long needed relevant ratio measures to analyze basic social processes. At present sociologists rely extensively on data derived from questionnaires and interviews which are founded on nominal categories. The analysis of social relations in contemporary research relies more on the cogency of argument than on well-accepted and undoubted measurements. In this book we develop and apply an extended array of mensural, graphic, and analytical techniques to direct dyadic conversation. It is our purpose to describe in detail the conversational relation by isolating and measuring its primary components.

The conversational process makes an excellent vehicle for the development of precise measures. It is rich in a variety of small behavioral elements which are readily recognized and recorded. These elements combine and recombine in certain well-ordered rhythms of action and expression. In the live two-person confrontation there results a more or less integrated web of communication which is the foundation of all social relations. Our task is to disassemble this web and to determine some of the regularities which give it structure.

We must begin with a parsimonious but sufficient description of the conversational bond. This demands recognition of the source skills of verbal articulation and audition plus the minimal requirements of the social relation in which two persons can oscillate as emitter and receiver. Such a discussion could extend indefinitely into socially relevant factors, but we have tried to confine ourselves to a few of the most essential considerations which immediately affect ongoing conversation.

We identify two distinct kinds of components in face-to-face conversation, of which the verbal output is primary, and somatic behavior is secondary. We have selected intersyllabic loudness variation as a phonic property to analyze as the communication conditions vary, and have identified conditions associated with variable shifts in loudness and variation in gaps between vocal elements. We also identify vocabulary characteristics related to temporal parts of conversational contacts and to the different sex structures of the dyad. A separate analysis is applied to variation in the stream of verbal components to identify characteristic cycles of assertions, agreements, fragmentation, interjection, and laughter. Another analysis is applied to the sequence of facial acts generated in both partners, including ocular contact, facial contortion and smiling, head nodding and shaking, and head tossing.

From the close examination of the components of the conversational relation we are in a strategic position to develop a trial theory of conversational bonding. We believe that the strength of the bond varies in a fairly complex way in relation to gap, fragmentation, agreement, assertion volume, facial contortion, smiling, and head movement. We support our contentions as well as we can from data developed in the analysis of the components.

The problem of measurement is anchored in a complex phenomenon which contains thousands of discrete elements within a short time span. Even in this initial exploration, we have identified some twenty types of basic elements in the action matrix of two-person conversation. The analysis of such a mass of articulate elements calls for both statistical and accretive measures, and for the application of high capacity recording and processing. In developing these measures we have consistently attempted to apply empirical criteria to the internal properties of the phenomena based on time, intensity, and frequency. We have used external properties — those relating to the emitter of conversation rather than conversation itself — only as a test vehicle for the internal measures. We have been particularly concerned to identify dynamic processes which fluctuate in real time and which can be described exponentially as a uniform curve of increase or decrease. Consistent measures of the conversation process, if meaningful, would provide a most valuable tool for researchers and clinicians who work with or through the verbal bond.

The most challenging part of this investigation has been to develop a satisfactory theory of the bonding process inherent in the conversational encounter. What really goes on during actual conversation is the accumulation and creation of a communicative union between the partners. The quality of this union varies both in general and in specific ways. We believe that fluctuation of the component elements in the conversational emission stream are indicative of the quality of the contact. We recognize that the momentary quality of bonding has a direct bearing on more remote outcomes, but feel that it is necessary to confine the theoretical treatment to the process of bonding itself. The bonding concept refers to the bipolar action system which unites two social actors in a process of sharing and elaborating meaningful symbol streams. Bonding is both dependent on and productive of consensus which is basic to the development of a community of understanding. It is important to identify and evaluate those elements which contribute positively or negatively to this fundamental social process. This theory of bonding is necessarily tentative, and hopefully will lead to more adequate treatment in the future.

It is difficult to fix the limits of application of information about the conversational bond. On the professional level, the process of oral communication is an important concern to the sociologist, psychologist, speech therapist, economist, political scientist, lawyer, psychiatrist, and teacher. In a general way the efficiency of oral communication is of interest to everyone who is active in contact with others in his daily life. Both success and failure in social relations is often closely linked with the ability to communicate verbally in face-to-face relationships. Meaningful analysis of the varying components of the conversational stream must depend on three basic tools: the video-audio (TV) recorder, the analog-digital converter, and the computer. All of the professionals mentioned above can get access to this equipment. Specimens of conversation can be analyzed to evaluate conversational efficiency, extent of communication, equilibrium between partners, the degree of personal involvement in the relationship, the amount of energy invested, and the degree of affect and acceptance between the partners. Such analysis can be helpful in research, diagnostic, and applied fields.

We hope to have accomplished two results with this book. The first is a somewhat more exact description of the conversational relation than has been available in the past. We regard this as a small beginning on a challenging process which has great significance for analyzing more extended kinds of social relations. The second aim was to illustrate a series of measures and descriptive techniques which we hope will be of further use in research in the social sciences.

TABLE OF CONTENTS

1

THE PROCESS OF CONVERSATION

THE SOCIAL CHARACTER OF CONVERSATION

Conversation is the primary basis of direct social relations between persons. As a process occurring in real time, conversation constitutes a reciprocal and rhythmic interchange of verbal emissions. It is a sharing process which develops a common social experience. This shared experience necessarily implies an equivalence of viewpoint and a tendency toward consensus. This consensus is not necessarily to be seen as agreement but as an increased understanding. Through a continuing sequence of verbal action, identical word strings are generated by the emitter and replicated more or less perfectly in the receiver's mind. Over time, the exchanges build up a mental union which we call the conversational bond.

As a bond the conversational relation manifests mental, physical, and social properties. For the establishment of a mental bond, there must be a shared language and a vocabulary in common. In conjunction with the shared vocabulary there must be mutually coherent associations among the words and a shared focus of interest. It should also be recognized that the shared vocabulary expands through mutual transfer and new modifications of usage. This means that the mental union leads to an enrichment of language skills and the development of new perceptions. The mental union may be more or less perfect, but insofar as it is genuinely achieved, a common consciousness is developed in which each participant comes to see the viewpoint of the other and to take in fully what the other is saying. This is a primary ingredient of a shared consciousness in the conversational bond. The mental bond is not a passive end-state. It is developed through action, and it consists of an integrated oscillation of verbal action which over time tends to converge toward a consensus of meaning. The physical bond in the conversational relation consists in the mutual spatial oriental of the participants and the restrictions of distance which the conversational union imposes upon them. For optimum interaction in face-to-face conversation the participants need to be oriented in view and at a conventional distance (Hall 1959: 187). Communicators tend to group themselves into a mutually facing group at a distance which permits hearing over ambient noise. For the duration of the verbal contact the participants are confined to relatively fixed positions and to a limited range of movements. The physical anchorage in the conversational posture may be supplemented by transient bodily contact through touching, tapping, striking, or stroking with the extremities as a communicative gesture.

The conversational relation is regarded as a social bond because it involves two or more persons in a predefined relation. The relation is essentially a bridging phenomenon which for short segments of time ties pairs and larger social systems into a genuine social contact. The contact is achieved and maintained through conventional rules of interaction. It requires respect, social recognition, and mutually permissive and cooperative sharing of the available time. It is supportive of temporally extended social relations such as friendship, colleagueship, and familial institutionalized relations. The conversational unit establishes recognized boundaries of inclusion and exclusion while the contact is operating. Intrusions and interruptions are resisted or repelled and persons outside the conversing group tend to respect these restrictions. Participants are similarly constrained by the boundaries to remain within the group during the action and their attention and social resources are preempted by the communicative needs of the group. When the bond of active conversational interaction is dissolved it becomes a part of the social history of the individual actors. They retain elements of the informational exchange, new associations between the verbal elements, and a somewhat modified relationship to each other. In other words, the interpersonal contact has contributed to the more general social relation between the participants and to their involvement in other social groupings. And in the process, their behavioral and verbal repertoires have been somewhat expanded. Sociologists have long recognized the fundamental importance of verbal and gesticulatory interaction in social process (Mead 1934; Chapple 1939; Goffman 1961; 1963; 1967; Blumer 1969; Bales 1950; 1970). However, there has been insufficient investigation of the components and basic mechanics of the conversational union (Scott and Lyman 1968). One factor has been the lack of agreement on any fundamental theoretical model which is based on the actual give-and-take or agreement regarding what operational models might be applicable. Finally there has been a widespread tendency to theorize in the broadest and most general terms at the level of a universal culture with limited reference to the empirical world (Hall 1959: 217; Cooley 1909: part 28; 1966: chapter 17).

THE SOCIAL FUNCTIONS OF SPEECH

As noted by Vygotsky, speech is essentially and primarily social. Vygotsky takes issue with Piaget's contention that speech becomes basically social only in later childhood at seven to eight years of age (Vygotsky 1962: 19). While recognizing the value of Piaget's concept of the developmental stages of language use in the child, we agree with Vygotsky that the social base of vocal relations between adult and child is established in the first interchanges in the parent-child dyad. From his earliest days the neonate uses his cry to start an interaction with his mother. The mother, in responding to the cry returns vocal reactions, usually in conventional language. The neonate also emits sounds which indicate contentment to the mother. The baby's cry is punishing not only to the mother, but also to everyone within hearing, so that a social pressure, built up through a variety of indirect paths, impels mother to respond to the message (tend to the baby) and stop the crying. It also has the effect of firmly establishing the baby as an active member of the familial social system.

The social action process initiated so intensively through the vocal interchange in the infantile period continues to bring about the progressive integration of individuals into fixed and repetitive social action systems. This takes place in large part in the elaboration and extension of verbal exchange capability. The vocabulary becomes differentiated and specialized. The individual, through repeated contacts and some integrating experience between contacts, develops a flexibility of thought and action which permits him to engage in precise verbal interchange with a wide variety of others. By virtue of his ability to enter into precise verbal interaction with different kinds of others, the individual is able to enter as a regular participant into socially and functionally distinguished groups. He can interact both as an undifferentiated member and as an actor with a defined position and some set of specified tasks. His defined position in the interaction system also requires restrictions and specifications regarding the interaction patterns between persons in the group. This provides the primary requirements for the social role. The organization of the social role specifies the make-up, technology, values, norms, and rules of relationship among the members. The discrete roles are defined in explicit language in terms of duties, tasks, and functions in the system. The role and system specifications require social conformity (Merton 1959: 178; Coser 1961: 28). All of the elements in the operating social system and the roles which it incorporates are verbally defined with specialized vocabularies. They are verbally transmitted and generated and are operated in large part in a directed network of vocal interaction.

Language and verbal definition are central in the organization of the elements of an ongoing social system (Morris 1955: 36). Specific verbal formulations are used to define system components, related action sets, sequences of action, criteria of evaluation, and goal orientation. These definitions are temporarily fixed for some particular cycle of action (Pike 1967: 32). However, they must be redefined as membership or components of relations within the system change. Hence verbal formulations provide a basis for indefinitely extended adaptation of members and operational components in the action system. A part of the action consists of the continuing reaffirmation of the definitions of the system among the members.

Language is used to establish functional and operational boundaries of social systems of all sizes from the fixed family group to the large national community. The boundary-related language includes particular identification of name, unique properties, specific structure, and it specifies the boundary itself. The boundary essentially marks the limits of community membership. The boundary is also marked by the extent of the specialized language and vocabulary of the community. Extended verbal interaction within the community tends to maintain the community as an integrated system of social action.

NEURAL FUNCTIONS

Language interchange is a dynamic process of action made up of temporal strings of events. The events are modified vocal pulses recognizable as syllables which combine into words and sentences. The transactional element in conversation is the word which is somehow vocally emitted by the speaker. We therefore need to consider the process of word acquisition and word association in the individual. This will involve a limited discussion of neural processes primarily concerned with speech.

The basic active element in the nervous system is the neuron. The unit of action in the neuron is the transmission of an electrical pulse. The electrical pulse, an input on a short dendrite fiber on one side of the cell nucleus, is transported through the cell body and a longer output fiber called an axon. The axon terminates at the dendrite of another neuron or in a muscle cell which it activates. The electrical pulse has a duration of .0005 seconds or 0.5 milliseconds. The neuron recovers its original negative electrical charge of −70 milli volts in about .0005 seconds (Deutsch 1967: 39). This recovery period establishes the upper limit of discharge rate at about 1000 pulses per second. This rate is required in auditory nerve cells, although the typical working rate of neuron discharge in mammalian fibers ranges from 5 to 100 pulses per second (Hodgkin 1964: 19). The action of the enzyme acetylcholine leads to immediate recovery in the dendrite which permits the nerve to respond to the next stimulus in less than a millisecond (Nachmansohn 1960: 230). The rapid succession of neural pulses should be thought of as a stimulatory current, and not as an isolated pulse. The pulse propogates along the neural fiber at the rate of 100 meters per second (Hodgkin 1964: 18). Neural associations in networks are therefore facilitated by grouping them closely together.

Neural processes are carried out in the cortex of the brain by three specialized forms of neurons. Pyramidal neurons have a pyramid-shaped nucleus, relatively short local dendrites for input, and a relatively long axon which carries impulses to other areas of the cortex or to more remote areas of the body. Axons have multiple endings, permitting them to stimulate a number of cells simultaneously. Stellate cells, named for their star-like shape, have a much larger number of dendritic input fibers and a relatively short axon which carries impulses to nearby areas within the outer stratum (the gray matter stratum) of the cortex. Granular neurons, so termed because of their grainy appearance in pictures of cortical cross sections, have short, dense branchings of dendritic fibers and axonic branchings of similar length. The granular neurons serve to diffuse impulses in the immediate area (Hausman 1961: 120).

A functional distinction must be made between exciter neurons and inhibiter neurons (Deutsch 1967: 39). The exciter neuron transmits a series of pulses to other neurons and excites them to a similar sequence of pulses. The inhibiter neuron blocks excitation of the exciter neurons to which it is connected, and hence excludes them from the network while it is sending its series of pulses. The inhibiter function is carried out by reducing the electrical charge in an excitor neuron from −70 millivolts to −90 millivolts. This negative shift in voltage neutralizes the effects of the normal exciter impulses received from other neurons. The unit of action in the neural system consists of an operating network of morphologically differentiated excitor and inhibitor cells. It is the pulsating neural network which constitutes the pattern of action. However, the network pattern is apparently not dependent on a specific collection of cells (Penfield and Roberts 1966: 246). This means that isolated sets of cells are not exclusively reserved for specific patterns of neural action which are involved in repeatable elements of memory or behavior (Penfield and Roberts 1966: 226). The patterns are not stored in fixed neural nets. Rather, the pattern is regenerated in nearly identical form through a process of complex and extensive associations. It appears that the patterns of neural action can readily be regenerated through a wide variety of alternative associative pathways which could connect innumerable combinations of behavioral and verbal association. It is this feature which permits immediate access as opposed to serial access in selecting among alternatives where creating organized behavior or neural action in the form of thought. The operating neural network includes thousands of neurons working in concert, but such basic neural nets do not operate in isolation even in most simple coordinated behavior. Rather an extensive collection of more elementary neural networks is generated through neural association. In fact the entire central nervous system with its ten billion neurons (Penfield and Roberts 1966: 6) is essentially a high capacity associative system of neural action.

Surgical evidence indicates that there is some general localization of speech function in the cerebral cortex. Such sensory functions as vision, audition, and associated motor functions show indications of localization in both hemispheres of the cerebrum. Moreover, each eye and each ear has extensive connections through neural bundles to both hemispheres. The dual connection from both cerebral hemispheres is also found in the motor centers which can be stimulated along the lower part of the anterior side of the central fissure or "fissure of Rolando" (Penfield and Roberts

1966: 201). There are three verbal centers which are found only in the dominant hemisphere of the brain and usually in the left hemisphere (Penfield and Roberts 1966: 204). The superior speech area is named for its location just forward of the central fissure on the top of the left hemisphere. The Broca area, named for the physician who identified it as a speech area, is located in the third gyrus (convolution) of the frontal lobe. The most extensive speech area, sometimes called Wernicke's area, occupies most of the left temporal lobe.

MEMORY

There is no universally accepted theory or body of empirical evidence which indicates how the process which we call memory occurs in the neural system. It has been assumed since the time of Locke that the mind functions like a blank tablet on which information is written. The present tendency is to assume distinct levels of memory. Feigenbaum recognizes three duration levels of memory: (1) immediate memory in brief time intervals; (2) working memory which is slightly longer and in which immediate associations are made; and (3) permanent storage in which internal representations are organized and stored for long-term retrieval (Feigenbaum 1970: 467). Bjork recognizes two duration levels of memory in his discussion of temporally spaced-repetition as a factor in the transfer of information from short-term to long-term memory (Bjork 1970: 319). Other authorities also utilize this theoretical model in considering memory capacity and processes of memory search and retrieval (Sperling and Speelman 1970: 190; Shiffrin 1970: 442). Deutsch, in discussing the memory process, hypothesizes that only one syllable is stored in each neuron (Deutsch 1967: 190). These treatments suggest implicitly or explicitly that remembered elements often referred to as memory traces are permanently stored in fixed neural networks in the brain. These assumptions do not agree with surgical evidence which denies the fixed permanent relation of the neural processes in speech to specific neuron nets. According to Penfield, "Any limited previously damaged area of the left cerebral hemisphere may be excised with transient aphasia but without immediate or permanent dysphasia so long as the remaining brain functions normally. All parts of the hemisphere may be removed with only transient effects." (Penfield and Roberts 1966: 181). It should be noted that when cortical stimulation in a particular location produces an identifiable reaction, this need not be taken as evidence that the function is fully localized at this location but only that some part of the neural process passes near the stimulated area.

We return now to the neural process in memory. As Penfield states, no neurally fixed pigeon holes exist for the recording of words in the cortex, because after aphasia due to cortical excision there are never any groups of words to be learned over (Penfield and Roberts 1966: 226). Moreover, it has not been possible through cortical stimulation to elicit the production of any particular word. Available evidence seems to indicate that memory is a neural process rather than a neural condition. An element in memory consists of a highly discriminant pattern established in an extensive neural network which has its being in continuing intranet neural excitation. Any single neural network can function in more elaborate mental processes only through neural linkages to a wide variety of other active neural nets. We must therefore reject the concept of a simple linear function or a Markov-type chain in the temporal sequences of neural activity. It is evident that organized mental activity involves thousands of neural nets acting simultaneously in self-selecting and thereby organized patterns of association.

THE HEARING PROCESS

The neural process of audition starts in the cochlea of the inner ear. The cochlea consists of a double tube ending at the center of a flat spiral. Sound waves enter the inner tube, travel to the center of the spiral, and return via the outer tube. Resonance occurs along the length of the tube proportionate to the pitch of the sounds, and the resonating areas cause the tectorial membrane to vibrate against the projecting hairs of the auditory nerves. This mechanism provides distinct areas of excitation for the auditory tonal range. According to Walsh the cochlear nucleus is a more complicated structure than the retina. He indicates that all afferente of the cochlea make synapsis with at least thirteen distinct subdivisions of the cochlear complex and each fiber ends on a large number of cells (Walsh and Marshall 1957: 247). Both ears have connections with both temporal lobes of the cortex. Allport believes that "pitch is mapped on the cortex in such a way that as we go from one end of the auditory region the cells in the receptive layers represent continually higher pitches" (Allport 1955: 506). Allport suggests that there is a neural scanning mechanism performing a sweep at intervals of one-tenth of a second which permits the identification of tonal intervals. The organization of neural patterns corresponding to sounds permits the development of associated neural nets in which sets of sounds are ordered into syllables and groups of syllables. These neural nets are connected to more remote neural nets which represent other kinds of associations which are selectively tied in to such related processes as reading, writing, listening, thinking, and vocalization (Sapir 1921: 17).

Word acquisition results from an initial presentation of a new word plus some series of repetitions of the word. New words always occur in a situational context which provides associative cues to the word. New words usually occur in conjunction with already known words which provide additional associative cues. As the word is repeated in other contexts, it is both recognized as a somewhat familiar word and it is involved in enriched associations so that it becomes accessible from a wider variety of cues. A prime variable in word learning is word frequency and word recall (Kintsch 1970: 334).

LISTENING

The listening function is a complex activity which the receiver undertakes when the emitter projects a vocalized syllable string. The listening function includes the reproduction of the syllable string in the receiver's mind as a meaningful proposition, according to the verbal resources of the receiver. The listening process can be described in four parts: (1) intake of the temporal sequence of sounds, (2) reactivating a neural network corresponding to sounds previously experienced, (3) linking the sound combinations into integrated sets of words, and (4) relating the resultant message to other mesasges. This series of processes constitutes an ordered hierarchy starting with the first and progressing, as far as the listener is able, to the fourth. The four steps involve a learning adjustment both individually and collectively.

The first element of listening involves sound intake as a temporal series of auditory events. The formation and grouping of sounds, including their tempo, are a part of the experience. There is always an increment of learning, whether these sounds are heard for the first time or for the thousandth time. In the case of sounds heard for the first time, the auditor will have difficulty recalling the event since he has no basis for comparison. For the same reason he would experience uncertainty if he attempted to approximate the sound he has just heard. But he has learned something on first hearing the sound which, on repeated audition, becomes more and more familiar and hence more recognizable to him. In human speech, of course, we are dealing with a system of sounds called phonemes which must first be learned, and thereafter must be recognized by the listener. The phonemes or conventional sounds of the language are grouped into an extensive variety of sets called morphemes which constitute vocalized words and conventional affixes to words.

The second process of matching sound combinations to similar combinations already known through repeated hearing allows the listener to recognize what he has heard as an interpretable syllable string. This second step in listening more or less faithfully reproduces the intake string if all elements are sufficiently well-known. Imperfection in internal reproduction of syllable strings results from vocalizing morphemes indistinctly and through interference with parts of morphemes, which cause the listener to misrepresent and thus to mistake some words in the string.

In other words, when a listener hears a syllable string which has a missing element, he reincorporates what is left in similar familiar words, and thus he incurs a chance of error. The essential point in the second step in listening is that the auditory intake is ordered into recognized syllable strings insofar as it can be reproduced as already known words and groups of words. This permits the listener to hear the syllable string approximately as delivered. An increment of learning is also involved at this step because the listener has another experience of assembling a meaningful syllable string which either reinforces a familiar pattern or somewhat expands the existing variety of statement forms.

The third step in listening requires that the syllable string as received be integrated into a meaningful message. The listener recognizes the relations among the word elements in the syllable string and interprets their apparent meaning. It is at this point that a unit of information is acquired in the form of what was said. If we attempt to retrieve this element of information from the listener, he may approximately repeat the syllable string, or he may reformulate it as a conclusion, a condensation, or a consequence. Since the listener must generalize some fairly definite meaning from some small range of alternative interpretations, he may well hear something other than what is being said to him. The magnitude of the discrepancy varies, but successful listening requires some means of keeping it at a reasonable minimum for most syllable strings. The increment of learning at the level of interpreting messages represents a higher order of magnitude than those at the two preceding steps, where the learning element is regarded as significant only while new verbal elements are being acquired or when a language is being learned. It is at the message level that the listener is commonly motivated to understand and incorporate distinctive units of information. If asked what he has learned during a verbal contact, he is likely to repeat or encapsulate selected messages out of the syllable strings which he has heard. The accumulation of such messages builds up a partly organized body of knowledge which provides additional alternatives for future action to the listener.

The fourth step in listening is to integrate sequences of messages into more generalized propositions which may or may not be vocalized. In the process of developing more generalized propositions, the listener may assign specific symbols to classes of statements presented to him in syllable strings, and then may combine these symbols into propositions to reflect the derived meaning of an extended sequence of syllable strings. In generalizing the relation among sets of messages from discrete syllable strings, the listener organizes a complex set of events into a simple unity which he may generalize or use as a basis for meaningful response (Hayakawa 1963: 73; Roethlisberger 1962: 46).

It must be recognized that the syllable strings which the listener recognizes as organized sentences composed of specific words do not fall on a blank recording surface as they are reproduced in the listener's mind. Rather, they regenerate neural network facsimiles which the listener has previously experienced. Moreover, the listener's vocabulary set is organized into connected series of related words. It is due to the order and relation among groups of words that the listener readily forms associations, since these relations were already established in earlier experience. Words are the tags or initiators of ideas which can be formulated into conventional word sequences. Therefore, the listener can readily branch in any of hundreds of alternative associations from any word or any sentence that he hears. If he branches in directions generally consistent with the intake sequences, he can follow the theme of conversation effectively, and can emit well-integrated statements which sustain the conversational contact when it is appropriate for him to carry on the conversation.

The learning increment at the fourth level may be economically expressed as the conclusion or outcome of a series of statements. As a more final interpretation of what has been said, it affords a basis for making something more than a transitory contribution to a social relationship. It also allows both emitter and receiver to recognize the new element of understanding and the new element in the social relation.

VOCALIZATION

When a complex vocal pattern has been established in the cortex, and certainly in more than one area in the cortex, it can be matched by a variety of external sources at later times. The individual who has retained a vocal stimulus pattern from external sources is now in a position to duplicate the pattern through his own vocal system. He can then match back through his auditory system for comparison with the original pattern of neural discharges. Of course the conversion from audition to oration is an equally complex process as regards neural organization, since the vocalizer must marshal an extensive neural network from cortical speech areas to motor areas where the impulse message system must be generated and established. The expressive system requires synchronized pulse systems to muscles in the chest, pharynx, vocal chords, velum, tongue, cheeks, and lips, coordinating an expired air stream with muscular modifications to approximate the given stimulus pattern. Moreover, the matching pattern, once developed, must also be retained in a neural network which thereafter retains potential for regenerating the same or similar complex of neural impulses to reproduce the vocal event. When this process is complete, we would say that the individual "knows" the word, first, in the sense that he can recognize the phonic pattern from whatever source when he hears it, and, second, in the sense that he can vocally express the word when he wants to.

For speech capacity, the individual must develop the cortical networks for recognizing and reproducing hundreds and, later, thousands of unique phoneme sets representing words based on variable combinations of some forty distinct sounds, if he speaks English. Extended neural networks similar to those which constitute the potential for hearing and expressing words also become established for combinations of words, so that the individual retains both separable word elements and an indefinitely extensible system for combining them. Verbal combinations are thus also remembered both as input and as output, so that specific word strings can be remembered, repeated, and modified. Initially, successful learning both in audition and oration tends to be limited to what has come from external sources, although we would grant that the infant learns from his own unique vocal outputs. Early in the process of speech acquisition, however, the individual finds that he has considerable latitude in combining the verbal elements in his lexicon, and that he can indeed express many verbal sequences which he has not acquired from any external source. In this process we can identify innovative speech, and can associate with it creative or imaginative thought.

FEEDBACK AND INTERACTION

Interaction is used here as a generalized concept referring to a complex exchange of directed behavior distributed through time between two or more persons who serve as generators of action. It is a reciprocal process incorporating a variety of verbal and somatic components which are organized into meaningful action segments transmitted from one actor to the other in an oscillatory pattern. Previous research on this conversational process has tended to concentrate on a single actor in this dual system (Watzlawick, Beavin, and Jackson 1967: 35; Ruesch 1961; Pittenger, Hockett, and Danehy 1960; Laffal 1965).

Any veridical consideration of interaction as a system of action must recognize the functional equality of all participants in the system. This simply asserts that they are full and equal participants apart from the precise pattern of inputs from each actor. We are then in a position to recognize the sequential emergence of each unit of action together with the shifting source of action through time (Murray 1951: 439). A primary property of interaction is the time dimension, particularly in view of the fact that organized verbal interaction is a linear function of time. This imposes a requirement for temporal coordination of emission segments, and close, continuing cooperation among actors for genuine interaction. If temporal coordination fails, verbal interaction breaks down and vanishes.

The concept of feedback is useful for describing an interaction system (Ruesch 1957: 175-80). For simplicity we will consider the two-actor system. We can identify four levels of feedback in a two-actor verbal interaction system. The first level of feedback consists of self-monitoring by the emitter of a series of vocal outputs. The speaker attends to his own output and judges how it will sound in terms of what he wants to say. Each verbal segment prepares a logical path for the next. The second level of feedback consists of direct short cue responses from the receiver which serve to support the emission stream. The emitter incorporates the feedback from the receiver in his monitoring process and thereby further modifies his emissions. The third level of feedback is the reversal of the emission source, in which the new series of verbal outputs becomes a response to the preceding series of outputs from the other emitter (Goldman-Eisler 1968: 1). It is at this point that we can identify a complete circuit of communication. The cycle of communication consisting of two related emission series have now been incorporated into the experience of both actors. As a result of the cumulative effect of a series of cycles of communication, a fourth level of feedback can be identified. Essentially the fourth level of feedback consists of generalized outcomes resulting from the interaction in the form of conclusions, agreements, affects, contracts, and behavioral modification of the relations between the actors. These are regarded as feedback because they are manifested in each actor as a response to the shared series of communicative cycles and as a response to the other actor. The fourth level of feedback results in behavioral and conceptual reorientations of each actor toward the other (Keltner 1970: 29). This feedback may be more or less immediate.

DYADIC INTERACTION

The dyadic relation involved in vocal interaction is a two-person system of action extending over some specific period of real time. The conversational dyad begins when two persons concentrate attention and behavior on their mutual verbal interchange and terminates when the focus of action of either participant is transferred to something outside the system of immediate verbal intercourse (Goffman 1967: 34). Termination of the dyadic contact can occur through mutual agreement of the participants that the communicative goal has been reached, through the unilateral action of one actor, or through the intrusion of an external event (Becker and Useem 1942: 13; Goffman 1963: 88). The conversational dyad as treated here is a social system of continuing action the duration of which is typically measured in minutes. The communicative goals of many dyadic contacts can be achieved within a fraction of a minute, and more complex conversations can readily be completed in perhaps thirty minutes. The member of a social system in the course of a day generates multiple dyadic and group conversational contacts. As defined herein, he typically does have repeated dyadic contacts with the same individual. These contacts, both repetitive and unique, make primary cumulative contributions to the operation of the social system (Ruesch 1957: 189).

Sustaining the dyadic contact imposes two requirements. First, an action boundary must be established and maintained which excludes intrusion on the interaction chain. Goffman calls this engrossment (1961: 43). Second, at any point in time, there must be a joint concentration in a common area of interst and a continuing generation of successive cycles of verbal interchange. Conversation in the dyad manifests full engagement and follows the exclusion principle. Participants during the contact resist distractions from whatever source. Outsiders respect the boundary and refrain from interfering with the union. For both participants, the rhythmic sequence of communicative cycles has a rewarding effect which Berne has compared to stroking (1964: 15). As cumulative elements of information, verbal exchange is satisfying and rewarding to both actors because it tends to reduce dissonance, give social support, and provide further information for future action.

The core of the conversational dyad consists of the mutual

transfer of information between partners. The prime carrier of the information is the elaborated and highly definitive verbal emission stream. The great communicative power of the verbal stream lies in its unlimited flexibility. The first element in verbal flexibility is a wide choice of words available to each partner for expressing his messages to the other. A second element is the wide variety of alternatives for ordering words in communicative statements. Finally, each participant has great freedom in redefining, repeating, modifying, and referencing his own and his partner's preceding statements. This process establishes new chains of association for each participant. This process of verbal exchange is a creative flux in which the two partners can generate and adjust their verbal interchange up to the point where some level of understanding has been reached. Understanding here does not mean agreement but rather a modified orientation toward the communicative content. A secondary carrier which clearly could reinforce or modify the verbal communication stream consists of somatic behaviors and postures. Somatic behavior having some communication significance includes capital behavior such as ocular contact and avoidance, smiling and facial contortion, nodding and shaking the head, and tossing the head (Birdwhistell 1952; Bales 1950; Matarazzo, Wiens, and Saslow 1965). General body movements occurring are of course subject to some interpretation by the partner, but they are basically a repositioning of the body to relieve the tensions resulting from physical confinement of prolonged conversational contact. These body movements are peripheral. They can readily be distracting and are subject to multiple interpretations. Indeed, one of the challenges for the listener in successful verbal communication is to overcome the distracting influence of body movements and behavior and other mannerisms of the emitter. The speaker does restrain body movements within well-defined conventional limits and may impair the success of his communication if he exceeds the limits. Hands do have some specifically communicative functions including pointing, displaying affection or hostility, emphasis, and signaling that the verbal output is not finished by means of a grouping gesture. During conversation the hands are also used for self-manipulations, such as holding the head, patting hair, adjusting clothing, and clasping the hands.

The communicative efficiency of the dyad varies in terms of the rate of information transfer per unit of time. The unit of information transfer is an organized syllable string which can be interpreted by the receiver. The rate of output in organized verbal statements fluctuates within fairly definite limits. Acceleration or deceleration beyond these limits impairs the information transfer process, probably because the emission rate departs too far from the habitual verbalization rate of the receiver. The optimum density of message sending is associated with an ideal tempo for each receiver successfully matched through tempo adjustments by the emitter.

The conversational bond is generated initially by sharing nearly identical verbal sequences in the minds of both partners in the talk-listen process. The bond is elaborated and extended through the progressive addition of associative verbal elements and by verbalized mental associations developed in the mind of each partner during the process of exchange. The bond is developed by supporting cues from both the listener and emitter which creates a trend toward a common understanding. The relation requires some minimum level of balance between the two actors. A conversational relation in which one actor preempted all of the time in speaking, permitting no organized verbal response within the capacity of the receiver, violates the minimum requirements of balance in the conversational contact. As the two partners approach equality in sharing the available time for verbal emission, the communicative relationship tends to approach maximum efficiency in developing common understanding between the partners.

Every conversational contact is oriented toward some communicative goal which supports its continuity. An immediate objective in the conversational engagement is for the emitter to keep going in an organized stream of verbal emission. A closely related objective is to generate relevant responses from the partner and to maintain a reasonable rate of cycling in the exchange. A final objective is to get the idea across and emerge with consensus and some improved understanding. Both participants will thereby have gained something which they could add to future contacts. Their social and mental resources will thereby have been increased. This implies that every conversational contact constitutes a unique event in the social history of the individual. It also makes its own contribution to the shared relation of the two individuals to each other.

One of the basic properties of the conversational contact is the phenomenon of bridging across the social space between two individuals. By social space we mean essentially the range of shared or similar social experiences between any two actors. Some of the elements which contribute to social distance are differentials of age, education, occupation or social function, social routine, and the orientation of action. One of the vital tasks in the conversational contact is to overcome the combined effect of the conversation differentials. The generalized nature of language and the breadth of social experience and interest are prime factors in overcoming the combined effect of such differentials. Successive and repetitive episodes of bridging between pairs of persons constitutes a process of temporally distributed binary fusion. Among a collection of individuals in a social group this process distributes a series of communicative and social relationships which become more generalized through time and more widely shared in the society. The cascading effect of pair relations provides the basis for more complex and enduring relations which constitute the order and structure of society.

THE PROCESS OF CONVERSATION

Conversation is a continuing and social process which fundamentally involves verbal exchanges between two persons, although more than two persons may participate. It operates through speech, which Whorf defines as the best show which man puts on (Whorf 1956: 249). Conversation links individuals by twos and larger groups in a verbal interchange which ranges potentially over an infinite variety of vocal assertions. At the same time the conversational relation is strictly bound to a conventional system of usage and to an extensive but finite shared vocabulary (Whorf 1956: 221). At the same time it is impossible for people to be together in the waking state and not communicate in some minimal form (Watzawick 1967: 51). In the conversational relation, organized verbal emission requires careful control of verbal and expressive behavior. As Goffman notes, the social relation imposes limits on conversation which, once exceeded, must be restored (Goffman 1963: 173). All participants in conversation must be concerned about the impressions which they make on the others (Goffman 1967: 33). This behavior falls naturally in two parts, including the verbal assertions which are readily controlled, and the varied expressions and impressions which the actor creates which are difficult to control (Goffman 1959: 7). Finally, the maintaining of a conversational relationship requires a cover of selective attention whereby both the speaker and the listener successfully concentrate on their own verbal stream and exclude generalized environmental sounds and sound sequences (Sullivan 1956: 50). Morton (1970: 231) has demonstrated the power of selective attention by simultaneously feeding one of two different recorded messages by the same speaker into each ear of a subject: he found that the subject could attend to either message.

ZIPF PRINCIPLE OF LEAST EFFORT VERSUS SUFFICIENT UNION

Zipf has set forth the principle of least effort to explain the tendency to shorten words and expressions in speech. He also suggests that this enables the speaker to attain the maximum communication for the least cost. This principle, we think, goes beyond the simple economy of effort for the individual. Most real people actively seek out occasions where they can expend their energy in talking to others. The need for economy of effort lies in the problem of establishing a sufficient conversational union. Limitations of a single channel, of time, and of the kinds of unions any two persons can effectively establish, tend to constrain each contributer to use his time segments to the best advantage. The problem is also affected by the partners' definition of a "sufficient union" and how well the partners agree on what constitutes a "sufficient union".

Problems of composition, editing, coordinating, and convincing resolved concurrently and jointly between the two partners places a premium on optimal selection of terms and phrases within the limited time available in intermittent and time segments. It is the complexity and pressure of time during engagement which forces the speaker to make the most of his opportunities. This is an external constraint which tends to reduce or to minimize the size of words, phrases, and sentences. Opposed to this is an internal constraint for adequacy of expression for each emitter. While he has the channel, he wants to express sufficiently (as he judges it) what he is trying to inject into the mind of his partner. Both partners need an agreement on what constitutes an adequate union — how long the conversational episode must be continued, how much and what kinds of elaboration, redundancy, and validation are necessary, and, in short, when the conversing pair are satisfied with their exchange.

The conversational relation is the basic element of organized action which ties individuals together in groups. The tightness of bonding of individuals in groups is a direct function of the range and quality of conversation among the members. This is well illustrated in Marshall's description of the intensive and continuing conversational tie among friends and within families of the Kung tribe (1968: 181). The social ties maintained through conversation serve to organize action, generate consensus, and distribute information through a community. Maintaining the conversational relation requires tolerance, friendliness, acceptance of the partner and his statements, and sociability (Argyle 1967: 98). The ongoing process of conversation in a group consists of a highly active sequence of somewhat disjointed verbal segments. There is a freedom and spontaneity of give and take, for example, in the well-bonded family. Disruptions in the flow of communication and variation from ordered complete sentences were found to be more likely in families manifesting good communication than in similar families with a schizophrenic child which had poor communications (Mischler and Waxler 1968: 164). The conversational relation also incorporates a supportive system of positive and negative sanctions. A preponderance of positive sanctions is essential to the maintenance group (Bales 1950; Thibaut 1959: 12). Both explicit and implicit sanctions emerging within the conversational relation also serve to modify and sustain the social norm of the community.

Verbal communication on the interpersonal level is essential to the maintenance of society and culture. It provides the basis for interstimulation, reciprocal response, and establishment of common meaningful conceptualizations (Hertzler 1965: 26). The inability to recognize this basic function results in cultural and social lag, relative to technological advancement, and with grossly inadequate mastery of face-to-face speech communication processes (Keltner 1970: 12). Social integration and social distintegration alike arise and diffuse in the society through the process of direct verbal conversation. Conversation also incorporates an element of play and enjoyment which provides an element of warmth and vigor in daily human associations (Meerloo 1967: 145).

2

PROBLEMS OF ANALYSIS

The conversational bond is a prime object of research for the social scientist. For the sociologist the conversational bond represents the basic social relation in real life. This is not only the basis of all social relation but is in fact the actual substance of all social relations. To develop proper understanding of social interaction, the sociologist would be particularly well employed to investigate with precision and rigor the broad range of conversational links and active social units which recur so universally and continuously throughout a highly active society. The range of conversational involvements can be identified in four modal types which may predominate and intermix. The first modal type is affective and emotional. It serves to convey and distribute levels of excitement and positive or negative orientations between participants. The second modal type, information sharing, is the core function of communication between two or more persons. Unlike the affective mode which merely sets the tone, the information sharing mode incorporates the indefinite incrementation of knowledge and the continuing elaboration of detailed and specific associations. The third modal type is resolution, focused toward an acknowledged goal which requires some reorganization of viewpoint and some accommodation by each participant to arrive at some level of agreement. Resolution process includes agreement, conflict, debate, discussion, and an integration of the expressed ideas which emerge in the exchange. The fourth modal type is sociable interaction which includes permissiveness, friendliness, consideration, responsiveness, and spontaneity. The sociable contact serves to establish rapport, sustain the relationship between participants and develop a diffuse but persistent bonding affect within the broader social group. Each of these types calls for incisive and penetrative investigation. The socialization of the individual comes about through a continuing series of verbal contacts with a wide spectrum of social others. Luria notes that the process of the child's social intercourse with the adult is a powerful means of systematic organization of mental process (Luria 1961: 144). Through the process of acquiring speech both the child and the adult are able to modify environmental influences through motor and verbal responses (Luria 1961: 20). The relationship constitutes the fundamental process of socialization, the dynamics of which are only vaguely understood. Face-to-face social relations are usually carried out in the process of activating social roles. These episodes of social engagement establish a wide range of kinds of social action. There has been some investigation of the operation of roles in the social encounters (Weinstein, Wiley, and De Vaughn 1966: 210).

The phenomenon of conversational engagement is readily accessible for scientific investigation. It is by nature a broadcasting process which is directly experienced by the participants and anyone else within hearing, and with suitable provision can be reliably recorded for research. A large part of these social engagements occur in public places such as schools, factories, stores, churches, and recreational facilities. More private occasions of conversational engagement involve some problems for data collection, but their problems can be overcome by clinical arrangement, a well-devised laboratory procedure, or by consent within the natural private setting.

It is highly desirable to develop an improved understanding of the mechanisms involved in the conversational relation. According to Shannon the elements included in conversation are (1) a source, (2) a transmitter, (3) a signal, (4) a receiver, and (5) a destination (Shannon and Weaver 1949: 5; Raisbeck 1963: 2). These components work together in a rhythmic process of information exchange. The information transfers in strings of identifiable verbal units in real time. In the succession of steps we can identify the density of information, the temporal efficiency, and the success in accumulation of related elements. Within this process of interchange there is explicit evidence of interactor facilitation and disruption. As a topic of conversation becomes established, it is progressively organized and structured (Weiner and Mehrabian 1968: 11). The sequence pattern between communicative verbal elements in the dialogue has been identified as a four-state Markov model (Jaffe, Feldstein, and Cassotta 1967: 285).

The Markov model seems inappropriate because each succeeding communicative element can hardly be defined as a chance event. The interelement association is likely to be constrained by a logical requirement or by a response requirement. Within the interaction stream our concern is to identify and define regularities, constants, and primary variables. We also wish to subject recorded data to repeated examination and thorough scrutiny of small segments of the interaction process (Lennard and Bernstein 1969: 50).

We have to recognize that research objectives should initially be concentrated on the basic tasks of description and variable identification in the conversation process. Complexes of elements which require thorough description include intensity variation, word usage, verbal characteristics, and those somatic outputs which appear to be veridically related to communication. Real progress in science can be obtained only through replication of a variety of research designs to the point where reasonable doubts are thoroughly resolved. The conversational relationship requires concentrated research from a diversity of techniques and theoretical and technical approaches.

CATEGORIES

The purpose of the category system for the scientific investigator is to order data in some consistent way. A categorical system is selected to fit the analytical tasks for which it is designed. Therefore, any categorical system must have some basis in the theory according to which data is being analyzed. The most primitive class of categories is that which involves the arbitrary assignment of names to classes of phenomena with no fixed logical relationship among the names. This can be illustrated in the field of sociology by Park and Burgess types of interaction (1921). The types of social interaction include competition, cooperation, conflict, accommodation, and assimilation (Sutherland and Woodward 1940: 636). Other sociologists have freely modified this list by expanding, contracting, and redefining the terms in the category set. The first level of refinement in categorizing is the assignment of a set of names bearing a fixed logical or functional relationship among themselves. A prime example of logically related categories is Bales' Revised Category System for Interaction Process Analysis. This is a dichotomous set of six processes with three types involving functional opposition, namely friendliness, dramatization, and agreement, and three types involving directional opposition, namely giving suggestion, giving opinion, and giving information (Bales 1970: 96). Bales uses the first three as a social-emotional component and the second three as a task-performance component which is functionally dependent upon the first. In the first two levels of categorization we have discussed nominal categories which permit the consistent discrimination of data into named classes.

A higher level of categorization which permits a comparison on a quantitative basis is a system of ranked categories constituting an ordinal scale. The comparison is based on a substrate quantity which varies continuously in the same direction. Osgood applies the ordinal scale in the development of the semantic differential in which he provides for an odd number of scale divisions (5 to 11) between two conceptually opposed adjectives such as bad-good, pleasant-unpleasant, or like-dislike.

A categorical system based on an interval scale permits more precise mathematical analysis. The interval scale applies to quantities which may be presumed to increase by amounts which can be measured in equal intervals. This is well illustrated by a process which occurs over time, in which the time point of origin is not identified. A given conversational process can be measured in temporal duration. The minute serves as a unit of measurement and may be treated as if it added an equal increment to the inter-action process and to the total conversational experience of the participant. The zero point of the total conversational experience occurs in the early infancy of the individual but it has not been identified in the analysis of the total conversational experience. When the research framework will permit the definition of a zero point, it is possible to establish a categorical system which can be stated in terms of a ratio scale. The point of initiating conversation between two strangers meeting for the first time identifies the origin for the analysis of the exchange. Frequency counts of analy-tically identical events can be measured by a ratio scale if the frequency counts are relatively high. Ratio scale measure can be ideally applied to continuous variables which range between mathematically definable limits. Examples of continuous variables in the conversational relation include loudness variation, syllable density, physical distance, tone, and pitch.

There have been a wide variety of categorical systems developed by theorists and researchers in the social sciences, which incorpo-rate all these categorical types (Hertzler 1965: 407; Howes 1967: 133; Cherry 1957:226; Ruesch 1957:180). For purposes of analysis, however, some of the more informative applications have arisen through the combination of two dimensions of measure to provide a derived category of measurement. These applications are usually implicit in measures of rates in which time and frequency or time and distance are combined to provide a derived measure such as velocity or slope. These measures are particularly useful in ana-lyzing variation in the internal functioning of an organized system, changes of the system with respect to an external reference point, or relative changes between systems.

THE SELECTION OF VARIABLES

The most critical task of researchers who are interested in the analysis of ongoing verbal interaction is an evaluation of the full range of highly relevant variables. Once the family of relevant variables is identified, there is a basis for selective exploitation. The process of the scientific examination and exhaustion of the relations among variables must be seen as a long term process which would take decades to complete. It seems reasonable at this time to recognize four kinds of variables which provide an initial basis for research in live conversation. These include muscular behavior, intensity variation in vocal contact, vocabulary, and verbal characteristics.

Three kinds of muscular behavior can be defined. The first of these is the muscular coordination concerned with the direct production of speech. Muscular control of speech centers primarily in the operation of the vocal cords imposing selected tones on the pneumatic air stream which produces the basis for vocalization. Muscular control of the lips, jaws, tongue, glottis, and velum are coordinated with variation in tonal production in the vocal cords to produce a limited number of distinct sounds in fixed sequences recognizable as language. This study of language is included under the study of phonology. For the English language, the individual speaker employs some 45 phonemes, and the English language in general has fewer than 100 sounds including variants (Brown 1965: 247-48).

Muscular behavior related to the communicative process and normally accompanied by vocalization includes deliberate movements which have conventional semiotic significance. The clearest examples of this behavior is the nodding and shaking of the head which provide a visual signal of agreement for disagreement. Another kind of bodily behavior is a shrug of the shoulders which signals a lack either of knowledge or of concern. Conventional movements of the hands are used to indicate direction and emphasis of a verbal output. From the viewpoint of the speaker, ocular contact is not primarily a semiotic act. Rather, eye contact serves as a continuing source of information regarding the target of his vocal outputs, and provides a basis for adjusting further communicative behavior. Similarly the act of contorting the face is a reaction which reveals the state of the speaker although it is not a deliberate attempt on his part to signal this internal state. Facial contortion does indicate tension, doubt, anxiety, and discomfort. Functionally, the smile is the opposite of the facial contortion although it also basically reveals the internal state of the speaker. The smile reveals an internal state of gratification, contentment, and happiness. The partner in conversation does observe these revealing behaviors and can incorporate them into his communicative behavior along with other environmental events. Other generalized body movements such as shifting of the torso, movement of limbs, and posturing of the head are not originated for the purpose of conveying messages although they could be interpreted by the observer as indicating restlessness, boredom, or discontent with the communication if it occurs with greater than normal frequency or energy. The communicative function of overly frequent bodily movements is distractive rather than contributory. Their function for the emitter is to counteract tension and discomfort. To date there has been no reliable method of measuring the communicative effect of paralanguage variables (Gottschalk 1969: 15).

The pattern of variation in loudness provides an ideal source for precise measure and analysis. As elements in this pattern of variation are identified, they can be used for more general analysis of the conversational bond. Loudness variation fits the concept of continuous variation over an infinite range of values. It can be readily translated from voltage analog to digital form for computer processing. Voluminous data in this form can be economically analyzed in terms of amplitude, gap or silence, density or syllable rate, and wave character forms in real time (Gottschalk 1969: 15). As loudness varies, one can observe variations in the wave length, area under the curve, number of syllables per emission, and intensity intervals. These variations are suggestive of longer of shorter vocal utterances, of more or less dense vocal utterances — two concepts which are related to the information transfer.

The element of reciprocity refers to the give and take relationship in terms of vocalization upon the part of the two partners. If, for example, one encounters a dyadic contact in which one person does the majority of talking, then certainly reciprocity is considerably reduced. Equal participation on the part of both subjects, however, does not necessarily indicate reciprocity. A dyadic contact dominated in the first half by actor one and dominated in the second half by actor two does not suggest reciprocity. By reciprocity we mean a fairly regular looping of vocalizations between the two partners in a rhythmic manner. Equilibrium refers to the ratio of less to greater vocal outputs on the part of the two actors. This particular property is extremely important to the bonding process. Transfer of information is a two-way process. Information must pass from one individual to the other and vice versa. For this reason the concept of equilibrium offers a powerful index for determining whether or not this type of transfer occurs. There is a limited range within which the syllable stress points can vary. The intensity interval is defined as the measured difference in loudness between adjacent syllables. Vocalization of too great or too little intensity impairs communication. The regularity of the proportional distribution of the intensity intervals provides a basis for analyzing the underlying characteristics of the conversational bond. A consideration of the vocabulary list affords certain advantages in studying the conversational relation. The vocabulary list in itself gives abstract evidence of vocabulary range. This measure standardized for time could demonstrate differential effects of types of social situation, communicative goals, age, and power. Differences of vocabulary range also should relate to the efficiency of communication and the efficiency of task performance. The distribution of vocabulary according to syllabic word length affords an index of verbal elaboration which is probably indicative of level of education, degree of technical involvement, degree of formalization, degree of social involvement, and level of socialization. Indexes based on variables such as syllabic word length are consistent over time and over a wide range of research applications. The frequency of word use affords a basis for examining the distribution of words in the vocabulary and a basis for weighting classes of words in actual use. Individual words can be indexed by mean frequency. Low frequency words are of special interest as indicators of topical range and topical focus. The frequency of word use also affords a measure of parallelism or lack of parallelism between two speakers. We would normally expect similar relative frequencies for high frequency words and a high degree of relationship between low frequency words. It should be possible to assign low frequency words to a common shared topic. It is the low frequency words which tend to give the conversational contact its special character.

There are several variables which can be applied to a vocabulary list which are confined to a restricted conceptual orientation. Such variables need not be exhaustive of the list. The vocabulary list could be interpreted in terms of action words, object words, and relation words. It is likely that sex and age manifest differences in the indicated concern with action as contrasted with concern to objects. Such an indicator permits assessment of the activity level within the dyad and in reference to the social environment. The vocabulary list can be assessed in terms of the distrubution of the social references implicit in the employment of personal pronouns, proper names of persons, and names of social groups, and generalized references to persons. Examples of the last category include man, child, person, fraternity, school, church, town, and nation. The reach of reference from self into society is indicated by the distribution and frequency of pronominal and nominal references to persons and groups.

The verbal characteristic refers to the natural sequencing of vocal outputs into intelligence bearing units. The elementary components of the verbal stream include seven types of verbal acts. These are: assertion, question, agreement, laugh, interjection, fragmentation, and simultaneous speech. These verbal acts have major functional differences. The assertion and question are complementary to each other and they carry virtually all of the information transfer. It is important to recognize that the information transfer is mutually additive for both participants in the actions of sending and receiving. Therefore the study of communication and social relations involved should center here. Agreement is an action which seemingly must be regularly injected along the stream of verbal emission. It should be measured in terms of frequency by source and in terms of the variation in the span of verbal outputs between the supports which agreement provides. Laugh sequence, interjection, interruption, and fragmentation are negatively associated with information transfer and provide a basis for assessing the noise factor in the conversational exchange. The pattern of verbal interchange can be measured through various dimensions of reciprocity. The unit of action in reciprocity is a communication cycle in which both actors have entered one sequence of verbal acts. If a consistent convention is developed for unitizing integrated syllable strings as discrete verbal acts, they can be ranged sequentially so as to produce a graph of reciprocal action which produces a wave-like form dependent on the syllable length of unit acts and the ordering of these acts into groups.

There are a wide variety of methods of content analysis (Weiner and Mehrabian 1968: 28; Berelson 1952; Stone, Dunphy, Smith, and Ogilvie 1966; Pool 1959). The content analysis can range from a broad recognition of topical areas to a minute consideration of indicative elements based on psychological factors, political reference, social relations, or other arbitrary orientations. A possible approach to the analysis of verbal characteristics involves the evaluation of levels of interrelation between verbal elements. This kind of evaluation ranges from identification of coherence between adjacent elements to a complex analysis of the possible relation between all groupings of verbal elements.

THE PROBLEM OF SAMPLING

The sample is used in research to represent some property which can be reliably used to represent the total population from which the sample was drawn. How well a given sample can represent a general population with respect to a property depends on how uniformly the property is distributed in the population. If a property is universally distributed in the population in a single form, then a sample of one case is representative and adequate for research. Any property which is characteristic of all segments of a population can be sampled sufficiently for research purposes with a small number of segments. A property which is irregularly distributed in a population requires sufficiently extensive random sampling to assure a high probability of representativeness. If a sample is representative of an irregularly distributed property, the same degree of irregularity will occur among samples as that which exists in the total population. A property which has an indefinitely large number of forms distributed in a population can only be sampled representatively by large samples which incorporate a major portion of the population.

In the conversational relation we think of the substance which is being sampled as the aggregate of all segments of face-to-face verbal interaction which occur in an extended social group. The temporal flow of verbal interaction consists of discontinuous segments of conversation between participants in dyads or slightly larger groups. For a larger extended social group the multiplication of conversational segments constitutes an aggregate of communicative action which continues through time and constitutes a major part of social action. Their properties which characterize all conversational action can readily be examined by sampling these segments of conversation.

Properties which are characteristic of conversations generally include vocabulary extension, word sequencing, pausing between verbal emissions, loudness variation, the mixing of kinds of verbal action syllable rate, variation in temporal or syllabic length of speech, and oscillation of action between partners in speech (Goldman-Eisler 1968: 14, 17, 23, 76; Gottschalk and Gleser 1969: 9-10, 67; Mishler and Waxler 1968; Weiner and Mehrabian 1968: 59). A limitation in the sampling of these properties is the temporal length of the vocal interaction. Although some authors argue that weeks or months must pass before characteristic patterns of verbal behavior are revealed, Birdwhistell (1952), Gottschalk and Gleser (1969: 9), and Pittenger, Hockett, and Daneby (1960) maintain that characteristic patterns of interaction are revealed within a few minutes or less. All of the properties mentioned above recur within a five minute sample of conversation several times

and it is not unusual to find close to 1000 conventionalized syllables and 750 vocally stressed syllables in five minutes of conversation. Their properties have been found to be well distributed in
the records of conversation both in our research and in that of
others who have investigated the mechanics of conversation. The
description of these properties both in mathematical and conceptual
terms is a basic and important task in understanding the conversational process. The explanation of variance in each of their properties should be undertaken initially in connection with the other
properties in this set.

A second level of analysis involves consideration of the relevant
characteristics of the actors who engage in conversation, for this
level we identify action characteristics and social stratum characteristics. Although there are no well-accepted conventions among
sociologists as to what these characteristics of social action are,
in general they include reciprocity, information, affect projection,
social energy, and action rate. Their properties in general become
manifest in segments of verbal behavior extending well beyond
the unit of counting and will usually include two or more verbal
emissions. Reciprocity involves the general pattern of give and
take between two partners. The information involves the net
transfer of information recognizing that specific assertions and
verbal acts have been ignored by the participants. Affect projection
establishes the tone of the relation involving friendliness and
hostility. Social energy refers to the degree, extent, and activity
level of participation in sustaining the action. Action rate incorporates the larger units of action and the rapidity with which they
emerge. All of these action characteristics are to be derived directly
from the record and not from the subjective impressions or post
hoc generalizations of participants or observers. The source data
consists of the action itself.

Social stratum characteristics are those most habitually and
conventionally supplied in contemporary research. They can be
directly related to either the descriptive properties or to the social
action properties. Social stratum characteristics include such properties as sex, education, age, social class, and power. They can be

used to help to interpret differences identified in the data or in the properties related to it. At the same time relation of the characteristics to the verbal and action properties contributes to an improved understanding of the social stratum properties.

RECORDS AND RECORDING

Research on the conversational process depends much on the quality of the record of verbal interaction. Recollection of conversational encounters previously experienced or observed provides an approximation which can be only loosely verified in its outcomes. The element of doubt and uncertainty in attempting to work with this kind of record is at a maximum. A somewhat better record can be developed by a trained observer who approximates the verbal exchange by written notes (Barker and Wright 1954: ch. 6). Even if this type of recording is verified by a second observer, it is generally recognized that the note taker using regular script cannot readily record all the complete sequences of verbal emission. More complete and accurate recording of verbal behavior is possible through the use of stenography. Such records are conventionally used in the verbatim recording of courtroom procedures.

Magnetic tape recording provides the most efficient and reliable means of recording the conversational interaction. There are several major advantages in the taped record. The first advantage is the accurate representation of real time in the record. The relation of real time of the original action to the time taken in playback is close to 1:1 depending on the relation of recording speed to replay speed. The ratio of time relations in the record is identical to the ratios in the original action. Sound recording provides a faithful record of variation in loudness, tone, pitch, and the exact sequencing and spacing of sounds. The utility of sound recording is that it can be applied regardless of language or setting with portable self-powered equipment. Video recording adds a visual dimension which can simulate the positioning of the observer's eye and can record the rich detail of a complex scene. The video record preserves the complex elements of physical and social action. The flexibility of video recording equipment permits the simultaneous recording of action sequences from several experimentally selected points of recording, and their views can be recorded on a split screen. The video recording studio permits a wide variety of experimental controls over the environmental setting and the action elements which are injected into it. The experimental effect of the setting can be varied by isolation with movable panels and the selection and arrangement of furnishings. Video recording permits a more accurate identification of the source of each verbal action. Therefore, the experimenter has a wider range of alternatives for injecting actors into the experimental setting. In the study of two-person interaction it is possible to examine the effects of a third actor on the relation.

The disadvantages of audio and video recording of social interaction are chiefly in the expense and effort involved. The cost of video tape is much greater than the cost of audio tape and both become very costly if extended records are made. Recording in a television studio on a university campus incurs expenses for operating and supervisory personnel and the problem of scheduling around the regular production schedule. The ideal, of course, would be to provide a fully equipped television studio solely for research purposes. A voluminous amount of data is generated within a few hours of recording time both on video and audio tape. Their records require a great expenditure of time if they are repeatedly reviewed in real time in order to produce verified protocols of verbal and physical action sequences. This time cost is further compounded by the requirement of typing, stenciling, coding, and entry on IBM cards. Major economy of effort can be obtained through the machine processing as through an analog digital converter to a computer. The equipment, particularly for video recording, is expensive and the research organization necessary to support intensive research into the social relationship could necessitate financial outlays far in excess of those currently made available for research in face-to-face social interaction. This level of action demands intensive study because it is the basis for all more extended levels of social relations.

Aside from experimentally generated records, there is a vast amount of recorded material in both audio and video format which has been recorded for other purposes. This material is free of bias as regards the researcher. These include news interviews, panel discussions, reactions of ordinary people to contrived situations, and clinically recorded material of both informative and therapeutic interviews.

MEASUREMENT

The level of measurement most frequently encountered in sociological research is based on a putative ordinal scale made up of a range of responses to a verbally stated question (Cancian 1964; Lennard 1969: 57). Typically the researcher must develop an aggregate score from a set of questions grouped according to an underlying concept. He then assumes that the score measures the variation in the conceived property in a consistent way. The collection of data which can be more precisely related to an underlying continuum would permit much more meaningful mathematical analysis. Measurement involves a consistent mapping of data in relation to a well-defined extended scale. The level of measurement improves as the extension of the scale can be quantitatively expressed in equivalent units of measure and related to an underlying continuum (see Coleman 1964: ch. 2).

Meaningful analysis of the conversational relation requires that the action can be broken down into component parts for precise measurement and analysis. Wiener and Mehrabian note that such analysis may not be possible with our current methodology (1968: 24), and some theorists feel that it destroys the reality of social interaction to decompose it into parts. In recent centuries empirical scientists have ignored such strictures and have applied a wide variety of conventional and applied measures. All measurement involved a transformation from a property observed in nature to some quantification expressed in standardized units. Direct measurement involves a simple transformation of the extent of a property in standard units' which incorporates the property being measured. For exemple, the length of a table may be measured in the standard inch, and the inch incorporates the property of length. Variations in the physical distance of speakers can be measured in units of length. Length is a property which fits the mathematical property of a continuum in that it is infinitely divisible. Time is a core property in the measurement of conversational action because it must be exclusively and sequentially allocated between the two partners. Speech is bound to a time continuum (Chapple 1948-49; Cherry 1957: 77-78; Goldman-Eisler 1968: 11; Martinet 1960). Time is a direct measure because the clock minute has the same property — duration — which is the core property of time as a continuum. Indirect measurement involves the transformation of an underlying property to an analog scale which is thought to vary consistently with variation in the substrate property. This can be illustrated by measurement of loudness variation in which voltage variation is regarded as the analog of loudness variation. Amplitude is a special case of loudness variation which measures the loudness interval between any two points on the scale. The frequency dimension depends on the concept of unity applied by definition to some segment of a collection of elements. The unit of measure is the defined case or occurrence. The frequency range is thought to extend indefinitely with the addition of cases, and to provide a basis for comparison between measures based on the frequency count. In conversational encounters, there are many conceptual bases for applying this frequency count including syllables, words, agreements, encounters, sentences, and vocabulary range (Wiener and Mehrabian 1968: 2; Iker and Harway 1969; Howes 1967: 189).

The derived measure by definition combines two or more properties in a single measure. It has the advantage of combining and simplifying a group of properties for more precise analysis. It may provide the basis for a simple coefficient which serves as a measure for a set of properties acting together. Usually some analytical concept is associated with such a measure. Slope is a derived measure based on the ratio between a vertical and horizontal interval between two points simultaneously defined by two measurements. It indicates a rate of change between the two points. In vocal speech, slope can be defined as a joint function of intensity and time, and constitutes a measure of the increase or decrease in intensity. Syllabic rate can be identified as a density function measured in syllables per unit of time. The area concept can be reflected as an integral function of amplitude and time, to provide an index of energy variation. Pitch is a derived measure defined as the dominant frequency of a sound wave perceived by the ear, ranging from a low tone of about 20 cycles per second to a maximum high approaching 30,000 cycles (Funk and Wagnalls 1963). The regularity of verbal cycling between partners can be measured by the dual functions of syllabic amplitude and the temporal sequence of verbal acts. Such phenomena can be graphed by source into a wave-like form above and below a line of origin.

For purposes of identifying the verbal pattern, taped information is generally recognized as a valid record of verbal action if the noise level is sufficiently low to permit unambiguous identification of all verbal elements on the record. The validity of video material is limited by the control of lighting sufficient to discriminate the subjects clearly and by the location and field of view of the cameras. The video record cannot be a full record of all action from all viewpoints, but it does provide a valid record from at least one viewpoint, providing ambient noise is held to a low level to permit accurate discrimination of action. Good quality electronic recordings of conversational behavior generally provide valid records of conversational action (Gottschalk and Gleser 1969: 49).

Reliability of data transformation depends on the number of transformations of data and the degree of control over the transformation process. As the transformations become more remote from the original record, reliability becomes more difficult to control. Maximum reliability is obtained through electronic conversion as in the conversion of voltage values to digital values at some fixed sampling rate. A high degree of reliability can be obtained through the repeated comparison of the written protocol to the original taped record. Further transfers of data, such as the typing of protocols, introduce further chance of error which can be reduced by careful review.

In the conversational process, the control function applies primarily to the verbal emission stream and to the series of messages which they contain. If the conversational process is complete there is a second control function associated with the receiver who must listen and attend to the verbal stream. Therefore control in the conversational process resides in two complementary forms in two places. The control process in both the emitting action and the receiving action is neither uniform nor constant. The emitter has to assert two kinds of control: (1) somatic control which includes the mustering of energy for bodily action and verbal output, and (2) editorial control which incorporates the sorting and developing of words into sentences. The emitter loses control from time to time as he breaks into laughter, sobs, stuttering, or fragmentation. He also sometimes breaks down momentarily in doubt and confusion. The listener has somatic control which is less pressing than that of the speaker because it requires less effort. The listener has the problem of controlling listening and concentration in the receiving process. He will experience distraction if the emitter loses control, if the channel is noisy, or if the listener wanders too far afield in his series of mental associations with what he has previously heard. The control function is further complicated by the fact that the control modes must alternate between partners as the emitter source cycles. These internal controls in the conversation process involve the bulk of the control which is inherent in the action (Mischler and Waxler 1968: 2).

When the experimenter attempts to apply controls to the experimental relation, he must recognize that they can only be partial and peripheral. The experimenter can establish boundaries within which the action occurs. He can establish a time limit more or less successfully and he can control the physical positioning of the speakers through an arrangement of the furniture. Limitations are imposed on the range of conversational action between the two partners by social conventions including those stressed by the experimenter. Topical control may be imposed by task specification but it is difficult to maintain rigid limitations as the conversation readily shifts to related but tangential topics. This recognizes that the efforts of the experimenter to impose control are frustrated by freedom of action and freedom of association which is implicit in verbal expression. Therefore evidence of control within the system must be sought in the relations among the components of action. This requires an atomistic approach to the analysis of conversational action as a basis for constructing tentative hypothetical models for the detailed study of well-defined components of verbal exchange. It should be reiterated in considering the operation of control in the conversational relation that it is grossly affected by variation and uncertainty in all of its applications.

RANGE OF ACCESS LEVELS

The exhaustive study of the conversational relation in society incorporates at least seven distinct levels of analysis, each of which has its own unique range elements, relations, and laws. We will describe these levels in terms of the size of the time frame. The level of action is defined as the relation among the events occurring within a second. This range is appropriate to a consideration of neural functioning, relations between adjacent syllables in time and intensity, and the production of individual words and small groups of words. Verbal acts such as fragmentation, agreement, and laughter are completed within one second. The process of composing and integrating both in emission and reception occurs on a second by second basis. The second level incorporates the complete information-bearing statement as a unit of analysis. The information-bearing statement is defined as a sequence of syllables which conveys information by virtue of the relation among the syllables. Here the concept of syntax as perceived by Chomsky becomes relevant (Mehta 1971). Statements can be described in terms of syllable length, temporal length, coherence with adjacent statements, word analysis, vocabulary range, and the unit of information. The third level of analysis is the cycle involving one complete verbal exchange between two persons. The cycle begins at the initiating point of the first partner's speech and ends at the terminal point of the partner's following speech. A series of such exchanges constitutes a set of interaction cycles. The analysis of the cycle permits measurement of the equilibrium between the actors, assessment of their participation rates, and a comparison of the relation between half cycles regarding form and composition. The periodicity and rhythm in the flow of the verbal exchange process can be identified and assessed through measures of the regularity of cycling.

The total conversational episode in a single contact provides a fourth range of access. A conversational episode is defined as the verbal exchange which occurs between the time of the first statement by one speaker and the time when the conversational exchange is terminated by the intrusion of an external event. In sociological analysis we would treat the conversational episode as a unit of social action. It could be assessed as an association and in terms of how it is generalized by each participant. Here we are concerned not with the verbatim content but with the social effect. The analyst would be concerned with what was said, the net impression gained by the participants, and the social outcome accruing to each party gained from the experience of verbal contact. In the conversational episode we are primarily concerned with the fundamental unit of social action.

In the analysis of the development of specific social relations between a given pair of persons, we can incorporate the fifth level which is a series of conversational episodes distributed over a considerable period of time. In the acquaintance process the relation develops between a pair of individuals through the incremental effects of a series of conversational contacts in a stable relationship. The sixth access level in the investigation of the conversational relation is identified in the gross outcome of specific pair relations which can be identified by a change of direction in the life pattern for one or both partners. Such outcomes include the choice of an occupation, the initiation or termination of habitual social contacts, and entering a marital or task partnership. Finally we are concerned with the long-term relations based on continuing conversational contact. By long term effects we mean those social characteristics and orientations which result from long enduring contacts between pairs of persons. This is dependent on a large aggregate of specific shared episodes and the assumptions which each can make about the social reactions of the other which is the basis for an intimate association.

DYADIC MODELS

The theoretical model is of utmost importance to the researcher because it explicitly or implicitly imposes certain limitations on observation and definition. It determines both the field of view and the direction of analysis. The ability to apply quite different theoretical models to the same class of phenomena affords a powerful tool for developing information and insight in an unknown area. There is no such thing as the correct theoretical model but there are alternatives of applicable theoretical models. We would expect that each theoretical alternative would have some advantages for the analysis of certain aspects of a class of phenomena. We will present four illustrative models for the two-person conversational contact while recognizing that various other models would be equally applicable. The theoretical model of reciprocating action asserts a social unity between the two persons and stresses the uniformity and equivalence of the successive phases of action. Regardless of the variation in the content of action, this model presumes an operational equivalence between the actors. An advantage of the reciprocating system model is that it is consistent with a time series analysis of the sequence of action. It gets at the moment by moment process of action, and affords a basis for examining the underlying process of social action. It affords an approach for examining the nature of the social union. By implication the reciprocal model affords a good basis for the evaluation of the equilibrium process in the conversational dyad. Goffman

(1967) seems to have this kind of model in mind in his discussion of face-to-face behavior.

A theoretical model based on the exchange of transactional payments has been suggested by Thibaut and Kelley (1959: ch. 3). This model can be made dynamic by recognizing the sequence of payments in which each partner in the dyad alternately extends rewards in relation to payments which he has received or payments which he anticipates. This is a linear model with bidirectional causality. It tends to exclude the precise analysis of time and to require the transaction as the unit of analysis. It permits a systematic accounting of the rewards and costs between the two actors and the ratio between these. This model is well suited to an investigation of the cooperative process in communication. It is also helpful for recognizing the competitive factor in social exchange since the experienced participant is presumably aware of the possibility of more profitable alternative associations. The transactional payments model provides a means for identifying the source in which social utility is originally generated. Social utility could well be treated as the basic energy source for social action in general, including its more extended forms.

The theoretical model of mental conjunction departs from the linear approach incorporated in the preceding models and views the conversational contact as a holistic entity created by the superimposition of mental fields of interest held in common by the two partners. This model is consistent with Lewin's field theory (1951: ch. 2). Field theory employs the concept of a unique life space for each individual in which component elements are pictured in a planiform array. The individual moves among the elements in patterned action. In the model of mental conjunction we could describe the conversational approach between two individuals as an attempt to bring areas of their life space into conjunction. The expression of a statement on the part of one actor represents an attempt to establish a link between the life space of the emitter and that of the receiver.

If there is congruence between the life space components which the statements represent, then the link is successfully established.

A collection of such links would build up an area of conjunction between the two actors and their life spaces are more or less conjoined. If the related components in the two life spaces are incongruent, the link fails. If there is a sufficient proportion of such failures, the conjunction cannot be established. The two partners talk past each other. The life spaces remain discrete and the union is nonexistent. This theory is helpful for applying the concept of the fitting together of social personalities in active relations. It incorporates the notion of mapping the components of personality in the life space of each actor. The problem of conjunction between areas of the life space of two persons requires both congruent elements and the organization of a sufficiency of the elements into an accessible area.

The theory which underlies what we shall term the discrete personality model assumes that the personality is a self-contained system which cannot extend beyond itself into another personality system. This assumption about the human personality seems implicit in the works of Freud (1923), Fromm (1947), and Allport (1960). It stresses the importance of maintaining and defending the boundaries of the personality and of excluding intruding influences. In the discrete personality model we view each of the two actors in the dyad independently and separately. We are impelled to analyze the conversational action as a unilateral process. Ego is the center of reference and alter is an opposing external force against which ego reacts. Ego may adjust or reorganize but only autonomously and after a time lag. The discrete personality model is not very helpful for exploring the social process since it presumes a fundamental independence of the actors. It could be used for the study of personality — its integrity and development — and the lag effect of verbal inputs. It is also helpful for focusing on the processes by which the individual acquires and expresses verbal action. It helps to understand the organization of the personality.

THE DYAD AS AN EXPERIMENTAL CHAMBER

The experimental technique of isolating selected pairs of persons in the conversational contact opens the way for the exploration of a vast variety of social actions and social processes. Useful information can be obtained in nonisolated settings (Gamson 1961 : 572), but isolation brings a desirable reduction in the rather intricate complex of variables in the simple dyadic contact. The conversing pair is relatively easy to isolate and record, provided that care is taken to establish optimum recording conditions. If incident noise is reasonably well controlled a relatively rich veridical record of verbal interaction is readily obtainable over varying time periods. As a data source the verbal record contains analogs of energy, information, speech rate, and action sequences, all of which can serve as uniform measures of other variables. We can illustrate only a few of the possible applications of the conversational dyad as an experimental chamber. Intensive exploitation of the technique would certainly disclose others.

The isolated conversational dyad could be used in the study of types of social interaction (Dunnette, Campbell, and Jaastad 1968; Lennard and Bernstein 1969). The experimenter can readily impose a decision requirement, reached through discussion, which allows one partner to triumph and defeat the other. From a set of records of the argumentative situation, the experimenter can search for the elements and their combined effects in studying the process of social conflict. The vital process of information transfer is implicit in the record of verbal intercourse. The investigator can evaluate variability in the success of explication of single items of knowledge, measuring illustrative, graphic, hortatory, and definitional techniques against time and retention. The social process of verbal persuasion can be measured through assessment of the series of assertions and responses emanating from the persuader and his client. Many kinds of decision problems and success criteria can be included in such experimental research. The conversational dyad provides a medium for studying the acquaintance process. The experimenter can treat the acquaintance process in terms of social mapping and social fixation as each partner serially makes assumptions about his interests, connections, and history in the social world. Finally there is a need for a definitive study of ritualistic and culturally prescribed statements and their function in maintaining the conversational relation.

Many kinds of significant experimental differentials can be applied to the isolated conversational dyad. To a certain degree the interaction is affected by variations in the social context (Lennard and Bernstein 1969: 32). Verbal practices can be conditioned by selective reinforcement (Lewin 1951: 229). There can be systematic exploration of the nature of the social differentials as age, sex, power, cultural differences, relevant knowledge, roles, money, control, and time. We can explore the effect of the differences in the magnitude of the differential and the operational techniques of overcoming its barrier effects. Boundary phenomena also deserve extensive investigation (Goffman 1961: 35). First, what is the evidence that the defined boundary exists? How is it maintained? Is the boundary permeable or impermeable with respect to external factors? How does the boundary deteriorate? We believe that the conversational chamber is suitable for the examination of the development of social union between various kinds of participants in terms of the integration of action and the coherence of adjacent acts.

3

INTENSITY

Varying energy investments defined in terms of intensity variations and their temporal distribution relate to the core properties of the conversational bond (Lieberman 1967: 144). The first core property is defined as the interlock between conversational partners. Interlocking is manifested in the nearly simultaneous emission and intake of syllable strings where the thought of one partner becomes the nearly identical thought of the other. Interlocking is directly related to characteristics of the syllable string which include intensity, time, and joint functions of these two and can be identified in the pattern of loudness variation (Bloomfield 1933: 110; Gottschalk and Gleser 1969: 15). Variations in energy investments are partly a function of variations in loudness in which one can note variations in temporal wave length, number of syllables per vocal utterance, intensity intervals between adjacent syllables, and the temporal gain between utterances. All of the factors are directly accessible from the audio tape record.

The analysis of intensity as an indicator of the conversational process has been undertaken from a data source of 70 unique dyads each generating a five minute sample of conversation. The sample included 47 upper level college students with 27 females and 20 males. The students, who were only slightly acquainted, had been instructed to talk about anything they wished. They were fully aware that their conversations were being recorded.

Operational Definitions

Amplitude — range in loudness variation for each vocalized syllable.

Area — summation measure of energy investments, an integral function of intensity and time.

Density — the number of vocalized syllables per second.

Equilibrium — ratio of the vocal participation between actors.

Hesitancy — ratio of gap time to speech time.

Interactor gap — the length of the temporal pause between actor emissions.

Interrupt — simultaneous vocal emissions from both actors.

Intra-actor gap — the length of the temporal pause between adjacent mesowaves (see below) emitted by the same actor.

Interactor mesowaves — series of mesowaves including actor transmissions of both actors.

Intra-actor mesowaves — series of uninterrupted mesowaves emitted by the same actor.

Mesowave — two or more microwaves — an uninterrupted or continuous string of vocalized syllables terminated by a period of silence or by vocalized emissions from the other actor.

Microwave — a wave of action in time marred by the peak loudness of one vocalized syllable.

Point interval — the length of time between vocalized syllables regardless of actor.

Slope — the ratio (y/x) of intensity variation (y) and time (x).

Spectrum — range of loudness levels.

Wave length — time duration of a mesowave in seconds.

Method of Analysis

For analysis of intensity variation it was necessary to convert the audio record to digital values. A rectifier and filter system was connected between the type recorder and an analog-digital converter. The rectifier system converted the alternating current in full-wave and thus eliminated negative values. The elimination of the negative values simplified the data without loss of information as the positive and negative values are simply mirror images. The filter damped fluctuations in tone so that only loudness variation remained. This manipulation eliminated error attributable to the interdependence of these two factors.

The analog digital converter was set to sample 50 times per second, producing 3-digit values as an analog of loudness. The digital output was stored on a computer disc unit in one minute segments by a 1620 IBM computer and was machine punched on IBM cards. The input to the converter was held to a maximum of 5.0 volts. The maximum digital value was 965, approximately equivalent to 5.0 volts. Vocal output was sampled fifty times per second to obtain a sufficiently dense sample to insure the most maximum values of each vocalized syllable. This produced a digital record of approximately 15,000 values for each five minute dyadic contact. In the graphic depiction of these conversations, intensity is plotted on the vertical axis and time on the horizontal axis, to create a visual image of the auditory patterns. The plots proved extremely valuable as a first step toward recognizing differences and identifying segments of action, and afforded a basis for selecting measurement parameters and criteria of discrimination.

The next step was to condense the data by abstracting from each record those maximum intensity values indicative of each vocalized syllable and the associated time interval. The computer program chained these syllables together in their natural sequence thus identifying syllable strings or mesowaves.

Lennard and Bernstein note that there has been considerable controversy concerning how the flow of interaction should be segmented. The problem appears to have become polarized around the issue of "natural" versus "artificial" units (1969: 53). Barker argues that "natural" behavioral units represent self-generated parts of the stream of behavior (1963). Bales' research (1950) also places emphasis on the "natural" unit. The following design proposes use of the natural unit referred to as a syllable string. By definition, a natural syllable string, called a mesowave, can be terminated by two conditions: (1) time filled with silence, or (2) vocalization created by the other partner. For the latter, the program terminated one mesowave and began another when one actor ceased talking and the other actor commenced. It was necessary to establish a criterion span of time for terminating a mesowave. Goldman-Eisler (1968: 11-15) uses one-tenth of a second as time lapse sufficient to denote a pause. Her research indicates that pauses were never longer than three seconds and that ninety-nine percent were less than two seconds. For the current research effort, the time segment selected was four-tenths of a second. The literature on the concept of syllable rate tended to indicate that normal speech rate is between six and eight syllables per second. With a rate of fifty samples per second, each record has approximately eight digital values representing each syllable. Four-tenths of a second would correspond approximately to the amount of time needed to vocalize between two and three syllables, a sufficient amount of time to mark a functional gap and the end of a syllable string.

In addition to the mesowave controls it was necessary to establish controls for locating the maximal intensity value representative of each vocalized syllable. The first control needed was a control establishing the minimum interval between syllable maxima. This minimum limit was set at 0.12'' based on the research on speech rates. With a maximum speech rate of eight syllables per second this limit screens out the effects of small fluctuations due to machine noise.

For the same reason it was necessary to establish the minimum intensity level at 100 millivolts. Inspection of the digital record indicated that lower intensity values are attributable to machine noise.

For each mesowave having three or more syllables, six measures were abstracted: (1) slope, (2) amplitude, (3) wave length, (4) area, (5) density, and (6) number of points per mesowave. These measures were not acquired for mesowaves consisting of only one or two syllables due to the instability associated with such short vocalized emissions. In addition to these six measures obtained uniquely for each mesowave, several summary measures were retained. Summary measures were retained independently for each actor in the dyad to facilitate the analysis of differences which might be attributable to actor make-up. In addition to summary measures obtained for each actor, summary measures were also retained for the first and second half of each dayd for analysis of the contact in real time. The data in Figure 1 illustrates the design of this output. The six columns are summary measures for actor one and are to be compared with a similar layout for actor two. The first three measures of Row 1 indicate the number of mesowaves comprised of one, two, three, or more points. The last three measures in Row 1 represent total time in seconds for silence, short emissions (mesowaves of two points), and long emissions (mesowaves of three or more points). Row 2 delineates the overall mean slope, amplitude, wave length, area, density, and syllables per mesowave. Rows 3 and 4 delineate the means of each of these variables for the first temporal halves of each sample. The summary measures of Row 5 include total area, area by halves, total number of vocalized syllables, and total number of mesowaves for each half. Row 6 represents an analysis of positive and negative slopes analyzed independently. The last gives frequency counts.

	1 Syl	2 Syls	3+ Syls	Gap	Short	Long
	35.0	21.0	48.0	50.2″	4.3″	54.4″

	Slope	Ampli	Length	Area	Density	Syls
Means T	−2.6	3.5	0.9	3.1	5.9	4.9
Means 1	−2.3	3.5	0.9	3.3	5.8	4.9
Means 2	−3.2	3.4	0.8	2.7	6.1	4.8

	Area T	Area 1	Area 2	Syls T	Waves 1	Waves 2
	150.1	110.0	40.1	104.0	33.0	15.0

	+Slope 1	−Slope 1	+Slope 2	−Slope 2	+Slope T	−Slope T
Means	4.2	−6.0	2.9	−7.2	3.8	−6.4
Counts	12.0	21.0	6.0	9.0	18.0	30.0

Legend: First Half 1
Second Half 2
Total T
Seconds ″

Fig. 1. Mesowave properties of a Dyad (Dyad 1, First Actor)

The set of 84 indices (42 for each actor) was factor analyzed to determine the association among the indices and to reduce the data to a more manageable form. The factor analyses were run by dyadic structure producing three main analyses: (1) male-male set, (2) male-female set, and (3) female-female set. A similar structure was applied to the other analysis. The t values and associated probabilities were calculated for paired actors by dyad and by paired temporal halves. The conversational bond can be pictured as a veridical social system in real time. A mental coherence is created between the two actors as the information cycles within the system. It cannot be assumed that each actor's responses are independent of the other. Likewise, it cannot be assumed that an actor's response patterns in the first two and one-half minutes are independent of his response patterns in the second two and one-half minutes. Therefore, the t test assuming dependence between samples was chosen.

An examination of the pictorial plots revealed that slope divided naturally into four categories: (1) monotonic positive, (2) monotonic negative, (3) polytonic positive, and (4) polytonic negative. A monotonic slope is one which does not change the sign of its direction; a polytonic slope is one which does change the sign of its direction. Monotonic and polytonic mesowaves were analyzed by actor and by halves, and the mean number of syllable maxima per mesowave in each of the above was retained. Other indices include density, amplitude and time; t tests for paired data with associated probabilities were calculated.

To analyze the intensity intervals between adjacent syllables a frequency count and proportional distribution means, and standard deviation of the point intervals was made by actor and by halves. The calculations included the maximum and minimum point intervals within mesowaves of three or more points, the mean interval within the two-point mesowave, the mean interval within the long mesowaves, and the relationship between intensity and point interval size by actors and by halves. The gap concept affords two applications: the intra-actor and the interactor gap, with a frequency count and proportional distribution of the occurrence of all gap sizes between any one actor's adjacent mesowaves for the first, and termination due to vocalization on the part of the other actor for the second. The proportional distribution of intersyllable intensity intervals suggested a curvilinear function which could be described mathematically. Exponential curve fitting was applied to assess this function.

The clustering of loudness levels is expected to appear as a banding effect in the distribution of intensity intervals. The intensity levels at which the banding effect occurred were described in terms of the mean interval between bands by actor, by temporal half, and by dyad structure. There was an effort to determine if any given band pattern was characteristic of a given sex or dyad structure.

Hypotheses

The following hypotheses were formulated prior to the emergence of the test data:

H_1: There is a significant relationship between the dyadic structure and the level of energy investment.

Corollary: Differences in energy investments will be more noticeable in sexually heterogeneous dyads.

H_2: The initial phase of the dyadic contact manifests greater energy investments than the terminal phase.

H_3: There is a positive relationship between equilibrium and the similarity of actors.

H_4: There is a spectrum of loudness indicated by a scale of loudness levels identifiable from the natural groupings of intensity variation.

H_5: The mathematically ascertained variables descriptive of conversational bonding can be condensed into clearly discriminant factors.

H_6: There is a positive correlation between intensity intervals and time intervals. An increase in the vertical interval shifts will be accompanied by an increase in the intersyllable interval.

H_7: Gap varies significantly by dyadic structure.

H_1 Sex Structure and Energy Investment

The energy investment is that evidenced through the following indices: slope, amplitude, wave length, area, density, and number of syllables per mesowave. For this hypothesis, results of a series of t tests are given in Table 1.

TABLE 1

Comparison of energy investments by
actor within each Dyad structure

Index	Male-Male		Female-Female		Male-Female	
	t	p	t	p	t	p
Slope	−.692	.504	.802	.559	1.472	.146
Amplitude	.163	.866	−1.179	.255	3.990	.001
Wave Length	−.148	.878	−.302	.763	2.381	.021
Area	−1.614	.122	−.045	.963	4.628	.001
Density	−.752	.531	.053	.957	−.413	.684
Points	−.091	.925	−.432	.674	2.195	.032

In the homogeneous dyad structures, there are no significant differences by actor in energy investments as ascertained by the selected indices. In other words, in the homogeneous dyads the energy investments of the two actors on these indices are quite similar. An examination of the t's obtained in the heterogeneous set reveals considerably different results. There is a significant difference by actor for energy investments as measured by amplitude, wave length, area, and number of syllables per mesowave. The implication is that sex is a significant factor in describing energy investments in the dyadic contact. Thus, the first hypothesis is supported. There does appear to be a significant relationship between the level of energy investment and the dyadic structure, since differences in energy investments are noticeable only in the mixed dyad structure.

H_2 *Temporal Structure and Energy Investment*

Hypothesis two states that the initial phase of the dyadic contact manifests greater energy investments than the terminal phase. The tests compared each actor's performance in the first half of the five minute contact to his performance in the second half as shown in Table 2. In the male-male structure, three significant statistics can be noted. There is a significant difference between the density index for both actors moving from the first to the second half. The t values are positive indicating a decline in speech rate as the contact progresses in time. Comparing the summed area in the first half to that in the second half for actor one, the negative t value also suggests a substantial increase in energy investment. In the female-female structure, it is interesting to note that the only significant statistic is the amplitude index. The t is positive suggesting a significant decline in amplitude during the five minute contact.

Examination of the male-female structure reveals the greatest differences. For the male actor in this dyad structure, significant differences between the first and second half can be seen for wave length, number of maxima per mesowave, summed area, and number of mesowaves. The t values of the latter two indices are negative indicating an increase in the summed area and the number of mesowaves per half. However, the positive t values obtained by comparing halves for the wave length and the number of points per mesowave suggest a decline in the mean number of points and the mean wave length as time progresses. Because the number of points per mesowave, mean point density and mean wave length decrease from one half to the next; the fact that an increase is observed in the area and number of mesowaves by halves might appear to be a contradiction. The implication suggested by this pattern is that although total energy investments are greater, the male's speech patterns become more fragmented. In other words, speech utterances are significantly more fragmented in the second half of the dyadic contact for the male actor in the heterogeneous dyad structure. For the female participant in the heterogeneous

TABLE 2

t Scores comparing energy investments between first and second half by actor

Index	Male-Male				Female-Female				Male-Female			
	Actor 1		Actor 2		Actor 1		Actor 2		Actor 1		Actor 2	
	t	p	t	p	t	p	t	p	t	p	t	p
Slope	-.08	.932	-1.08	.30	-1.70	.105	-.80	.562	-.37	.720	.24	.810
Amplitude	1.49	.152	.64	.54	2.25	.037	1.52	.144	1.28	.210	3.94	.002
Wave Length	-1.44	.165	-.70	.50	.95	.645	1.51	.146	2.07	.040	2.95	.006
Area	-.93	.633	-1.79	.09	.45	.657	.45	.661	.95	.650	2.77	.009
Density	2.16	.044	2.86	.01	1.76	.094	1.63	.119	1.28	.210	1.84	.070
Points	-1.36	.187	-.52	.62	1.23	.236	1.48	.154	2.12	.040	2.96	.005
Summed Area	-2.84	.011	-1.90	.07	-.55	.592	-1.21	.242	-2.69	.010	.37	.710
Mesowaves	-1.65	.114	-1.31	.21	-1.19	.247	-2.08	.052	-3.73	.001	-1.60	.120

d yad structure, four significant *t* values emerge. There is a significant decline in energy investments between the first and second half as measured by amplitude, wave length, area, and number of points per mesowave.

The performance of the two actors in the first half was compared to their performance in the second half to determine if differences in energy investments between halves could be ascertained. No significant differences were found in the homogeneous dyad structures. However, in the heterogeneous dyad structure, several differences appear (Table 3). On the amplitude and area indices, differences were found in both the first and second half. The *t* scores obtained in the second half of the contact indicate greater differences between actors in the second half. This suggests that on these indices, in the first two and one-half minutes of the contact, there was little difference between the energy investments of the two partners. Movement into the second two and one-half minutes establish significant differences, with increased energy investments on the part of the male and decreased energy investments for the female participant. The implication is that as the interaction progresses in time, the two actors move away from an equilibrium model rather than approaching one.

The data suggests some support for the hypothesis if reference is made specifically to the heterogeneous dyad structure. If reference is made to the homogeneous dyad structure, the hypothesis must be rejected as the data indicates only chance differences.

The third hypothesis states that there is a significant relationship between equilibrium and dyadic structure. Equilibrium has reference to the ratio of lower to higher output frequencies by actor, where the ratio of 1.00 indicates equal participation. As shown in Table 4, equilibrium is highest in the homogeneous dyad structures indicative of more equal participation on the part of both actors in the homogeneous dyads. Equilibrium is lowest in the heterogeneous dyads suggesting that one partner is significantly more active than the other. The data indicates that the greatest participation is attributable to the male actor in the mixed dyads.

TABLE 3

t Scores comparing energy investments between actors by halves

Index	Female-Female				Male-Male				Male-Female			
	Half 1		Half 2		Half 1		Half 2		Half 1		Half 2	
	t	p	t	p	t	p	t	p	t	p	t	p
Slope	.43	.670	.68	.510	−.08	.930	−2.01	.060	.61	.550	1.53	.130
Amplitude	−.74	.520	−1.10	.290	1.39	.180	−.45	.660	2.07	.040	4.23	.001
Wave Length	−.07	.940	.00	.990	−.14	.880	.49	.640	1.27	.210	2.78	.009
Area	.00	.990	−.06	.960	−1.40	.180	−1.60	.130	3.05	.004	5.49	.001
Density	−.30	.760	−.03	.970	−.74	.526	−.44	.670	−.83	.590	.09	.920
Points	.05	.960	−.26	.800	−.15	.880	.46	.660	1.25	.220	2.68	.010

TABLE 4

Equilibrium ratios in the three Dyad structures

Female-Female	Male-Male	Male-Female
.88	.96	.68

From a theoretical point of view, the implication is that bonding is tighter in the homogeneous dyad structure. Both actors' short and long emissions were compared together within each dyad structure. Here short emissions refer to utterances consisting of either one or two stress points. Long emissions refer to mesowaves of three or more stress points. Short and long emissions refer to mesowaves of three or more stress points. Short and long emissions simply refer to a summation of the time spent in vocalizing each type. Within the homogeneous dyad structures as shown in Table 5, no significant differences were found, suggesting that the two actors' vocal performances were similar. In the heterogeneous dyad structure, significant differences were found to exist for all of these factors without exception, which suggests the two actors' vocal performances were dissimilar, and that there is greater participation by the male actor, which supports the third hypothesis. There appears to be a significant relationship between equilibrium and the dyad structure, with seemingly better equilibrium in the homogeneous dyad structure.

TABLE 5

t *Tests comparing vocalization patterns between actors*

Index	Female-Female		Male-Male		Male-Female	
	t	p	t	p	t	p
2 Points	1.05	.31	.39	.70	2.19	.03
3+ Points	.96	.65	.23	.81	3.44	.002
Total Points	1.33	.20	.04	.97	2.60	.01
Phrases Half 1	1.38	.19	.08	.94	2.43	.02
Phrases Half 2	.43	.67	.32	.75	3.70	.001

Hypothesis 4 states that there is a spectrum of loudness indicated by a scale of loudness levels identifiable from the fairly regularly spaced concentrations of intensity levels (Chomsky and Halle 1968: 59; Greenberg 1968: 69). It was thought that the frequency of the occurrence of these intensity levels formed a regular pattern which could be mathematically described. To test this hypothesis a table was built distributing the frequency count according to the size of the intensity shifts between adjacent syllables within meso-waves. The regularity of the pattern can be observed in Table 6, and does suggest support for the fourth hypothesis.

If we describe the proportional distribution of all intersyllable intensity shifts representing scale levels by the subscript X on a scale increasing from 1 to 100, it can be shown that the observed distribution proportions are closely approximated by the exponential function:

$$p_{x+n} = p_x e^{-(\text{Log } p_x + nL)}$$

where: p = proportion of intensity shifts at a scale level

e = 2.71828, the base of the natural log system

x = some level on the intensity shift scale

n = some number of scale steps such that $1 \leq (x + n) \leq 100$

L = $(\ln p_i - p_j) / (j - i)$, the log increment for one step on the scale

i = a scale step near the lower end of the scale

j = a scale step at least 10 steps higher on the scale

The difference between observed and predicted proportion of intersyllable intensity shifts is reduced if the proportions are pooled, say over five consecutive scale levels at the lower end, and five consecutive levels ten or twenty steps higher. The values reflected in Tables 7 and 8 result from such pooling over 12 sets of data summing scale levels 1-6 for the mean proportion p_i and levels 21-26 for the mean proportion p_j. The mean error in the predicted proportions for 97 scale levels was approximately .0001 for the 12 sets of data incorporating 40,347 measures of intersyllable intensity shifts.

TABLE 6

Distribution of intensity shifts for 70 Dyads
N = 40,347

Shift Size	Ob- serve	Predict	Error	Mean Error	Shift Size	Ob- serve	Predict	Error	Mean Error
0	.0826	.0826	.0	.0	45	.0037	.0029	−.0008	−.0000
1	.0687	.0607	.0080	−.0080	46	.0036	.0027	−.0009	−.0001
2	.0555	.0566	.0011	−.0035	47	.0032	.0025	−.0007	−.0001
3	.0477	.0528	.0051	−.0006	48	.0028	.0024	−.0004	−.0001
4	.0452	.0493	.0041	.0006	49	.0029	.0022	−.0007	−.0001
5	.0428	.0460	.0032	.0011	50	.0025	.0020	−.0004	−.0001
6	.0407	.0429	.0023	.0013	51	.0026	.0019	−.0006	−.0001
7	.0371	.0401	.0030	.0015	52	.0021	.0018	−.0003	−.0001
8	.0351	.0374	.0023	.0016	53	.0019	.0017	−.0002	−.0001
9	.0319	.0349	.0030	.0018	54	.0019	.0016	−.0004	−.0001
10	.0311	.0326	.0015	.0017	55	.0020	.0015	−.0005	−.0001
11	.0293	.0304	.0011	.0017	56	.0014	.0014	−.0000	−.0001
12	.0271	.0284	.0012	.0016	57	.0018	.0013	−.0005	−.0001
13	.0259	.0265	.0006	.0016	58	.0016	.0012	−.0004	−.0001
14	.0246	.0247	.0001	.0015	59	.0014	.0011	−.0003	−.0001
15	.0234	.0230	−.0003	.0013	60	.0012	.0010	−.0002	−.0001
16	.0207	.0215	.0008	.0013	61	.0010	.0010	−.0000	−.0001
17	.0190	.0201	.0011	.0013	62	.0014	.0009	−.0005	−.0001
18	.0188	.0187	−.0001	.0012	63	.0012	.0008	−.0004	−.0002
19	.0176	.0175	−.0002	.0011	64	.0011	.0008	−.0003	−.0002
20	.0169	.0163	−.0006	.0011	65	.0010	.0007	−.0003	−.0002
21	.0146	.0152	.0006	.0010	66	.0009	.0007	−.0003	−.0002
22	.0144	.0142	−.0002	.0010	67	.0007	.0006	−.0001	−.0002
23	.0138	.0133	−.0006	.0009	68	.0008	.0006	−.0002	−.0002
24	.0130	.0124	−.0006	.0009	69	.0007	.0006	−.0001	−.0002
25	.0123	.0115	−.0007	.0008	70	.0006	.0005	−.0001	−.0002
26	.0127	.0108	−.0019	.0007	71	.0005	.0005	−.0000	−.0002
27	.0119	.0101	−.0019	.0006	72	.0002	.0004	.0002	−.0001
28	.0108	.0094	−.0015	.0005	73	.0005	.0004	−.0001	−.0001
29	.0109	.0088	−.0021	.0004	74	.0004	.0004	−.0000	−.0001
30	.0093	.0082	−.0012	.0004	75	.0004	.0004	−.0000	−.0001
31	.0090	.0076	−.0014	.0003	76	.0003	.0003	−.0000	−.0001
32	.0078	.0071	−.0007	.0003	77	.0002	.0003	.0001	−.0001
33	.0071	.0066	−.0005	.0003	78	.0004	.0003	−.0001	−.0001
34	.0067	.0062	−.0005	.0002	79	.0004	.0003	−.0001	−.0001
35	.0065	.0058	−.0007	.0002	80	.0003	.0003	−.0001	−.0001
36	.0062	.0054	−.0008	.0002	81	.0002	.0002	.0000	−.0001
37	.0065	.0050	−.0015	.0001	82	.0003	.0002	−.0000	−.0001
38	.0058	.0047	−.0011	.0001	83	.0002	.0002	.0000	−.0001
39	.0053	.0044	−.0009	.0001	84	.0002	.0002	.0000	−.0001
40	.0051	.0041	−.0010	.0001	85	.0001	.0002	.0001	−.0001
41	.0051	.0038	−.0013	.0000	86	.0001	.0002	.0000	−.0001
42	.0045	.0036	−.0009	.0000	87	.0002	.0002	−.0001	−.0001
43	.0037	.0033	−.0004	.0000	88	.0001	.0001	.0000	−.0001
44	.0037	.0031	−.0006	.0000	89	.0001	.0001	−.0000	−.0001

An examination of the data in Table 6 reveals that for the most part the highest proportions are at the lower levels with a steady decline in the proportional distribution as one moves from level one to ninety. There are some regular exceptions to this, however. In order to assess the effect of irregularity on error and banding, the data was smoothed by reordering the proportional distributions from highest to lowest. The data was analyzed in both its un-smoothed original form and in its smoothed form, and the level mean error and the absolute mean error were calculated for each level. This error measure allows one to determine if the error is relatively well distributed above and below the mean. Hypothesis 4, predicts a fairly regular occurrence of some higher frequencies out of order slightly modifying the basic trend of decline. This tendency is referred to as a banding effect. A comparison of the absolute mean errors of the smoothed and unsmoothed data reveals the error attributable to this banding effect. If the banding effect is functioning, it was thought that the absolute mean error should be higher in the unsmoothed data set (Table 7). As predicted, the absolute mean error is greater in the unsmoothed data set.

TABLE 7

Comparison of absolute mean error in smoothed - and unsmoothed distribution of intensity shifts

Actor and Half Characteristic	Female-Female		Male-Male		Male-Female	
	Smoothed	Un-smoothed	Smoothed	Un-smoothed	Smoothed	Un-smoothed
	Error	Error	Error	Error	Error	Error
Actor 1 Half 1	.0004	.0015	.0014	.0019	.0007	.0010
Actor 1 Half 2	.0008	.0014	.0014	.0018	.0012	.0013
Actor 2 Half 1	.0007	.0011	.0019	.0022	.0007	.0011
Actor 2 Half 2	.0006	.0013	.0020	.0023	.0007	.0010
Unit of Measure:	.0004		.0004		.0002	

Note: Unit of measure represents the single occurrence of one shift.

The banding effect, the tendency for certain loudness intervals to be used more frequently than others, accounts for a portion of error which can be explained but not readily eliminated. The absolute mean error is higher for the male actor, suggesting that his intensity pattern is somewhat more variable than that of the female participant.

Since the absolute mean error is larger for the male actor, logically one would predict the absolute mean error to be largest in the male-male dyad. The data indicates this to be the case. The absolute mean error is lowest in the female-female dyad structure. There is a reduction in the absolute mean error of the male actor as one moves from the male-male dyad structure to the male-female dyad structure. However, the male still has the highest absolute mean error. This suggests that the proportional distribution of intensity intervals is affected by both sex and dyad sex structure. The fact that the male actor has the most variable pattern in both the male-male and male-female dyad structures suggests

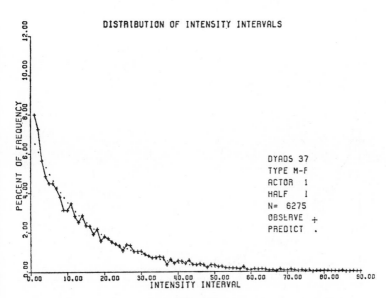

Figure 2

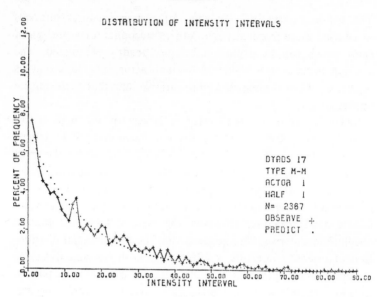

Figure 3

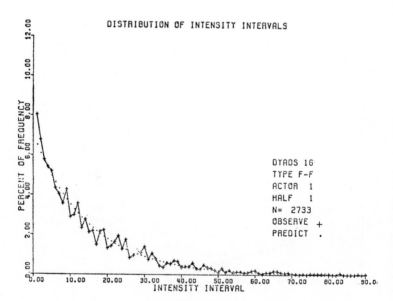

Figure 4

that sex is certainly creating some of the differences. However, if sex were the only factor creating this difference, the absolute mean error for the male should be the same in both the male-male and male-female structures. The tendency for this error to become smaller suggests that the male actor is attempting to adjust to the intensity pattern of his female partner. Consequently it appears that both unmixed and mixed sex dyad structure are significant factors.

In addition to developing the mathematical function, a plot routine was executed which offers a pictorial representation of the proportional distributions. Figures 2, 3, and 4 illustrate this function for each dyad structure. The graphs of the proportional distribution of intensity shifts exhibit a decreasing exponential trend. The banding effect is also clearly represented in the graphs. Thus it was desirable to determine if additional structure evident in the banding could be mathematically described as a periodic component.

The frequency of the occurrence of any given intensity shift level may be assumed to be selected from a Poisson distribution. The mean of the Poisson distribution is different for each shift level and is unknown. The standard deviation (square root of variance) of a Poisson distribution is equal to the square root of the mean. Since the mean is unknown, the statistical error in the population of each shift level is taken equal to the square root of the population, as is common practice. If the population is zero, the error is taken to be 1.0. Thus s_i, the error in y_i, the population, is taken to be: $s_i = \max(y_i, 1.0)$.

A weighted least squares fit to the data was made using an exponential function. Using standard methods, the values of A and B were calculated that minimize the weighted sum of squares:

$$S_i = \sum_{i=1}^{n} (Ae^{bx_i} - y_i)^2$$

where: n = the number of shift levels considered
A = the vertical axis intercept

b = the declining distance between any two coordinates by a factor of $e = 2.71828$

x = shift level being considered

y = population within any shift level

The fitted value obtained by this mathematical technique was subtracted from each data point leaving a set of residuals. The residuals are positive and negative numbers of generally decreasing magnitude that contain the remaining structure, if any. In order to adjust the later residuals to a magnitude comparable to the preceding residuals and thus make more obvious any periodic component, the residuals were multiplied by the exponent $-bx_i$, when b and x_i have been previously defined.

At this point two methods of analysis were pursued. First, the autocovariance function, $c(2)$, of these "detrended" and magnified residuals was computed. The autocovariance function can be defined as $r(t) = c(t)/c(o)$

where: $c(t) = 1/n \sum_{i-1}^{n-t} (Y_i - \bar{Y})(Y_i + t - \bar{Y})$

$$\bar{Y} = 1/n \sum_{i=1}^{n} Y_i$$

If the Y_t consists of a sine function plus random noise, the autocovariance function will be a damped sine function plus noises, as shown in Figure 5.

Figure 5

If there is no periodic component, the 'autocovariance function will consist mainly of noise for $t \neq o$. $r(o)$ is unity by definition (Figure 6).

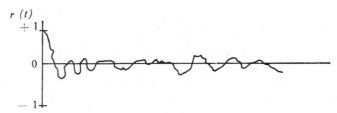

r (t)

$+1$

0

-1

Figure 6

The autocovariance function is limited in that exact statistical tests regarding the significance of the oscillations are difficult to make. Consequently a least squares fit of a general sine function was applied to the modified residuals Y_i:
The error in Y_i is equal to t_i: $t_i = s_i e^{-cb x_i}$ where c is a constant slightly less than unity.
The sum of squares which is minimized in this second fit is

$$S_2 = \sum_{i=1}^{n} \frac{(d \sin (w x_i + \emptyset) - Y_i)^2}{t_i}$$

where: d = amplitude
w = angular frequency
$\emptyset$ = phase

In a nonlinear least squares fit, there may be more than one set of parameters, d, w, $\emptyset$, that give a "local minimum" in S_2. Consequently fits were performed using two starting points for w.

Data analysis reveals that in most cases, the first one or two intensity shift levels lay above the fitted exponential values by two or three times the corresponding s_i. The value of s_i is approximately distributed as a chi-square variable with n-2 degrees of freedom. The approximation arises because the fitted function is nonlinear in the parameter b. Testing the value of s_i on this basis, an acceptable fit was obtained to the exponential in five of the twelve cases ($p > .05$). In the other seven cases, the distribution s_i is exponential, but the chi-square probabilities suggest that perhaps there is additional structure. The autocovariance functions were examined for evidence of structure, however none was identified.

A second test using the chi-square was performed in an effort to describe additional structure. Since chi-square variables are additive, the sum of two chi-square variables with $m_1 + m_2$ degrees of freedom respectively equals a chi-square variable with $m_1 + m_2$ degrees of freedom. For this reason the quantity $S_1 - S_2$ can be tested as chi-square variable with three degrees of freedom. If the chi-square probability is small, then the value of S_2 is significantly less than the value of S_1, indicating that there is a significant amount of sine function structure in the modified residuals. This was not found to be the case in any of the proportional distributions. From the data analysis it can be concluded that the proportional distributions of the intensity shift levels are fairly well represented by an exponential function, particularly if the first level is not fitted, and that although there may be further structure, it is not of a simple periodic nature.

The banding effect refers to the occurrence of peak frequencies of loudness intervals preceded and followed by lower frequencies. The mean number of steps between bands shown in Table 8 is extremely stable regardless of sex or dyad structure. The means range between intervals of 3.03 and 3.95 with a standard deviation of 2.00 or less. The bands were represented graphically to determine if certain bands are characteristic of a given sex or dyad structure. However, no consistent pattern was identified.

Scores were calculated to evaluate differences in the banding patterns for actor, half, and dyad structure. If the banding effect were similar for all actors, time periods and dyad structure, small z scores and large probabilities would indicate it. The observed z scores are extremely small thus suggesting no significant differences in banding by actor, half, and dyad structure. The banding pattern is relatively uniform, though not identical for all twelve data sets (Table 9).

Hypothesis five states that the mathematically ascertained variables can be reduced to a smaller number of common dimensions. The question concerned the identification of those variables which were measuring the same attribute. To test the hypothesis, a factor analysis was made for each dyadic structure. In the male-

TABLE 8

Banding effect in three Dyad structures

Actor and Half Characteristics	Female-Female			Male-Male			Male-Female		
	Number of Bands	Mean Band Width	σ	Number of Bands	Mean Band Width	σ	Number of Bands	Mean Band Width	σ
Actor 1 Half 1	25.00	3.56	1.63	26.00	3.23	1.25	24.00	3.63	1.75
Actor 1 Half 2	24.00	3.50	1.61	26.00	3.35	1.27	25.00	3.56	1.70
Actor 2 Half 1	23.00	3.78	1.84	26.00	3.31	1.43	24.00	3.63	1.28
Acotr 2 Half 2	22.0	3.95	2.08	29.00	3.03	1.22	26.00	3.42	1.21

female dyads 84 variables were loaded on thirteen factors. In the male-male and female-female dyads, there were eleven unique factors, suggesting two factors might be associated with sex. Although eleven factors in the homogeneous dyads and thirteen factors in the heterogeneous dyads were found, several of the factors were ambiguous, as was evident in the weak loadings, however, in all three dyadic structures, there were five factors which emerged with a degree of clarity. Examination of the loadings in the heterogeneous dyad structure reveals marked dissimilarities from those found in homogeneous dyads. Factor one, energy, is composed primarily of variables calculated as a function of time and intensity. Factor two, frequency of act emissions, is composed primarily of counts. They are an intensity summation measure of time or speech units. The third factor is primarily amplitude and slope. The fourth and fifth factors has been labeled density and are based primarily on density measures. The additional factors are ambiguous. The factor analysis tends to support the fifth hypothesis.

Hypothesis six states that there is a positive relationship between intensity intervals and time intervals between adjacent syllables. Table 10 indicates the mean intensity interval for shifts up to 5000 millivolts. For all twelve dyadic combinations there appears to be a consistent tendency for the size of the time interval between syllables to increase as the intensity interval increases. The implication in this finding is that the greater the intensity shift is, the greater is the time needed to produce the shift as indicated by Hypothesis 6.

Hypothesis 7 states that there is a significant relationship between gap size and dyadic structure. There was no significant difference between the actor's gap indices in the homogeneous dyad structures The calculated probabilities are far from significant. However, in the heterogeneous dyad structure different results were obtained. This indicates a significant difference between the gap indices of the two actors in the heterogeneous dyad structure, thus supporting the hypothesis. For the examination of intra-actor gaps and the interactor gaps, interactor gaps were grouped into three categories:

z scores for band difference

		Female-Female				Male-Female				Male-Male			
		Actor 1		Actor 2		Actor 1		Actor 2		Actor 1		Actor 2	
		Half 1	Half 2	Half 1	Half 2	Half 1	Half 2	Half 1	Half 2	Half 1	Half 2	Half 1	Half 2
F-F	Act 1 H1 1	1.00											
	H2 2	−0.13	1.00										
	Act 2 H1 3	0.44	0.56	1.00									
	H2 4	0.72	0.82	0.29	1.00								
M-F	Act 1 H1 5	0.13	0.26	−0.30	−0.58	1.00							
	H2 6	0.00	0.13	−0.43	−0.71	−0.13	1.00						
	Act 2 H1 7	0.16	0.30	−0.34	−0.64	0.00	0.15	1.00					
	H2 8	−0.34	−0.19	−0.80	−1.06	−0.47	−0.33	−0.57	1.00				
M-M	Act 2 H1 9	−0.81	−0.66	−1.21	−1.43	−0.91	−0.79	−1.10	−0.56	1.00			
	H2 10	−0.52	−0.37	−0.95	−1.20	−0.64	−0.51	−0.77	−0.22	0.33	1.00		
	Act 2 H1 11	−0.59	−0.44	−1.00	−1.23	−0.70	−0.57	−0.82	−0.31	0.21	−0.10	1.00	
	H2 12	−1.33	−1.17	−1.68	−1.85	−1.40	−1.29	−1.71	−1.18	−0.59	−0.93	−0.76	1.00

z score probabilities

		Female-Female				Male-Female				Male-Male			
		Actor 1		Actor 2		Actor 1		Actor 2		Actor 1		Actor 2	
		Half 1	Half 2	Half 1	Half 2	Half 1	Half 2	Half 1	Half 2	Half 1	Half 2	Half 1	Half 2
F-F	Act 1 H1 1	1.000											
	H2 2	0.865	1.000										
	Act 2 H1 3	0.662	0.583	1.000									
	H2 4	0.520	0.585	0.762	1.000								
M-F	Act 1 H1 5	0.863	0.786	0.758	0.570	1.000							
	H2 6	1.000	0.867	0.668	0.513	0.864	1.000						
	Act 2 H1 7	0.850	0.760	0.732	0.529	1.000	0.852	1.000					
	H2 8	0.732	0.829	0.568	0.291	0.644	0.738	0.576	1.000				
M-M	Act 1 H1 9	0.575	0.518	0.224	0.149	0.633	0.562	0.272	0.581	1.000			
	H2 10	0.608	0.709	0.658	0.229	0.530	0.618	0.553	0.808	0.738	1.000		
	Act 2 H1 11	0.565	0.661	0.680	0.215	0.507	0.575	0.585	0.749	0.818	0.882	1.000	
	H2 12	0.182	0.241	0.089	0.061	0.159	0.195	0.084	0.235	0.563	0.643	0.544	1.000

TABLE 10

Mean intensity shifts

Type	Intensity Interval	Actor 1				Actor 2			
		Half 1		Half 2		Half 1		Half 2	
		Time	N	Time	N	Time	N	Time	N
Female-Female	< 50	.218	1193	.216	1110	.215	958	.219	1034
	50-95	.226	638	.223	675	.225	544	.230	631
	100-145	.232	351	.237	307	.237	275	.241	284
	150-195	.242	186	.240	158	.253	137	.236	176
	200-485	.262	174	.261	179	.268	154	.250	148
Male-Male	< 50	.222	917	.222	946	.227	925	.224	871
	50-95	.227	531	.231	600	.227	506	.231	480
	100-145	.233	344	.235	339	.225	362	.231	338
	150-195	.246	195	.253	202	.242	188	.242	202
	200-485	.268	188	.256	196	.265	226	.254	199
Male-Female	< 50	.221	2639	.223	2451	.222	1989	.222	1759
	50-95	.227	1476	.229	1399	.231	1007	.230	990
	100-145	.236	804	.236	874	.238	496	.236	453
	150-195	.245	426	.242	452	.251	290	.234	240
	200-485	.263	461	.256	487	.260	284	.269	237

Note: Intensity Intervals are expressed in millivolts divided by a factor of 10.

(1) gaps less than or equal to .4 seconds, (2) gaps between .4 and 1.00 seconds, and (3) gaps greater than 1.00 seconds. Table 11 illustrates the distribution of intra-actor gaps, taking .4 seconds as the limit for the natural break in the vocal emission stream. The differences become apparent in intra-actor gaps greater than 1.00 seconds. There is a distinct tendency for the proportion of gaps in this category to increase with the heterogeneous dyad structure (Table 12). Goldman-Eisler found that gap was not related to complexity but to uncertainty of utterances (1968: 32-33, 42, 71). The mean total gap for the female in the homogeneous dyad structure is 58 seconds. For the male actor in the homogeneous dyad structure, the mean total gap is 65 seconds. However, examination of the mean gap for the male in the heterogeneous dyad structure indicates a mean total gap of 75 seconds. The female total mean gap remains relatively stable in the dyad structure. As stated in Hypothesis 7, there does appear to be a significant relationship between gap and dyadic structure.

HESITANCY

Although the gap concept has been discussed in relation to the formal hypotheses, there are some related ideas which should be reviewed. It is significant to note the relationship of the total speech time to the total gap time. Using the index which Goldman-Eisler has labeled hesitancy, we can obtain the ratio of gap time to speech time. The closer this ratio is to 1.00, the more nearly equal are the two time segments. The implication for the bonding process is that bonding increases as this hesitancy ratio decreases. Examining the data, the hesitancy ratio in the female-female dyadic structure is .68. In the male-male dyad structure this ratio is .80, and is highest in the mixed dyad at .86. This would suggest that the loosest bonding is in the heterogeneous dyad. The tightest bonding appears to be in the homogeneous dyads and most specifically in the female-female structure. The female-female structure produces the least gap time and the greatest speech time; the mixed dyad produces the least speech time and the greatest gap time; and the male-male hesitancy ratio falls between these two. Contrary to Goldman-Eisler's findings in analyzing the interview situation (1968: 51), our analysis of equilibrium in terms of speech time indicates an inverse relationship between interactor equilibrium and hesitancy.

MEASUREMENT INDICES

It will be recalled that in attempting to describe each unique mesowave, six indices were developed: slope, amplitude, wave length, area, density, and number of points per mesowave. In utilizing these indices to test the formal hypotheses, one index — slope — failed to establish any clear significance. However, within each dyad in all cases, the mean slope is negative. A mean negative slope indicates that there is a consistent tendency for actors to begin their vocal emissions with greater intensity. Martinet (1962: 32) has suggested that speech organs build tension before vocalization and that the tension tends to relax toward the end of an utterance with a decline in intensity. With the passage of time there is a tendency for the mean slope to become less negative. This is true in all cases except for the female in the heterogeneous dyad structure. The mean slope of the female becomes more negative with the passage of time. In this dyad structure, the male dominates the conversational contact. The increased negative slope of the female may be her attempt to gain a larger time segment in the interaction.

Four of the indices — amplitude, wave length, area, and number of points per mesowave — have been found to be significantly related to the heterogeneous dyad structure. Amplitude, defined as the range in loudness variation for each vocalized syllable, was measured by two methods. Amplitude was calculated as the interval between the highest and lowest loudness in any one mesowave. The mean amplitude in the male-male dyadic structure was found to be 1900 millivolts. The mean amplitude was somewhat lower in the female-female dyad, being 1755 millivolts. An examination of the mean amplitude in the mixed dyad structure reveals a mean

TABLE 11

Intra-actor time gaps by actor and half
(percent)

Time	Female-Female				Male-Female				Male-Male			
	Actor 1		Actor 2		Actor 1		Actor 2		Actor 1		Actor 2	
Interval	Half 1	Half 2	Half 1	Half 2	Half 1	Half 2	Half 1	Half 2	Half 1	Half 2	Half 1	Half 2
$\geqq$.4-1.00	81	91	90	88	84	86	88	87	87	89	88	90
> 1.00	7	5	5	6	11	9	8	9	8	8	10	7
Interrupts	7	4	5	6	5	5	4	4	5	3	2	3

TABLE 12

Intra-actor time gaps by actor and half
(percent)

Time	Female-Female				Male-Female				Male-Male			
	Actor 1		Actor 2		Actor 1		Actor 2		Actor 1		Actor 2	
Interval	Half 1	Half 2	Half 1	Half 2	Half 1	Half 2	Half 1	Half 2	Half 1	Half 2	Half 1	Half 2
< .4	81	87	84	84	85	85	82	84	81	82	87	81
.4-1.00	17	11	14	16	12	13	16	13	17	15	10	17
> 1.00	2	2	2	0	3	2	2	3	2	3	3	2

decline of 80 millivolts for both the males and females. The mean amplitude is 1675 millivolts for the female and 1820 millivolts for the male. Second, amplitude was defined as the maximum intensity interval between adjacent syllables within the mesowave.

The mean wave length for a male in the homogeneous dyad structure was found to be .99 seconds. For the female in the homogeneous dyad, the mean wave length was 1.07 seconds. However, an examination of the heterogeneous structure revealed the reverse pattern. The female's mean wave length decreased to .99 seconds and the male's mean wave length increased to 1.04 seconds. Although the difference may appear small, it is great relative to variance, is statistically significant, and is characteristic of all syllabie strings.

Examination of the mean area for males and females by dyadic structure reveals a similar effect trend. The mean area per emission for the male in the homogeneous structure is calculated to be 5.21 square units. In the female-female structure, the mean area is 4.39. In the heterogeneous dyad structure, the mean area is 4.11 for the female and 5.09 for the male. There appears to be a steady decline in energy investments and a looser bond comparing the homogeneous to the heterogeneous dyad.

The mean number of points per mesowave reveals a pattern similar to that seen in the other indices. The mean number of points per mesowave is 5.44 for the male in the male-male dyad and 5.83 for the female in the female-female structure. In the heterogeneous structure, the pattern is reversed with 5.70 for the male and 5.47 for the female. These findings are consistent with Goldman-Eisler (1968: 17) who indicates that in a situation where speech is most unprepared and speakers least under social pressure, 50 percent of the speech is broken up into phrases of less than three words, 75 percent into phrases of less than five words, 80 percent into phrases of less than six words, 90 percent in less than ten words.

Correlations were run in an attempt to determine the degree of association between these six indices (Table 13). Slope does not appear to correlate with the other variables, but the correlations

TABLE 13

*Correlations of the six mesowave indices
by Dyad structure*

Female-Female

	Actor 1						Actor 2					
	Slope	Amp	WL	Area	Den	Pts	Slope	Amp	WL	Area	Den	Pts
Slo	1.00	-.18	.15	-.07	-.32	.09	1.00	-.15	-.43	-.30	.08	-.35
Amp		1.00	.58	.83	-.35	.58		1.00	.69	.93	.05	.76
WL			1.00	.81	-.71	.99			1.00	.77	-.19	.98
Area				1.00	-.46	.82				1.00	.01	.84
Den					1.00	-.66					1.00	-.13
Pts						1.00						1.00

$r_{.05} = .482$

Male-Male

	Slope	Amp	WL	Area	Den	Pts	Slope	Amp	WL	Area	Den	Pts
Slo	1.00	.10	.13	-.19	-.11	.13	1.00	-.09	-.14	-.20	-.37	-.17
Amp		1.00	.33	.63	-.08	.36		1.00	.24	.54	-.07	.23
WL			1.00	.63	-.26	.96			1.00	.83	-.50	.98
Area				1.00	.00	.70				1.00	-.38	.79
Den					1.00	-.02					1.00	-.37
Pts						1.00						1.00

$r_{.05} = .468$

Male-Female

	Slope	Amp	WL	Area	Den	Pts	Slope	Amp	WL	Area	Den	Pts
Slo	1.00	.01	.17	-.05	-.26	-.07	1.00	.03	-.25	-.27	.24	-.25
Amp		1.00	.49	.79	-.24	.47		1.00	.47	.73	-.29	.52
WL			1.00	.78	-.67	.97			1.00	.83	-.70	.97
Area				1.00	-.46	.77				1.00	-.48	.88
Den					1.00	-.57					1.00	-.55
Pts						1.00						1.00

$r_{.05} = .325$

between amplitude, wave length, area, and number of points per mesowave are positive. Density is the only factor which consistently correlates negatively with other variables, pointing to an inverse relationship. Density was calculated for both monotonic and polytonic mesowaves. In the monotonic mesowaves, the mean density was 6.5 syllables per second with a standard deviation of 1.5. In the polytonic mesowaves, the mean density was 5.3 syllables per second with a standard deviation of .9, contrary to Gottschalk (1968: 17). Goldman-Eisler (1968: 23) states that syllable rate stabilizes with an increase in the speech unit. Our findings are consistent with those of Goldman-Eisler.

Examination of these statistics reveals how the dyadic structure affects the interpersonal contact. The theoretical implications regarding the bonding process have suggested that a decrease in energy investments, an increase in gap time, and an equilibrium ratio diverging from 1.00 are obstructions to the bonding process. The reasoning is that these types of factors decelerate the transfer of information which creates the bonding. The fact that these various findings have occurred consistently in the heterogeneous dyad structure and rarely in the homogeneous dyad structure suggests that there is an element of commonality among the bonding factors.

We were interested in determining the effect of the passage of time upon the interpersonal contact. In all three dyadic structures, the mean amplitude and density reveals a decline from the first to the second temporal half (Tables 2 and 3). For wave length, area, and number of points per mesowave, this same trend is evident in the male-female dyad and the female-female dyad. In the male-male structure the pattern on these three indices is reversed. There is a slight increase in the wave length, area, and number of points per mesowave. These findings must be viewed in conjunction with the statistics on the summation area by halves and the mesowave count by halves. In all three dyad structures there is an increase in these two measures by halves.

In addition to observing the differences in the vocalization patterns by halves, a series of correlations were obtained measuring the degree of association between any given actor's responses in the first and second half (Table 14). As was expected, these correlations are positive and extremely high. This would suggest that there is a high degree of stability in an actor's speech patterns and

TABLE 14

*Correlation of an actor's responses
between halves*

Index	Female-Female		Male-Male		Male-Female	
	Actor 1	Actor 2	Actor 1	Actor 2	Actor 1	Actor 2
Slope	.909	.745	.878	.391	.829	.813
Amplitude	.954	.898	.885	.973	.943	.933
Wave Length	.876	.767	.961	.939	.815	.770
Area	.953	.919	.960	.993	.955	.895
Density	.861	.940	.900	.792	.918	.913
Points	.897	.782	.964	.976	.851	.805
	$r_{.05} = .482$		$r_{.05} = .468$		$r_{.05} = .325$	

in the related indices. In establishing the guidelines for extracting the stress point, a minimum intersyllable interval of .12 seconds is established, based upon published research on speech rates. In the male-female dyads and the male-male dyads, the predominant intersyllable time interval appears to be .18 seconds, suggesting that the minimum limit was adequate. However, in the female-female dyad, a bimodal pattern is observed. Two predominant intersyllable time intervals occur: .14 and .20 seconds. The fact that a unimodal pattern emerges in the male-female and male-male dyads and a bimodal pattern emerges in the female-female dyads deserves some consideration. The fact that the bimodal pattern disappears in the female's speech in the mixed dyad is noteworthy. The implication is that within the female-female dyads, the participants have two rates for transferring messages.

Interactor and intra-actor gaps have been analyzed separately. The termination of a mesowave has been defined as a gap of .4 seconds or the gap occurring with a change in speakers. The selection of .4 seconds was based upon research publications in the area of speech rates. Support for this criteria can be found by examining the frequency distribution of various gap sizes (Table 15). Two natural breaks appear to occur. One is a short gap where

TABLE 15

Frequency distribution of interactor gaps

Seconds	Female-Female				Male-Female				Male-Male			
	Actor 1		Actor 2		Actor 1		Actor 2		Actor 1		Actor 2	
	H1	H2	H1	H2	H1	H2	H1	H2	H1	H2	H1	H2
.02	26	26	42	33	49	50	67	53	22	17	26	15
.04	17	24	19	18	48	32	43	50	20	11	15	12
.06	14	10	17	9	40	29	28	30	13	12	21	14
.08	11	8	9	10	24	34	32	35	13	8	12	16
.10	8	9	11	8	33	16	19	29	12	9	14	7
.12	9	7	6	8	31	23	21	24	7	5	7	9
.14	13	11	12	6	12	27	19	19	10	8	10	6
.16	2	3	3	2	18	17	13	9	7	4	11	5
.18	7	7	2	2	6	7	7	5	4	5	6	3
.20	1	0	4	2	12	10	8	4	3	2	7	2
.22	5	0	4	1	7	10	4	5	3	2	4	1
.24	2	1	1	3	4	3	1	5	3	0	1	4
.26	0	0	0	0	3	3	2	0	1	2	1	0
.28	2	1	0	0	2	1	0	2	2	0	3	1
.30	0	0	2	0	2	1	1	0	1	0	2	0
.32	1	0	0	0	2	1	0	0	1	1	0	0
.34	0	0	0	0	1	0	2	0	1	1	0	0
.36	0	0	0	0	1	0	0	0	0	1	0	0
.38	0	0	0	1	0	0	0	0	1	1	0	0
.40	14	9	8	9	16	23	30	14	8	11	7	5
.46	10	3	8	6	16	13	14	12	8	3	5	4
.52	3	3	3	5	7	5	15	10	4	6	4	0
.58	4	0	1	3	2	3	8	5	3	2	3	5
.64	1	1	5	4	3	4	6	4	2	2	1	3
.70	3	3	1	2	3	2	6	4	3	2	0	0
.76	3	0	3	0	1	4	2	1	3	0	1	1
.82	2	4	0	0	3	3	3	0	1	1	0	1
.88	1	0	0	0	2	2	2	2	2	0	2	2
.94	1	0	1	0	1	3	1	1	2	1	0	1
1.00	0	0	1	1	4	6	1	4	0	1	1	4
1.10	2	1	1	0	3	2	3	1	2	1	1	0
1.20	0	0	0	0	2	1	2	2	0	0	0	1
1.30	0	0	1	0	2	0	0	2	1	0	0	1
1.40	0	1	0	0	0	1	0	1	0	0	1	0
1.50	1	0	0	0	0	0	1	1	0	1	0	0
1.60	0	0	0	0	1	0	0	0	0	0	1	0
1.70	0	0	0	0	0	1	0	1	0	0	0	0
1.80	0	0	0	0	1	0	1	1	0	0	0	0
1.90	0	0	0	0	0	0	2	0	0	0	0	0
2.00	0	0	2	0	1	0	0	1	0	1	2	0

termination of one actor's speech results within .06 seconds of the preceding stresspoint from the other actor. The other is a natural break of .4 seconds.

LIMITATIONS OF THE INTENSITY ANALYSIS

The important factor to keep in mind is the stability of the pattern which is emerging. The fact that the differences consistently occur in one type of dyad structure suggests a relationship to bonding. If, on the other hand, the established six core properties distributed randomly among the three dyadic structures, there would be considerable doubt concerning their relation to conversational bonding. The consistency and stability of the findings suggests some support for the bonding model. It would be relevant to replicate the intensity considering other differentials in two categories. The first category includes differentials which may act as inhibitors, such as race, social class, education, and age. The second category includes modifier differentials such as transaction, message sending, allocation, social organization, and problem solving. The present discussion appears to be a first step in an effort to study the conversational bond from the perspective of vocal intensity. Human interaction is a complex phenomenon which includes both verbal and nonverbal behavior, both structure and content. Though the research under consideration deals only with the structure of verbal behavior, the significance of other perspectives is recognized.

The intensity research has many limitations. If the sample is defined in terms of the subjects who performed, the study is based on a limited analytical sample. A replication of this study could expand the number of subjects involved and the number of dyads recorded while at the same time controlling for inhibitor and modifier variables. However, it should be stressed what is being studied is vocalization patterns. Therefore, the sample can also be viewed in terms of each unique vocal utterance in which case the sample is well extended.

A second limitation is the total length of each vocal interaction. The literature indicates a variety of opinions regarding the ideal length of an interactional contact. Some authors argue that weeks or even months must pass before characteristic patterns of behavior are revealed. Others contend only a fractional portion of time is necessary. Birdwhistell (1952) and Pittenger, Hockett, and Daneby (1960) maintain that characteristic patterns of interaction are revealed within a few minutes or less.

A third limitation of the study is the nature of the interactional contact. We have been primarily concerned with vocal patterning in spontaneous or natural interaction. There may be differentiated "thresholds" for interacting within given communicative environments specifically for the processing of given communications. Therefore it is not assumed that communication which is predominantly hostile, deceptive, demeaning, etc., is similar in all respects to communication which is spontaneous and mutually supportive. The research under consideration does not attempt to generalize all interactional situations.

A fourth limitation is the laboratory setting in which the research was conducted. Specifically, one must consider the influence or lack of influence of the subject's awareness of being observed. The literature considers both perspectives. The current research effort concurs with Lennard and Bernstein (1969) who argue that the experimental approach to the study of "natural" interaction should receive more encouragement.

Our method of studying verbal interaction through intensity has deviated from the traditional research approach in sociology. Though this might be considered a limitation, more probably it is an advantage as an effort to expand research applications through somewhat innovative techniques, and may help to describe learning as a creative process. The data suggests that intensity variation is an important variable in the dyadic contact and that this importance can be evidenced as time progresses. The evidence suggests a real relationship between intensity and variable bonding implicit in the transfer of information.

According to Goldman-Eisler (1968: 4),

What seemed the most promising aspect of measuring the duration of events in sequence was that by this method objective measurement and quantification of behavior in progress could be achieved without breaking up its continuity and temporal pattern.

In using it I found that it was possible to distill from the spontaneous and free flow of conversation temporal patterns of considerable invariance.

She concludes that there is more information to be got out of acts of speakers than the verbal content of the linguistic product. It is hoped that the value of this technique can be recognized and implemented in further research dealing with the communication process.

4

VOCABULARY ANALYSIS

1. THE VOCABULARY LIST

The individual word is the basic element in verbal communication. Standing alone, the individual word has its broadest range of meanings and provides the speaker the broadest range of alternatives in the use of a particular word. The five hundred most frequently used words have an average of 28 dictionary definitions according to the *Shorter Oxford Dictionary* (Fabrin 1968: 27). Words vary in degrees of definition. Words with only one definition are of the first degree of definitiveness and are not dependent on context or modification to convey meaning. The second degree of definition is words having two meanings. Further degrees of definition correspond to further specific meanings for a particular word. Words used in syntactical combination produce modification and restriction in the range of meanings and permit a wide variability in the degree of specificity or generality. The vocabulary list implies the limits to which the words could have been used.

The question of what a word means is generally satisfied by offering an alternate word thought to have the same reference. If an effort is made to offer additional alternatives for the meaning of a particular word, it soon becomes apparent that the additive alternatives become more remote from the exact meaning of the original word. It would appear logically that no alternative word is identical in meaning to the word being defined. In general each word has some element of meaning which is unique to itself and adequately expressed only by itself. Any alternative approximation of the word is necessarily less adequate for defining its meaning.

Language-in-use has served extensively as a basis for evaluating social and personal characteristics in psychological, anthropological, and sociological investigation through pencil and paper tests, questionnaires, interviews, direct observation, and personal documents. In recent years, more attention has centered on sociolinguistics (Grimshaw 1969: 312), the process of verbal interaction (Bales 1970), and the generation of social roles through speech (Bernstein 1964: Goffman 1961). Bernstein notes, for instance, that "If ... the communication system which behaviorally defines a given role is speech itself, it should be possible to distinguish critical roles in terms of the speech forms they regulate" (1964: 255). And the problems of resolving the implications of the speech process are not simple. There is a disagreement about what the word, the basic linguistic unit, is. Osgood states that "no generally accepted and satisfactory definition exists, and some linguists deny the validity of the word altogether, relegating it to folk linguistics" (1965: 66). Yet the word is accessible as a discriminable element in both oral and written word sequences, and the want of an acceptable definition need not inhibit research effort.

In the present context we define the vocabulary list as the alphabetically ordered set of words and word-like utterances emitted by a speaker in simple conversation. The vocabulary includes basic words and their variants, such as variation in number and tense, in conventionalized spelling, word fragments, proper names, laughter conventionalized as an exact series of "ha's", space fillers conventionalized as "ah" and "mm", and throat clearing conventionalized as "ghm". All of the variant forms have been included in order to provide a veridical vocabulary of oral conversation.

The word provides a consistent unit of measure. The list reflects the conventions of word use and the distribution of variant forms. Vocabulary range and diversity may be exactly identified. It is useful in specifying topical range and in generalizing on the particulars of topical reference. It is possible to identify the distribution of parts of speech, temporal reference, positional reference, and directional and motile references. Although vocabulary lists are often treated as a static list of verbal use, it is possible to reflect dynamic change in conversation through word lists. The gradual development and concentration of interest in conversation can be reflected in a series of word lists for discrete periods of time. Thus the developing concentration of thought and the evolution of a social relation can be graphed through the profile of a time sequence of word lists. A comparison of word lists generated by different actors conversing in similar or complementary roles would permit a definite assessment of the output in terms of precise reference. A loose type of assessment commonly applied in interviews involves a rather impressionistic conclusion based on the vocabulary used by the interviewer. The vocabulary list provides a means of assessing the appropriateness of the verbal outputs to the requirements of the social setting. Thus in the problem where one person is attempting to persuade another to a course of action, as in sales, recruitment, or simple argument, the vocabulary list provides exact evidence of the range of symbols used in the effort. This affords an avenue for evaluating relatively complex interchanges in ordinary social relations. Such a technique also permits comparisons between different cultures and subcultures.

The vocabulary list is readily extracted from the protocol of a conversation and can be computer analyzed without transformation (Paisley 1969: 283). Little is known about how people go about using words. The word count is useful when the analyst is primarily interested in specific references and images (Stone, Dunphy, Smith, and Ogilvie 1966: 97). The word as a unit of measure allows the use of statistical procedures such as factor analysis (Rapoport 1969).

Like many other areas of scientific research, the analysis of extensive samples of vocabulary which emerges in ongoing social relations presents problems of collection, transcription, coding, and condensation. Fidelity to the original verbal stream depends on the quality of recording, the positioning of the pickup device, and ambient noise. Ambiguity is sometimes cited as a serious limitation of a vocabulary list. It may make doubtful the listing of a word and it may present an unresolvable doubt in the listing of homophonous words.

2. INVESTIGATION ON VOCABULARY

Research on vocabulary characteristics has centered primarily on written language (Zipf 1935; Eldridge 1911; Dale 1948). This is due in part to the ready availability of a wide variety of written materials in most modern languages (Carlton 1950: 30). Written language is strongly influenced by formal convention of style and syntax and by editorial requirements. It should therefore be recognized as a specialized form of language which has been carefully cleansed of fragments and grammatical errors. Oral speech manifests the natural regularities and irregularities in the use of language. Therefore the analysis of speech elements relevant to social behavior should be concentrated on typical examples of oral speech, particularly in conversation. Several investigators have contrasted the components of written with oral speech. Comparison of error in written and oral speech has indicated a low negative correlation and reflected a much higher rate of error in oral speech (Lemon and Buswell 1943). A comparison of oral and written themes indicated superior composition in the written form in contrast to the oral delivery (Bushnell: 1930). Fea (1953) found significant differences between oral and written compositions including a greater number of total words, difficult words, and unique words in the oral form.

Children telling stories based on pictures tended to use the same words that they had heard other children use in the same exercise while a few individuals provided a large number of different substantive modifiers. The children contributing new words were thought to reflect the availability of more extensive reading material at home and more extensive contact with adults (Carlton 1950). Smith's (1927) study on the timing of oral vocabulary acquisition indicates that the child's first words are usually interjections or nouns followed at later times by verbs, then modifiers, and lastly connectives with a strong predominance of pronouns. Children at two years of age use verbs, nouns, and adverbs. From three to five years of age, they use verbs and pronouns more frequently. Awareness of vocabulary size is evident in the high school years and has been found to be directly related to class standing and social class (Levin and Stacey 1951).

Rapoport suggests that it is not possible to trace the acquisition of words and their variations in meaning from the start, and that it is therefore necessary to find more abstract ways of describing large scale verbal output (1965: 31). In conversational interaction, there is a continuing mutual awareness between speakers (Psathas 1969: 438). Words reflect both related ideas and the disposition and interest of the speaker in the current social situation (Stone, Dunphy, Smith, and Ogilvie 1966: 5). The one speaker establishes his identity with the other in a process which Denzin calls self-lodging (1969: 924). Self-lodging is indicated by variations in the use of personal names and changes in the forms of address and personal reference. Denzin believes that self-lodging rests on the affective bond between the self and its relevant others and that the affective bond can justify actions based on custom, love, hate, jealousy, or respect. The presence or absence of the affective bond can be evidenced in the types of words occurring within the vocabulary list. Postman found that pleasant words occur three to four times more frequently than unpleasant words in regular word usage (1970: 241). He attributes this frequency of word usage to reinforcing qualities and presents evidence to show that pleasant words are more frequent than unpleasant words (Postman 1970: 241).

One of the most rigorous studies of vocabulary characteristics in oral speech was undertaken by French, Carter, and Koenig (1930) on randomly selected samples of telephone conversations terminating in New York City. The investigators monitored daytime telephone calls of which 89 percent were business calls. The distribution of conversing dyads included (1) two men, 87 percent; (2) two women, 10 percent; and (3) a man and a woman,

3 percent. All common nouns were extracted from a sample of 500 conversations during one week. Verbs were extracted from a sample of 500 conversations during a second week and adjectives and adverbs were extracted from a sample of 500 calls during a third week. Finally, prepositions, conjunctions, pronouns, and articles were extracted from a sample of 150 conversations. Proper names, interjections, profanity, and nonverbal vocalization were excluded. This permitted an analysis of vocabulary characteristics without regard to syntax, content, or the personal relations of the conversants. Of the omitted material, 40 percent consisted of exclamations, interjections, laughter, and profanity; 25 percent consisted of letters and numbers; 20 percent consisted of proper names and titles; and 15 percent consisted of the sound which they conventionalized as "er" (also sometimes conventionalized or "uh" or "ah"). More than 80 percent of the roughly eighty thousand words are monosyllables, and only 2,240 are unique words. As indicated in Table 1, unique words account for only two percent of the total of words used. When variants of the unique words are included there are 2,822 unique words which expands the list by 26 percent of its original total. The pronouns "I" and "you" occur a total of 7,500 times or 9.5 percent of the total words. The vocabulary characteristics described in the Bell Telephone Study are somewhat affected by the fact that the sample is confined to telephone conversations primarily initiated for specialized business purposes. We would therefore expect that conversations sampled under less restrictive conditions might manifest a somewhat broader range of unique words.

Extensive analysis of vocabulary characteristics have been carried out by George Zipf (1935). Drawing on extended samples of written material from many languages, Zipf has attempted to identify regularities concerning word frequency and word length which could be consistently approximated in mathematical form. Zipf believes that the most striking feature of words is their difference in length and he sought to determine the significance of these observable differences (Zipf 1935: 20). His data indicates unequivocally that the longer the length of the word, the less likely it is to be used. In general the length of a word tends to bear an inverse relationship to its relative frequency. The tendency of a decreasing length can result from an increase in relative frequency, Zipf believes, may be tentatively named the Law of Abbreviation (1935: 38). Mandelbrot (1953) has expressed the Zipf Law of Abbreviation as follows:

$$\log p_n = A - B \log n$$
$$\text{given } p_n = P_n{}^{-B}$$

where: n = rank of word in an extended frequency list
 p = proportion
 P = total of all proportions
 A = Y intercept
 B = slope

This formula postulates a trend toward maximizing the average information (in Shannon's sense) which is conveyed by a word by holding the average cost (length) of the word constant (Rapoport 1969: 23). Thus, the more frequently a word is used, the shorter it is likely to be. This function can be plotted as a Zipf curve relating the frequency of occurrence of an event and its rank when the events are ordered with respect to frequency of occurrence (Zipf 1935: vi). He believes that in any extensive sample of connected English, the most frequent word in the sample will occur approximately every ten words and the nth most frequent word will occur approximately once in every 10 n words (1935: xii). Zipf states that there is no cogent reason for believing that the small magnitude of a word is the cause of its high usage, since a speaker selects words not according to length but according to the ideas which he wishes to convey (1935: 29). We can only conclude with Zipf that high frequency of usage has led to shortening of words.

3. GENERATION OF VOCABULARY LIST

The vocabulary lists which we are analyzing here were generated in a series of seventy-four, five minute conversation episodes involving unique pairs of upper level college students. Each recording was transcribed by a team of two persons, including one of the original participants and one nonparticipant for each five minute episode. Having only one participant in the transcriber team was necessary because when both participants attempted to transcribe they became reinvolved in the conversational interchange which seriously impeded the transcription process. One participant was required to establish sure identification of the speaker for each vocal output on the tapes. On four of the recordings, it was necessary to ask the second participant to help identify one or two doubtful passages. All words and portions of words were transcribed in conventional spelling, and literal conventions were applied to nonverbal vocalization such as "ha" for each syllable of laughter, "ah" for the hesitation sound, and "ghm" for throat clearing. This material was transferred to IBM cards and exhaustively rechecked against the audio tapes to reduce error, the primary source of which was typists' omission from the written protocol. A nonparticipant rechecked these protocols against the original tapes to recover omitted material.

With reasonable diligence a team of transcribers can convert a five minute sample of verbal material from the audio tape to manuscript form in ninety minutes. This rate of transcription can be obtained with suitable training and about four hour's experience. Speed and accuracy of transcription is maximized if the tape is played in short segments of no more than about six words, overlapping the preceding segment by one word. Extracting verbal material in longer segments greatly increases the probability of omission and misordering of words and particularly of nonverbal vocalizations since in normal hearing we edit out and ignore such elements. It is also quite common for the verbatim record from the tape to differ considerably from the words the speaker thought he used. It is necessary to replay each segment at least twice when the text is clear and readily intelligible and up to ten times if the text is doubtful. When both speakers talk simultaneously, it is necessary to attend to the two verbal sequences separately. Such material requires extra replayings to separate the overlaid segments but in practice it is not difficult to tune in and listen to each speaker separately.

In the manuscript, entries were made on separate lines for each actor in order to permit accurate sequential representation of simultaneous speech. Regular words were restored to conventional spelling in disregard of elision or slurring of syllables or occasional mispronunciations. Conventional abbreviations were retained as words such as "math" for mathematics and "Rotcy" for R.O.T.C. (Reserve Officers Training Corps). Widely conventional slang expressions such as "yeah", "uh huh" ,and "hu huh" were retained. Verbal fragments are retained in conventional spelling to the degree that the fragments could be recognized; examples include "fam", "sor", "sp", and "poli" and single initial letters which occur from stuttering. Proper names, including compounded proper names, were entered in the vocabulary list as a single word to maintain the correct unit of personal reference. The same principle was applied to place names so that "Dayton, Ohio" would be extracted as a single word if the speaker specified both parts of the reference. Similarly titles were retained with names in a single word such as "Dean Rogers" or "Doctor Smith". Numbers were retained in script form as single words such as "forty-five-thousand" up to twenty characters. Sets of initials used as names were recorded as single words counting one syllable for each vocal syllable identified in the set. This provides a correct syllable count, for example, when recording Greek letters for fraternities. Laughter has been exactly counted by the number of breath explusions entered as the number of syllables emitted.

The verbatim record of the 74 conversational episodes was entered on computer data cards incorporating actor identification codes and character codes for the identification of certain characteristics of speech such as laughter, interjections, fragments, assertions, and questions. Simultaneous speech was entered sequentially but coded for the appropriate actor. Alphabetized word lists with frequency counts for each of the two actors were developed by machine processing for each dyad together with total syllable counts, word counts, and frequency counts for verbal acts. Six master vocabulary lists were developed reflecting three sex structures, including 18 male-male dyads, 17 female-female dyads, and 39 male-female dyads, in two content halves. Proportional frequencies were calculated for all words in the list. Frequency of word usage was recorded by character length and syllable length; total word count, unique word count, and diversity ratios were calculated for each set. The estimate of error in the word list based on an input of 19,749 words is .0014, involving a total of twenty-seven errors all but one of which was correctable.

The analysis of vocabulary was carried out on the IBM 360 Model 65 Computer employing the Fortran and PL1 languages. The vocabulary extraction and alphabetizing was accomplished by a character compositing program (Allen and Accola 1971: 265). The calculation of frequency ratios, statistical tests, and mathematical functions was incorporated into separate programs, and computer programs were prepared for plotting mathematical functions using the Calcomp Plotter. The most extensive program used to extract the master vocabulary list for all 74 dyads required 350 K (350,000 bytes) of core storage analyzed 76,000 in 7.6 minutes or approximately 10,000 words per minute including mathematical calculations. The development of the programs required approximately two hours of computer utilization at an assessed cost of $10.00 per minute.

4. EXPECTED DIFFERENCES IN VOCABULARY

Vocabulary has two basic properties: the first is the extent of the word list, and the second is the frequency of word usage. In general an increase in the length of the word list for a given period of verbal exchange indicates an increase in the variety and richness of information shared. Increase in the number of words without increase in the length word list indicates an increase in the amount of interaction without a corresponding increase in the variety of the content of exchange. This is not simply a characteristic of the actor but rather a characteristic of the interaction. For any mature actor who knows the language, there are important basic differences between vocabulary range and vocabulary usage, which can be pictured in terms of two opposed pyramids. Picturing the frequency pyramid as an upright triangle, a small number of words provide the broad base of the greatest frequencies and the usage of less common words provides progressively smaller frequencies for the higher strata of the triangle. The usage triangle pictured in terms of word frequency gives the impression of a limited vocabulary. The actor's total vocabulary may be represented by an inverted triangle superimposed on the frequency triangle and consisting of an extended base of specialized and unique words with progressively smaller number of more frequently used words. The word pool at the low point of the vocabulary triangle has minimum extent and maximum frequency. The inverted base of the vocabulary triangle contains tens of thousands of specialized words of which some particular elements, although readily accessible, may not be used over a ten year period of verbal interaction until some unique situation calls for it. It is this extended available vocabulary which permits precision, definition, discrimination, and highly particularized information. It is easy to demonstrate that the highly educated and sophisticated actor commands vocabulary not accessible to the uneducated. Professional and technical areas can be identified precisely in terms of such specialized vocabularies. However, the ordinary active adult in any society also has an extensive specialized vocabulary appropriate to his special skills and social functions. Any given sample of a speaker's conversation extending for at least a few minutes would be an adequate representation of high frequency words but only a limited indicator of his total vocabulary.

We define the dictionary of a given conversational sample as a list of all unique character combinations transcribed as words or word equivalents from the audio record. The lowest analytical level for studying the dictionary is the output of the conversational dyad for a fixed period of time identified by actors. The second level of analysis relates to the dictionaries and word totals developed by aggregating some number of samples of conversations.

The total word count refers to the aggregate of dictionary items multiplied by their associated frequencies. A diversity coefficient may be developed by dividing the total number of words into the number of unique words in the dictionary. A diversity coefficient approaching zero indicates a high repetition of a progressively shrinking vocabulary and its reciprocal is equal to the mean number of uses of each word. If the total number of words is controlled, then the diversity coefficients between two conversants can be compared. We may also indicate the coefficient of equilibrium between actors relative both to the dictionary and to the total word count by dividing the larger total into the smaller total. An equilibrium ratio of 1.00 indicates exact balance between two actors while a coefficient approaching zero indicates an extremely unbalanced relation in terms of output between the two speakers.

The following analytical hypotheses are set forth to evaluate differences by structure, sex, and content half. Regarding the equilibrium ratio based upon total words, we expect males to have a greater total than females in heterogeneous dyads reflected by a lower equilibrium ratio in the heterogeneous structure. We expect the word output for males in the heterogeneous structure to be greater than the word output in the male-male structure. We expect the output rate for females in the heterogeneous structure to be lower than the output rate in the female-female structure. Since the initial half of the contact is a period of probing for subject matter, it is expected that there will be more references to the local setting than in the second half. Local setting refers to the recording area, the school, and academic elements associated with it. It is also expected that setting references will be greater in the heterogeneous dyads than in the homogeneous dyads. It is believed that the dictionary will be less extended in the first half than in the second, and that the dictionary for females will be less extended than for males. It is believed that the dictionary will be at a maximum for females in the female-female structure and for males in the male-male structure. The dictionaries for the homogeneous structures will be approximately equal assuming that the range of interest is approximately equal. Based on the expected differences in total word output and dictionary size, it is expected that males will have a lower diversity ratio than females in the heterogeneous structure, that females in the heterogeneous structure will have a larger diversity ratio than in the female-female structure, and that males in the heterogeneous structure will have a lower diversity ratio than males in the male-male structure. We expect a lower dictionary equilibrium in the second half as compared to the first half. This expectation is based on the belief that subject matter will be more diversified in the second half of the conversational episodes.

5. DIFFERENCES IN EXTENT OF DICTIONARY AND WORDS

As has been suggested above in the heterogeneous dyad structure, the males had a consistently larger proportion of the total word output both in the first and second halves of the five-minute contact. In the first half with a total of 19,744 words the male output was 55 percent and the male had the same percentage of the total in the second half with a total of 19,749 words. A similar pattern is manifested when we consider the size of the dictionary. The male makes considerably more specific references, reflecting a somewhat larger dictionary in verbal emissions than the female.

We have suggested that the dictionary in all structures should be smaller in content Half 1 than in content Half 2, as conversation during the introductory stage is somewhat more standardized while in Half 2 we would expect to find more specialized and focused discussion and consequently a broader range of references which suggest a more extensive dictionary. This expectation appears to be consistently supported in all dyad structures (Table 4). Although the difference is proportionately small, the dictionary size represents a more stable measure than the total word count. It is also more suggestive of the relative range of reference. Comparison of the dictionary size for the female in the mixed and homogeneous structures indicates that the dictionary is larger for

TABLE 1

High frequency words for all structures

a	.0213	got	.0027	my	.0038	these	.0010
about	.0058	guess	.0014	nice	.0055	they	.0116
after	.0011	ha	.0024	no	.0039	they're	.0019
ah	.0259	had	.0036	not	.0041	thing	.0016
all	.0039	haha	.0045	now	.0033	things	.0013
an	.0014	hahaha	.0023	of	.0148	think	.0057
and	.0313	hahahaha	.0010	oh	.0062	this	.0069
any	.0015	has	.0010	on	.0063	three	.0010
anything	.0016	have	.0100	one	.0044	time	.0031
are	.0044	he	.0063	only	.0011	to	.0266
around	.0016	he's	.0024	or	.0066	too	.0023
as	.0033	her	.0013	other	.0018	two	.0016
at	.0042	here	.0026	out	.0039	uhhuh	.0086
back	.0013	him	.0020	over	.0021	up	.0023
bad	.0011	his	.0014	people	.0024	very	.0016
be	.0057	home	.0013	pretty	.0015	want	.0018
because	.0034	hours	.0011	probably	.0016	was	.0096
been	.0022	how	.0027	real	.0014	way	.0015
before	.0010	I	.0456	really	.0041	we	.0062
but	.0102	I'll	.0014	right	.0033	well	.0099
campus	.0010	I'm	.0056	say	.0022	went	.0021
can	.0030	I've	.0022	school	.0032	were	.0031
can't	.0014	if	.0049	see	.0031	what	.0068
come	.0012	in	.0156	she	.0021	when	.0031
could	.0014	into	.0016	so	.0064	where	.0016
course	.0016	is	.0087	social	.0013	will	.0012
did	.0029	it	.0180	sociology	.0012	with	.0038
didn't	.0020	it's	.0086	some	.0027	work	.0021
do	.0068	just	.0058	something	.0058	would	.0021
doesn't	.0010	kind	.0013	take	.0012	yeah	.0108
don't	.0071	know	.0149	talking	.0010	year	.0016
down	.0014	last	.0017	that	.0138	years	.0012
first	.0012	like	.0070	that's	.0065	yes	.0020
for	.0062	little	.0016	the	.0302	you	.0317
from	.0032	lot	.0019	their	.0011	you're	.0024
get	.0053	me	.0034	them	.0032	your	.0025
go	.0042	mean	.0042	then	.0039		
going	.0035	mm	.0011	there	.0060		
good	.0027	more	.0019	there's	.0012		

Proportion of high frequency words: .7550
Total words: N = 75,843

TABLE 2

Vocabulary differences by actor pairs

	Male - Female		Male - Male		Female-Female	
	Half 1	Half 2	Half 1	Half 2	Half 1	Half 2
Dictionary						
t	2.29	2.80	−2.08	−.02	.45	1.22
Probability	.023	.006	.040	1.000	.662	.228
Degrees of Freedom	76.	76.	34.	34.	32.	32.
Words						
t	2.74	2.93	−.59	.01	−.28	.85
Probability	.007	.005	.116	1.000	.821	.599
Degrees of Freedom	76.	76.	34.	34.	32.	32.
Diversity Ratio						
t	−3.27	−2.37	1.08	.19	.56	.33
Probability	.002	.019	.284	.975	.582	.764
Degrees of Freedom	76.	76.	34.	34.	32.	32.

TABLE 3

Vocabulary differences by Dyad structure

	M-MM	MM-FF	F-FF
Dictionary			
t	.95	− .37	−2.95
Probability	.657	.719	.004
Degrees of Freedom	148.	138.	144.
Words			
t	1.80	− .54	−2.71
Probability	.070	.590	.007
Degrees of Freedom	148.	138.	144.
Diversity Ratio			
t	−2.72	.41	1.77
Probability	.007	.689	.074
Degrees of Freedom	148.	138.	144.

M = Male in the Male-Female Structure.
MM-FF = Male-Male Versus Female-Female Structure.
F = Female in the Male-Female Structure.

TABLE 4

Dictionary size by content half

Dyad Structure	Half 1	Half 2
Male-Female	2098	2155
Male-Male	1416	1476
Female-Female	1329	1361

TABLE 4a

Occurrence of parts of speech

(Modified from French, Carter, and Koenig, 1930: 294)

Part of Speech	Total	Proportion of Total	Different** Words	Diversity* Ratio
Nouns	11660	.1470	1029	.0882
Adjectives & Adverbs	9880	.1245	634	.0641
Verbs	12550	.1582	456	.0364
Auxiliary Verbs	9450	.1192	37	.0039
Pronouns	17900	.2258	45	.0025
Preps. & Conjs.	12400	.1563	36	.0029
Articles	5550	.0700	3	.0005
Total	79390	1.000	2240	.0024

* The ratio of diversity equals number of different words divided by categorical total.
** Different words exclude variant forms of the same word.

females in the homogeneous structure (Table 3). This is a function of the somewhat higher level of involvement of the female when talking to another female. It was thought that the male's dictionary would be at a maximum in the heterogeneous structure due to the high level of involvement. However, the data indicates that there is little difference in the dictionary for the male under the two conditions (see columns 1 and 2 of Table 3). As was expected, the dictionary sizes between actors in the homogeneous dyad structures are approximately equal. In general the relation gains of the total word count by dyad structure is similar to and consistent with the relations which we have discussed here in comparing dictionary characteristics. This would suggest that dictionary size is strongly influenced by total word output particularly as there is a wider range in topical reference. Although the word count in these samples tends to be about four times as great as the dictionary it appears to reveal no differences other than those manifested in comparison of dictionary size.

The expectation that the diversity ratio for males would be lower than the diversity ratio for females in the heterogeneous dyad structure was also supported (Table 2). The diversity ratio tends to decline as the total number of words increases since it is developed by dividing the total number of words into the dictionary size. Consistent with the prediction that the male's total output would be greater in the heterogeneous dyad structure, it follows that his vocabulary diversity ratio should be lower than that of the female. This effect was not expected between actor pairs in the homogeneous dyads. The predicted effect for the heterogeneous dyad is clearly indicated when replicating the comparison for both content halves. In accordance with the prediction that females would have a higher diversity ratio in the mixed structure rather than in the homogeneous structure, there is some indication that this is the case (Table 3). There is considerably stronger evidence for the hypothesis that males should have a lower diversity ratio in the mixed structure than in the homogeneous structure.

It was expected that the dictionary equilibrium would be lower in the second content half. However, this was not found to be the case except in the female-female dyad structure (t –2.86; p –.007). This indicates that in the female-female structure there is a consistent tendency for the dictionary of one partner to become considerably extended so that there is a greater flow of information from the one partner compensated by an increase in redundancy from the other partner.

6. PRONOMINAL REFERENCE

The employment of personal pronouns as a special research category has been undertaken by several investigators (Grimshaw

1969; Ervin-Tripp 1969: 100-11). Hertzler (1965: 85) defines pronouns as "substitutes for nouns, differentiated further as personal ..., demonstrative ..., interrogative ..., and possessive". The personal pronoun set varies somewhat among cultures, but person, number, and gender are usually incorporated. Most European languages distinguish a singular form for the "second person" (French *tu*, German *du*, Russian *ty*), and some languages have dual personal pronoun elements, such as the Sierra Miwok "thou-and-I" as distinguished from an exclusive "we" and an inclusive "we" (Freeland 1951: 39). The sociological significance of forms of personal reference is examined by Friedrich in connection with socio-economic change in Russia from 1850 to 1950. He notes a decline in kinship terms for more distant consanguineal relatives, and an increase in the use of terms for nonblood relatives (1966: 184). Rommetveit includes personal pronouns among words which "... serve primarily to introduce particulars of the speakers' and hearers' shared cognitive fields into the message" (1968: 197).

Brown, who has worked extensively on various psychological facets of language use and language processes (Brown 1957; 1958; Brown and Bellugi 1964), has also isolated the second person singular and plural pronouns as indicators of power differentials and degrees of intimacy in interpersonal relations in the European languages (Brown and Gilman 1960). Brown and Gilman note that "in terms of Freud's striking amoeba metaphor, the pronouns signal the extension or retraction of libidinal pseudopodia" (1960: 276). Such an idea applies most immediately in the choice of the singular or plural second person pronoun in addressing a single other person on the European continent, where the singular form is conventionally reserved for intimates and subordinates and the plural form is used in addressing superiors and in formal relations. A more diminutive order of social distance is implicit in what Vygotsky calls "egocentric speech" or "the phenomenon of the transition from interpsychic to intrapsychic functioning i.e. — from the social collective activity of the child to his more individualized activity" (1962: 133). The manifest form of such speech is talking aloud to oneself, sometimes treating the self as other and sometimes not. Silent verbalization of this kind is not directly accessible to the investigator, yet it operates as a form of self-address which has a social dimension. Evidence of social displacement between the basic sex identifications indicated in the masculine and feminine pronominal forms is to be found in Garfinkel's account of the trans-sexual passage of "Agnes". Agnes believed that she was "really" a girl, but the surgical, psychological, and social transformation from the rejected male sex to the adopted female sex identification was both complicated and time-consuming. Among other problems, the establishment of normal social relations with friends of both sexes and on the job was perhaps the most challenging (Garfinkel 1967: ch. 5).

The use of personal pronouns in natural conversation constitutes an implicit index of social reference and could provide an elementary topography of the social environment as reflected in the conversational relation. There is some problem, as Psathas notes (1969: 343) in identifying the antecedents of pronouns, but the personal pronoun conveys intelligible meaning even though the antecedent is not specified, and for some general research objectives it is not necessary to sort out pronominal antecedents. Generally the referents of pronouns, if not understood are provided initially, and only as often thereafter as needed. Thus nominal reference is usually at a minimum and pronominal reference is preferred. The general frequency of pronominal reference expressed in ratio form such as a rate per thousand syllables could provide an approximate index of personal reference. For example, the third verse of the White Rabbit's poem has eleven pronouns in twenty-five words (Carroll 1925: 116; cited in Watzlawick, Beavin, and Jackson 1967: 76).

I gave her one, they gave him two, you gave us three or more;
They all returned from him to you though they were mine before.

An excerpt from Goffman (1961: 183) of natural conversation between a nurse and an intern during surgery contains twelve pronouns in fifty-three words. French, Carter, and Koenig (1930) in their verbatim sample of telephone conversations counted

17,900 pronouns in a total of 79,390 words (cited by Zipf 1935:227). Their data yields a proportion of 225 pronouns per 1,000 words. Pronouns were the most numerous of all grammatical categories. Such samples of verbal interchange can be compared on the amount of personal reference by determining the density of personal pronouns in the samples.

Pronominal reference to persons may be ordered in a quasi-linear series if two principles of ordering are applied in sequence: (1) the principle of extension, and (2) the principle of proximity. By the principle of extension a reference to a group of persons is more "extensive" than a reference to one person, and represents a more "distant" application of personal reference. By the principle of proximity, a reference to a person who is logically or categorically more remote from the speaker also represents a more "distant" personal reference. Applying these principles in increasing order of distance from the speaker, it is immediately clear that a speaker's references to himself are the most proximate to the speaker. The second-person position is that with which the speaker is directly engaged in speech, the *included other*, verbally signified by the pronoun "you". The third-person position is the excluded other, a person with whom the speaker in the act of speaking is not directly engaged. Here it is assumed that the same-sex referent is more proximate, and that the opposite-sex referent is more distant. These two types of reference occupy the third and fourth positions in the series. The fifth position is the social group which inferentially includes the speaker. The sixth and final position is the social group which inferentially excludes the speaker. By this reasoning, the personal pronouns may be ordered in a scale of social projection, as indicated in Table 5. The fact that third person plural pronominal forms may have impersonal antecedents effects some contamination of the scale function. A full-text check of ten protocols selected by a table of random numbers from the seventy-four protocols of dyadic conversation disclosed 143 instances of the third person plural pronoun of which 123 (87 percent) had personal antecedents and eighteen had impersonal antecedents.

TABLE 5

Social projection scale by pronominal reference

| | Most Proximate, Male Speaker | | | | | Most Remote |
	1	2	3	4	5	6
Nominative	I	You	He	She	We	They
Accusative	Me	You	Him	Her	Us	Them
Possessive	My, Mine	Your, Your	His	Hers	Our, Ours	Their, Theirs
Reflexive	Myself	Yourself	Himself	Herself	Ourselves	Themselves

Hypotheses

Social projection might be expected to vary by sex of adult actor, by age, by degree of social affiliation, by social class, and by racial identification. Following Parson's differentiation of male and female functions, the male is socialized more in terms of instrumental functions. He is judged in terms of his ability to manipulate objects in the environment for the achievement of instrumentally defined goals. The female is socialized in terms of expressive functions. Her performance skills are less crucial than those of the male, but her expressive qualities of sociability and skills in direct social interaction are crucial (Parsons, Bales 1955: ch. 2). This basic functional specialization would suggest that females should project farther into the social environment and more into the world of persons than would the males. On this basis the following outcomes are hypothesized:

1. Female emitters will manifest more social projection than male emitters.
2. Female dyads will exceed male-female dyads in social projection.
3. Male-female dyads will exceed male dyads in social projection.

When fraternity members are compared to nonfraternity members, it is expected that fraternity members are more concerned with social relations and with persons and groups involved in such relationships. The circle of acquaintances tends to be extended for fraternity members and the frequency of contact among acquaintances is increased through meetings, daily association, and organized athletic and social events. This leads to the fourth hypothesis:

4. Fraternity members will exceed nonfraternity members in social projection.

The basis for predicting social projection in terms of social class is less definite than for sex and social involvement. Social class is defined for students in terms of the social class of the family of origin and depends mainly on the father's occupation and education. Generally, it might be reasoned that as educational and occupational levels increase, the family of origin would tend to have more contacts in the social environment. As a secondary effect, the children maturing in families of higher educational and occupational attainment would tend to share in the more extensive social contacts of such families. Since these effects derive from the father's characteristics and are modified by the mother's influence and by the social orientation of the child, less confidence can be placed in the hypothetical effect of the father's attained social class and the child's ascribed social class on the child's social position. However, the effect should be positive. The fifth hypothesis is:

5. Students from upper middle class homes will exceed students from lower middle class homes in social projection.

For a population of university students, students within the younger age bracket (20-25 years) are more fully incorporated into the student culture than are older students aged 30 years or more, who are more peripheral to student relationships and to student values. Students within the normal age span (20-25 for juniors and seniors) will have more meaningful social contacts in the university community, and will reflect more social projection in pronominal use than will older students. Therefore Hypothesis Six states that younger students will manifest higher social projection than older students. Black students, like older students, are expected to be more peripheral to the predominant student culture of a school where more than 95 percent of the student body is identified racially as white. According to Hypothesis Seven, in conversational exchange within a racially mixed group, it is expected that the white students would have greater social projection than black students.

The hypotheses regarding the difference in age and the difference in social affiliation are supported (Table 6). The predicted differences by sex and by race do not appear, and those hypotheses are not confirmed. The rank difference by social class fails to reach the .05 criterion but this sample had a relatively small social class differential. A retest comparing subjects of working class origin with those of upper middle class origin is needed before a satisfactory assessment of class effect can be made. The same test was applied to dyad sets, making three comparisons among male, female, and mixed dyad groups in all of which the hypothesis of a sex related difference in social projection is disconfirmed.

A tabulation of the rate of pronoun usage per thousand syllables by dyad sex type and by sex of actor was made to evaluate the

TABLE 6

Social projection by age, sex, class, social affiliation and race

Category	N_1	N_2	Z	p
Young-Old	128	20	−1.79	.035
Male-Female	75	73	.51	.192
Low Middle-Upper Middle	43	105	1.35	.088
Fraternity-Independent	62	84	−1.77	.037
Black-White	21	127	.89	.190

* Mann-Whitney Test, direction predicted.

TABLE 7

Rate of pronoun forms per 1,000 Syllables
by sex and Dyad type

	I	Me	He	Him	We	Us	They	Them	You	Pro-nouns*	Sylla-bles
Males	38.9	2.4	8.6	3.6	5.2	.5	10.1	2.1	24.0	95.5	52,966
Females	40.4	2.1	8.8	3.2	5.0	.6	8.8	2.9	27.8	99.7	46,710
Male Dyads	37.1	2.7	10.1	3.9	4.4	.2	10.5	2.1	23.9	93.0	24,339
Mixed Dyads	40.1	2.1	7.7	3.3	5.6	.5	8.7	2.2	26.5	96.7	52,123
Female Dyads	41.2	2.1	9.4	3.2	5.0	.9	10.3	3.7	25.9	101.8	23,214

* Includes forms listed plus possessive and reflexive forms.

relation of nominative to accusative employment for each pronoun offering these forms. From Table 7 it appears that the two sexes are closely similar in the rate of use for all of the listed pronominal forms. The fact that this similarity also holds for the three dyad types suggests some relatively fixed underlying principle governing the distribution of pronominal forms in casual conversation. About 95 percent of self-reference is in the nominative case, as subject or originator of action and about 90 percent of in-group reference ("we") is in the nominative case. For third person references this ratio declines to about 79 percent in the nominative, and 21 percent as the object or receiver of action. These dyads also seem to be dominated by the self-included-other ("I-you") linkage since about 65 percent of all personal pronominal references are in these two positions. Since pronouns make up about 10 percent of all syllables emitted, it seems that sustaining the conversational contact imposes a considerable requirement for explicit verbal reaffirmation through pronomination of both emitter ("I") and target ("you") in the dyadic conversational contact. The emitter renominates himself roughly each 25 syllables, his partner every 40 syllables, and one member of the interacting pair every 15 syllables.

The proposition that self-reference ("I, me") by one partner tends to vary directly with included-other reference ("you") by the other is not supported in this data. Correlations for the male, female, and mixed groups were within the limits of chance variation, and no consistent pattern was apparent. Although first person and second person pronominal references by far are the most frequent, their frequencies tend to vary independently, and hence do not appear to constitute an interactor response pattern. This tends to suggest that first and second person references may be an emitter requirement and probably are not an interaction or exchange requirement.

Slight sex related differences become apparent when factor analysis is applied to the correlation matrixes for male, female, and mixed dyad sets. A 12-by-12 correlation matrix reflecting the six pronominal forms for each of two actors was made for the

TABLE 8

Pronominal associations by factor analysis loadings

Structure:	Factor 1 Act 1	Factor 1 Act 2	Factor 2 Act 1	Factor 2 Act 2	Factor 3 Act 1	Factor 3 Act 2	Factor 4 Act 1	Factor 4 Act 2	Factor 5 Act 1	Factor 5 Act 2
Male-Male	You .82 He .78 She .93	She .90	They .88	They .88	We .53	I .85	I .71	We .91		You .82 He .74
Female-Female	He .91	He .89	She .91	She .82	They .89	I .84	You .85	You .59	We .80	We .58
Male-Female	She .84	She .65	I .86 You .72		We .68	We .79	I .61 They .59	They .84	He .55	He .93

three sex structures, and are shown in Table 8. The five factors identified for the male set tend to link two different pronominal positions. The first and largest factor has high loadings on "you", "he", and "she". The second factor loads on the combination: "they", "they". The third and fourth factors both load on: "I", "we". The fifth factor loads on: "I", "he". These are integrative combinations which indicate clusters of complementary pronominal positions.

The five factors identified in the female sex dyad structure include: Factor 1, "he", "he"; Factor 2, "she", "she"; Factor 3, "I", "they"; Factor 4, "you", "you"; Factor 5, "we", "we". Four of these factors include pronominal pairs which are parallel rather than complementary. Female conversants show pronoun clusters in which usage tends to repeat rather than to complement, to mirror personal reference orientation rather than to integrate it. Female actors then tend to orient in similar and parallel paths in personal reference while male actors tend to orient in complementary or integrative paths in personal reference.

In the male-female set the first six rows 1-6 derive from the male partner and the last six rows derive from the female partner. The first factor of the male-female set loads on (M) "she", (F) "she", which creates a parallel relation in which males and female partners tend primarily to use the third person feminine pronouns "she", "her". The second factor loads on: "I", "you" pronouns by the female partners, which is complementary and integrative for the two sexes. The third and fourth factors load on: (M) "we", (F) "we", and (F) "they", (M) "they" also a parallel type of cluster, manifested by both sexes. The fifth factor loads on: (M) "he", (F) "he". The pattern of personal reference suggests some polarizing of the two sexes and a marked tendency toward the female dyad pattern of parallel pronominal reference.

7. CHARACTERISTICS OF HIGH AND LOW FREQUENCY WORDS

The total word output in the 74 five minute samples of dyadic conversation was 75,843 including all vocalization and conventional words. The dictionary of unique words included 4603 entries or 6 percent of the total word list. When the word lists are separated by first and second actor, the first actors produce a total of 39,823 words and the second actors a total of 36,020. The first actor's dictionary includes 3334 entries and the second actor's dictionary includes 3159 entries. The difference between the first and second actor is attributable to the fact that the second actor is a female in 75 percent of the dyads and there is a similar proportion of males in the first actor position. When dictionaries are separated by actors the diversity ratios are 8 percent for the first actor and 9 percent for the second actor, dividing total words for the actor into the dictionary for that actor.

The high frequency word list is indicative of those words which occur constantly and regularly and afford clues to the makeup of the conversational output. The high frequency word list is also indicative of the range and variety of conventional words, integers, and connectors in the make-up of conversational speech. We have constituted the high frequency word list by including words which have a frequency equal to or greater than two times per thousand words. This listing produced a total of 154 words or 3.3 percent of the total dictionary. The overall mean proportion of total output accounted for by the high frequency word list is 75.5 percent. When we examine the proportion of high frequency words and total output by structure, a marked difference associated with the female sex becomes apparent. There is relatively little variation in this proportion for the males whether they are talking in the homogeneous dyad or the heterogeneous dyad. When the female is talking to the male, high frequency words account for approximately 91 percent of her verbal output, but when females are talking to each other this proportion declines to a mean proportion of .783, as compared to the male mean proportion of .699. Under both conditions the females have a higher proportion of their verbal output under high frequency words, but the effect is much more extreme when the female is talking to a male (Table 9).

We define a supporting word or any word used by the speaker or listener indicating direct affirmation or negation including

TABLE 9
Proportion of high frequency words by structure

	Half 1		Half 2	
	Actor 1	Actor 2	Actor 1	Actor 2
Male-Female	.737	.906	.733	.908
Male-Male	.723	.629	.720	.723
Female-Female	.746	.846	.761	.760

"no" and "huhuh" for negation and "yes", "yeah", "uhhuh", and "right", for affirmation. There is a heavy preponderance of at least four to one of affirmation over negation. The negation appears predominantly in the dictionary form "no". The affirmation occurs primarily (10 to 1) in the ungrammatical alternatives of the words "yes" or "right" (e.g. "yeah" and "uhhuh"). There are also significant sex differences which appear in the usage of supporting words. There is a marked tendency to use more positive than negative supports in the homogeneous structure (12 percent for M-M, and 18 percent for F-F). However, in the heterogeneous structure, the proportion of negative supports increases to about 25 percent of the positive supports. This suggests a better consensus and agreement in the homogeneous dyads.

The high frequency word lists are nearly identical for all dyad structures and content halves. Extraction of high frequency words unique to a given dyad structure produced unique high frequency words in the male-male set (e.g. "football", "fraternity", "game", "job", "try"); eleven unique high frequency words in the female-female list (e.g. "parents", "need", "find", "stay", "says"); and only three unique high frequency words in the male-female list (e.g. "sure", "even", "married"). We have identified nine categories of word types in the high frequency word list of which the great bulk are connectors such as conjunctions, propositions, and auxiliary verbs. Nouns and verbs other than auxiliary verbs account for a small percentage of the words (Table 10). Of the high frequency words, 85 percent are words of one syllable.

It is easy to get the wrong impression from the high frequency

TABLE 10

Word types in high frequency word list

Type	Count	Mean Proportion
Fragments	4	.03320
Supports	7	.02889
Laughter	4	.01036
Pronouns	26	.21765
Connecters	67	.27419
Articles	3	.05290
Nouns	15	.02549
Verbs	9	.03787
Adj. & Adv.	19	.07720
Total	154	.75505

word list since it accounts for a large proportion of total output. More important to the communicative function is the low frequency word list which indicates the wealth and range of ideational and topical reference. We define a low frequency word as one which is used only once in the entire list of 75,843 words. This list of once-only words makes up 53.2 percent of the total dictionary. The elements making up the low frequency word list include fragmentation, 3.0 percent; numbers, 2.5 percent; proper names, 10.5 percent; word variants, 17.5 percent; and unique words, 66.5 percent. The wide distribution of unique words suggests the existence of an extensive reservoir of specialized words which are available to the typical speaker. Highly definitive references to specific persons and places and precisely defined objects are readily available although rarely used. It is the broad range of unique specialized words which gives virtually infinite variety to content in conversation.

8. WORD LENGTH

As noted earlier, Zipf believed that there were regularities in the variations in word length and sought to develop mathematical descriptions of these regularities. Zipf identified an underlying tendency to abbreviate word length in both speech and writing in order to convey the maximum of meaning for a given amount of effort. Word length can be analyzed in terms of the number of characters or the number of syllables. The possible number of one, two, and three character words is severely restricted when observing the conventions of vowel use in English. Thus there are in English only two one-character words, approximately 50 two-character words, and a rapidly increasing number of words with three or more characters. The frequency plot by number of characters as indicated in Figure 1 is typical of twelve replications by content halves of the various dyad structures. The frequency by character rises to a maximum at the four character word. Analysis of the distribution of character frequencies from four to eleven characters indicates a consistent negative exponential curve which closely approximates the observed values (Table 11). This range was

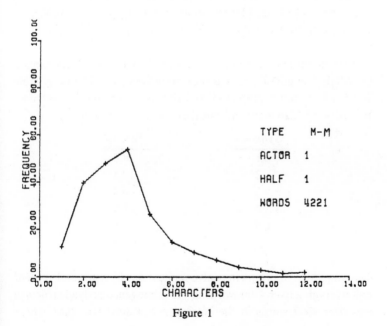

Figure 1

TABLE 11

Word distribution by character length (10,877 words)

Characters	Mean frequency		
	Observed	Predicted	Error
4	63.94	58.81	5.14
5	29.89	35.08	−5.18
6	20.56	20.92	.36
7	13.48	12.48	1.01
8	7.51	7.44	.07
9	4.89	4.44	.46
10	3.15	2.65	.51
11	1.46	1.58	−.12

Exponent X = −.517
Chi-Square 1.53 df 2 p = .40
(Male actor, Half 1, Male-Female set).

selected because it includes the great bulk of conventional words in conversational usage. Zipf's principle of the conservation of effort in terms of word length appears to be operating consistently and powerfully from the maximum frequency of four character words and on.

A similar distribution of frequency results when words are ranked by syllabic length. There is a maximum frequency of one syllable words which rapidly declines with words of more than one syllable. In a total of 4226 words a typical example is as follows:

Syllables	*Percent*
1	78.8
2	14.1
3	4.4
4	1.9
5	.6
6	.1

The same pattern occurs in twelve replications by actor and content half averaging over 4500 words in the homogeneous dyad structure and over 9000 words in the heterogeneous dyad structure. These results are similar to those found in the Bell Telephone Study (French, Carter, and Koenig 1930). An exponential curve was fitted to this distribution using the least squares technique. The basic pattern of distribution of frequency by syllables is illustrated in Figure 2. The chi-square test was used to evaluate the difference

SYLLABIC WORD LENGTH

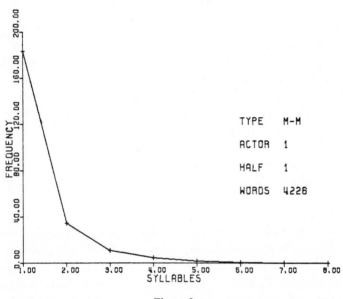

Figure 2

between the observed and predicted curve based on the exponential function. A declining value of chi-square indicates an increasing probability that the two curves are identical within the limits of chance variation. The high degree of similarity among the exponents of the curve and the low values of chi-square as shown in Table 11 over the twelve replications indicate that this is a highly stable and consistent pattern of decline of the frequency of words by word length when measured both by syllable length and character length. These distribution functions on word length provide strong support for Zipf's principle of the conservation of effort in the use of words. This is not to suggest that the shortest possible alternative is always selected but rather that there is a constant tendency to use the shortest alternatives consistent with the objectives of the speaker.

9. APPLICATIONS OF VOCABULARY ANALYSIS TO THE CONVERSATIONAL BOND

The degree of bonding between partners in the conversational dyad is reflected in various characteristics of the vocabulary which they generate. Conversational bonding is defined as an ongoing word-by-word social conjunction between two communicators who develop a consensus of mental experience. This does not necessarily mean agreement but rather the sharing of a common experience. We have hypothesized that bonding would be greater in the homogeneous dyads due to the wider range of shared values and experiences. Vocabulary analysis has provided support for this hypothesis in six different applications. First, the supports, defined as simple positive and negative words, were found to be more frequent in the homogeneous dyads (Table 11). In the heterogeneous dyads, along with a decline in the net number of supports, there was a marked relative increase in the proportion of negative supports. We interpret both of these effects to indicate a decrease in bonding in the heterogeneous structure since supports facilitate the emission of another assertion and seem to increase the sharing experience.

The second effect relating to bonding is the more diverse vocabulary which we have identified in the homogeneous sex structures. The more restricted vocabulary in the heterogeneous structure suggests that less information has been shared, and hence that there is less bonding. Third, the total word output of the female participant decreases consistently as one moves from the homogeneous female-female dyad to the heterogeneous male-female dyad. The female shares better with another female. This appears to be a one-sided effect since a similar effect does not occur when we compare the male in these two situations. Fourth, as a consequence of this difference, the word equilibrium between partners for both homogeneous structures is higher than the word equilibrium between partners in the mixed structure. Fifth, this same equilibrium difference may be identified in the dictionary equilibrium. A suggested explanation for this difference is that the male, by convention, has preference in topic selection and that he selects topics of interest to himself, disregarding the real interest of his female partner. The female will probably have less interest, less knowledge, and less sensitivity to the content of the male partner's verbal output. On the other hand, the female is far less likely to force one of her specialized interests on the male partner; this may in part account for the differences in vocabulary use. The sixth difference, relating to pronoun use, is much more difficult to interpret. We do not believe that the complementary and parallel use of pronouns sets directly relates to interpartner bonding. The pattern of pronoun use, whether it be complementary or parallel, is established by the partner who follows and the actor with the smaller output is essentially in the following position. This would account for our observed results of parallel use of pronouns being characteristic of the heterogeneous structure.

There are an indefinitely large number of specialized applications of vocabulary analysis for assessing social elements in conversation. Social elements, such as persons, collectivities, and kindred, can be precisely identified and discriminated if the relevant vocabulary characteristics are sufficiently well known and understood. The professional or the in-group member is recognized and validated as such by virtue of the specific vocabulary which he uses. Gradations of professional quality and adequacy may be established in part by vocabulary analysis. The distribution and frequency of kinship terms can provide a basis for analyzing the relative position and relations between persons in intimate groups. Gradations of intensity and meaning in oral vocabulary can be indicative of substrate factors which are important in analyzing social orientations and social relations. The variation and frequency in the use of superlatives and comparatives indicates relative shifts by the

TABLE 12
Affirmation and negation by sex structure
(Proportion of total words)

	Male-Female Half 1		Male-Female Half 2		Male-Male Half 1		Male-Male Half 2		Female-Female Half 1		Female-Female Half 2	
Total Words	10875	8853	10928	8822	4230	4923	4649	4646	4404	4514	4737	4262
Negation												
Huhuh	.0001	.0001	.0001	.0000	.0000	.0000	.0000	.0000	.0005	.0002	.0000	.0002
No	.0040	.0060	.0037	.0048	.0028	.0026	.0032	.0003	.0036	.0038	.0042	.0056
Affirmation												
Right	.0042	.0050	.0037	.0048	.0019	.0018	.0029	.0024	.0032	.0031	.0011	.0014
Uhhuh	.0066	.0086	.0043	.0053	.0092	.0077	.0069	.0071	.0161	.0162	.0165	.0185
Yeah	.0075	.0092	.0092	.0167	.0142	.0122	.0148	.0142	.0123	.0111	.0089	.0082
Yes	.0023	.0029	.0024	.0027	.0024	.0033	.0007	.0009	.0020	.0024	.0008	.0007
+	.0204	.0254	.0196	.0205	.0277	.0260	.0252	.0245	.0309	.0299	.0262	.0277
−	.0040	.0061	.0038	.0048	.0028	.0026	.0032	.0030	.0041	.0060	.0042	.0059
Total	.0244	.0315	.0234	.0253	.0305	.0286	.0284	.0275	.0350	.0359	.0304	.0336

TABLE 13

Incidence of affirmation and negation

| | Male-Male | | | | Female-Female | | | | Male-Female | | | |
| | Half 1 | | Half 2 | | Half 1 | | Half 2 | | Half 1 | | Half 2 | |
	M1	M2	M1	M2	F1	F2	F1	F2	M	F	M	F
Affirmation												
Right	.0019	.0018	.0029	.0024	.0032	.0031	.0011	.0014	.0042	.0050	.0037	.0048
Uhhuh	.0092	.0077	.0069	.0071	.0161	.0162	.0165	.0185	.0066	.0084	.0043	.0053
Yeah	.0142	.0122	.0148	.0142	.0123	.0111	.0089	.0082	.0075	.0092	.0092	.0017
Yes	.0024	.0033	.0007	.0009	.0020	.0024	.0008	.0007	.0023	.0029	.0024	.0027
Total Affirm	.0277	.0260	.0253	.0246	.0336	.0328	.0273	.0288	.0206	.0255	.0196	.0245
Negation												
Huhuh	.0000	.0000	.0000	.0000	.0005	.0002	.0000	.0002	.0001	.0001	.0001	.0000
No	.0028	.0026	.0032	.0030	.0041	.0039	.0042	.0058	.0040	.0060	.0037	.0048
Total Negate	.0028	.0026	.0032	.0030	.0046	.0041	.0042	.0060	.0041	.0061	.0038	.0048

speaker and suggests level of interest. Profanity, if selective and sharply focused, indicates the level of stress and the feeling tone of the speaker. The different orientation of profanation toward religious objects, parental objects, or somatic objects indicates variation in the underlying concerns of the profaner and the quality of social relations between social conversants. The use of absolutes in assertions indicates rigidity and a lack of discrimination associated with a poor aptitude for social adjustment. Such words as "definite", "never", "always", and "absolutely" illustrate the employment of absolutes.

Vocabulary sets relating in general to survival or security also afford indicators of the speaker's basic orientation and the quality of his bonding into a social relation. Variation in the hypochondriac's pessimistic expressions involving somatic functions, danger, pain, and death have a direct relation to the quality of his associations with others. Frequent reference to sexual and reproductive functions is also closely related to quality and the kind of association which the speaker reflects with both his own and the opposite sex. The vocabulary of the alcoholic gives extensive evidence of the underlying idea of assault or destruction on the body using such terms as "shot", "slug", "belt", and "being smashed", "soused", "bombed", and "plastered". In so far as these terms have a specific orientation it is away from the social bond and toward a kind of social isolation. The emergence of the baby vocabulary, particularly with the first born of the family affords a gauge of the concentration of family concern with the use of such terms as "love", "cute", the baby's name, "feed", "bath", "bottle", "crib", "Mama", and "Daddy".

The nature and quality of social processes is indicated in various ways by the manifest vocabulary. The range of information is implicit in the diversity of the vocabulary. The variety and definitiveness of nominal reference is a huge factor in such assessment. Discrete indicators of the persuasion process could be identified by such terms as "you know", "surely", "obviously", and others. Disputation could be evaluated in terms of the use of negatives, redundancy, and variation in pronominal reference to the self and the partner. Further conjectures may be made regarding the social process of dramatization in speech. Dramatization may be indicated by variation in the different forms of laughter, the variety of action verbs, and variations in temporal and spatial reference.

5

SOMATIC BEHAVIOR

THE RANGE OF SOMATIC BEHAVIOR IN CONVERSATION

The actions included in the conversational encounter extend well beyond the vocalization process. Each actor uses his whole body in a complex pattern of related actions in projecting his ideas and in sharing them with his partner. The complex and highly definitive elements of conversation must be carried by the verbal stream. However, the elements of somatic behavior modify and accentuate the vocal sequence. Movements of the body, limbs, and face are a varying, but continuing concomitant to verbal emission. Some of these actions are intentional and are used as communicative gestures. However, the majority of this massive stream of somatic behavior is unconscious on the part of the emitter though it may reveal things which he has no intention of communicating. Actions which could be taken as cues are not always noted by the partner. This total stream of verbal and somatic action is so rich that neither participant can be totally aware of details and their mutual implications. It should also be noted that the many elements of action are emitted in a rapid stream, many simultaneously so that it is difficult and distracting to attempt to interpret all of them.

Some somatic behavior, although not communicative, is associated with the requirements of conversation. For example, one usual requirement is to position oneself so that he is at least partially facing higs partner with as much comfort as the physical environment affords. As the conversation continues the onset of fatigue and muscular tension requires the frequent shifting and repositioning of the body. Movements of the hands and shoulders are often used to supplement or sometimes to substitute for verbal communication. The focal source of communicative behavior, however, is the head and particularly the mouth, eyes, and the musculature of the face.

The mouth, in addition to being the source of the stream of speech, also provides the primary means for smiling and contorting. We define the smile as a widening of the mouth and the lifting of the corners sufficiently that it can be recognized by two observers. The mouth may also be involved in contorting the face as in pursing the lips, screwing the mouth to one side, raising the upper lip, or biting the lip. Various other parts of the face may also be used in contortion. We define contortion as any perceptible muscular tension of the face other than smiling. This includes the raising of either brow, wrinkling the forehead, tensing the muscles in the cheek, chin, or jaw, or flaring or constricting the nostrils.

The eyes are the one part of the nonverbal action system which work both as receivers and emitters of information. The dynamics of the ocular shifts are such that the eyes are the most active and the most rapid in signaling and noting variation in the physical environment. We define eye position in two primary states: eyes focused on partner's face or eyes focused elsewhere. The focusing of eyes on partner's face is recognized by the return of one partner's eyes to the base position which the eyes maintain predominantly throughout the contact. The break in eye contact is noted when repeated observations verify the point in the verbal stream when the shift occurred. By this definition the break in ocular contact includes closing the eyes as well as looking away. The fact that the eyes are focused on the partner does not justify the assumption that the individual is taking note of what he sees.

There is an additional category of movements of the entire head which are controlled by the muscles of the neck. Since the head and neck represent a significant fraction of the body weight, much more energy is expended in movements of the head than in ocular and facial movement. The first type of head movement which we will consider is the nodding and shaking of the head, combined under the category of nodding. Our evidence for nodding is a perceptible movement of the head in either the horizontal or vertical plane. A horizontal movement of the head, in our culture, is generally interpreted as a signal of negation and movement of the head in the vertical plane is generally interpreted as a signal of acceptance. Both of these forms of head movement may constitute signs of agreement between partners. The second type of whole head movement includes a considerable variety of tiltings and repositionings of the head away from the vertical axis but not including nods. These movements may be slight head movements or they may extend up to about forty-five degrees from the vertical axis. The head repositioning may be incorporated with a partial turning of the head. The head may also be shifted in a circular motion sometimes referred to as a rolling of the head. We do not claim that the various head movements make any distinctive communication, and for the most part they do not. This can easily be verified by trying to assign meaning to all of the minor head movements of a conversing partner. If head tosses are not a part of the signal system, then what part do they play? We think it is a form of exercise which is inherently rewarding to the actor. It also provides variety and interest for the partner because he has a mobile object of attention.

The counting of events of nonverbal behavior may be based on a simple temporal continuum or a continuum of verbal action. The measurement of the distribution of somatic acts in seconds of time would be advantageous for measuring specific somatic acts in isolation. For relating the distribution of somatic acts to the verbal action stream it is simpler and more direct to use a verbal unit of counting, which is generally a close analog to the temporal continuum in freely flowing conversation. As our focus is primarily on the verbal action stream, we should take our unit of counting from the verbal action sequence. The most uniform element in verbal emission is the syllable and that is the unit of counting which we have adopted for measuring the duration of somatic acts. Using the word as a unit of counting would give similar results since the average length of the word is approximately 1.3 syllables. Frequency is also a useful means of measurement for relating nonverbal behavior to the verbal action stream. The recorded conversations in this research are all in a constant time frame of 300 seconds which permits approximation of the density of the verbal and somatic acts.

OCULAR BEHAVIOR

One of the functions of ocular contact is a monitoring function in which each partner maintains more or less continuous surveillance of the other and the local environment. There is a fairly heavy stream of incoming information in the form of movements, gestures, and environmental changes which arise in rapid succession. A second function of ocular contact is episodic in which the initiation or termination of eye contact signals some basic change for the channel. Goffman notes that the listener must usually give his visual attention to the speaker and to his face, and that the listener's inattention is an affront to the speaker (Goffman 1967: 123). Prolonged eye-break may signal readiness to terminate either the conversational contact or topic. Of all the somatic functions connected with conversation, eye contact is the most vital and the most closely incorporated in the exchange of communication. The predominant condition during conversation is for both partners to maintain eye contact about 70 percent of the time.

The conversational relation is a reciprocating process which during any segment of time requires two modes: one of these is the speaking mode and the other is the complementary listening mode. While successful conversation requires that these two modes be shifted with some regularity between the two partners, each mode has presumably distinctive requirements with respect to somatic behavior. Kendon, in discussing the role of ocular contact in conversation, asserts that eye-break functions to reduce the actor's load (Kendon 1967). It may be assumed that the speaker has the greater load of the two actors. First, he has the load of organizing, editing, and expressing his verbal stream. Second, he has the stimulus load of cues and other movements from his partner and environmental events, and he must integrate the two. If this is true, we would expect the duration of eye contact to be longer in the listening mode. We would also expect the frequency of eye-break to be greater in the speaking mode.

The sex structure is a well-recognized variable which is generally assumed to assert some influence on most of the components of conversational interaction. It is probably a cultural effect relating to the subordinate status of women in adult relations. In studying the relation between eye contact and sex, Rubin found that females maintain longer eye contact than do males when interacting (Rubin 1970). If this is true, we would expect females to maintain longer eye contact than males in the heterogeneous structure. We would also expect females to maintain longer eye contact than males when talking to a member of the same sex. Using this same reasoning we would expect a greater frequency of eye-breaks from males in both structures. Since the use of the eyes is a major element in maintaining the conversational contact and in maintaining environmental involvement, it may be that sex as a factor is less influential than other variables. That is to say that regardless of sex, the need for the use of the eyes may be similar.

A third variable which could affect eye contact is the content half of the conversation. Here we are talking about approximately the first two and one-half minutes of a five minute conversation between subjects who are only slightly acquainted. The logic of dividing this short episode into two periods is to determine if initialization of the conversational contact is associated with a heavier load. The effect of a heavier load in the initial period would probably be due to the need to search for a topic of mutual interest and to allow each to adjust his interaction patterns to a new partner. This would lead to the expectation of a higher frequency of eye-breaks and shorter periods of looking in the first half. It should be noted that in talking about the half of the conversational contact, we are actually talking about the initial minutes of the conversation and not about the half of more extended conversations, disregarding length.

To determine the effects of the mode on the duration of eye contact, the mean duration was calculated for the total set of 52 dyads after standardizing for variation in the number of ocular acts. Comparisons were made in four data sets as shown in Table 1.

TABLE 1

The effect of speaking and listening modes
on duration of somatic behavior
(Standardized by length of dyad by syllable count for 52 dyads)

Somatic	Half 1				Half 2			
Act	Speak		Listen		Speak		Listen	
	Actor 1	Actor 2	Actor 1	Actor 2	Actor 1	Actor 2	Actor 1	Actor 2
Contort	12.7	11.3	13.5	14.6	12.0	9.6	13.9	14.2
Eye	30.	27.5	48.0	45.	27.9	30.3	56.6	61.0
Nod	5.5	5.6	5.0	8.1	7.8	8.5	9.3	11.0
Smiles	15.4	16.6	21.4	25.2	16.5	18.1	19.5	22.5

In all four replications, the duration in the listening mode counted in syllables was greater by a factor which varied from 1.6 to 2.0. The average duration of ocular contact in the speaking mode was 29 syllables and in the listening mode it was 53 syllables. The magnitude of the difference is such as to indicate a major difference in the pattern of ocular contact between the two modes. This fact is also clearly indicated by an analysis of variance of the differences between actor, mode, and content half for ocular contact (Table 2). In three replications the modal phenomenon yielded F ratios which were highly significant ($p < .01$). There was no interaction between the three main effects of actor, mode, and content half. As would be expected, the data on frequency of eye-break is in agreement with the data on mean duration of eye contact. The frequency of eye-break in the speaking mode is appoximately twice as great as the frequency of eye-break in the listening mode (Table 3). Again the difference is quite substantial with an average

TABLE 2

*Effects of actor, speak-listen mode and
content half on duration of ocular contact*
(Standardized by length of dyad by syllable count)

1. Male-Female — 26 Dyads			
Source	df	F	P
Actor	1	.85	
Speak-Listen Mode	1	9.62	.01
Content Half	1	5.99	.02
2. Male-Male — 13 Dyads			
Actor	1	.33	N.S.
Speak-Listen Mode	1	25.73	.001
Content Half	1	6.84	.02
3. Female-Female — 13 Dyads			
Actor	1	.65	N.S.
Speak-Listen Mode	1	25.03	.001
Content Half	1	2.68	N.S.

TABLE 3

*Effect of speaking and listening modes on
frequency of somatic acts during conversation*
(Pooled mean frequencies for 52 dyads)

	Half 1				Half 2			
	Speak		Listen		Speak		Listen	
	Actor 1	Actor 2	Actor 1	Actor 2	Actor 1	Actor 2	Actor 1	Actor 2
Contort	3.2	2.0	1.6	1.4	3.0	2.0	1.6	1.6
Eye	8.4	9.4	5.6	4.8	8.0	8.2	4.0	4.6
Nod	5.4	5.8	3.8	4.3	5.8	6.1	3.8	4.6
Smile	4.8	5.4	3.7	3.7	4.6	4.5	3.2	3.5

of 16 eye-breaks per dyad (5 minutes) for the speaking mode, and an average of 9.4 eye-breaks per dyad in the listening mode. We can conclude then that the actor in the listening mode can maintain eye contact more continuously than he can when he is in the speaking mode.

Duration of eye contact is recorded under three sex structures (Table 4). If the female tends to maintain eye contact longer this

TABLE 4

*The effect of speaking and listening modes
on duration of somatic behavior by sex structure*
(Mean duration in syllables)

	Speak	1	Listen		Speak	2	Listen	
Male-Female — 26 Dyads								
	Actor 1	Actor 2	Actor 1	Actor 2	Actor 1	Actor 2	Actor 1	Actor 2
Contort	10.1	6.9	7.7	7.8	12.4	11.2	12.8	16.8
Eye	29.6	28.9	42.7	84.9	24.5	30.7	45.4	72.0
Nod	6.0	4.9	5.6	8.0	10.5	8.6	10.3	12.3
Smile	16.5	17.2	22.9	26.4	18.5	20.7	7.4	28.4
Male-Male — 13 Dyads								
Contort	11.5	4.5	14.5	4.7	12.2	6.7	20.6	4.9
Eye	31.0	25.8	49.3	34.9	34.6	33.9	54.0	38.4
Nod	2.8	7.0	2.7	9.1	3.1	7.4	3.7	6.6
Smile	12.4	12.1	21.7	23.0	12.3	12.9	22.0	12.5
Female-Female — 13 Dyads								
Contort	19.0	26.8	24.2	38.2	10.9	9.3	9.4	18.2
Eye	29.8	26.5	57.1	60.1	28.0	26.0	81.6	61.6
Nod	7.3	5.6	6.2	7.2	7.2	9.2	12.7	12.8
Smile	16.1	19.7	18.1	25.1	16.8	18.2	21.2	20.8

should become manifest in the male-female dyads. This difference should also become manifest when comparing the mean duration of eye contact in the male-male dyads to the mean duration in the female-female dyads. There is a major sex difference in the duration of ocular contact in the listening mode. In the male-female dyad, the period of eye contact for the female is approximately twice as long as that of the male. A similar effect may be noted in comparing homogeneous sex structures. When two females are conversing with each other, they maintain eye contact in the listening mode longer than two males conversing with each other. The males show no difference in the mean length of maintaining eye contact across dyad structures in the listening mode (44 syllables). Females listening to females maintain eye contact for an average of 63 syllables; when females are listening to males they maintain eye contact for an average of 78 syllables. From this it appears that the female is more attentive when listening. Insofar as eye contact contributes to bonding between the two partners the female appears to create a stronger bond. This may be evidence for the predominance of the expressive function of the female in her concentration on social relationships as theorized by Parsons (1955: 45-60). Since the male appears to be less attentive, he may be less concerned with the social relationship and somewhat less involved in the social action. The hypothesis of sex differences is not supported by the data regarding eye contact in the speaking mode. Females maintain eye contact for an average of 28 syllables while speaking and males maintain eye contact for an average of 30 syllables while speaking. This would suggest that the loading effect for the speaker is essentially the same for both sexes and that both reduce eye contact in order to reduce their stimulus loads in speaking. Therefore, the differences in eye contact by sex structure are primarily a function of the mode and are only secondarily related to sex.

The findings in regard to the duration of eye contact in comparing the first half to the second half of the dyad are inconclusive. Although the differences between the two halves are statistically significant in the male-female dyads and in the male-male dyads (Table 2), the differences are in the opposite direction. Males maintain eye contact longer in the first half in the male-male structure and longer in the second half in the male-female structure. This appears to be due to the influence of females maintaining longer eye contact in the second half. When mode and actor is held constant, the relationship between ocular contact and content half disappears (Table 4). The effect of the modal difference is far more powerful. A comparison of the first actor with the second actor indicates small differences which are well within chance variation. Analysis of variance also indicates no interaction between the main effects of the actors, the speak-listen mode, and the content halves.

Eye contact is an important supplement to the conversational encounter. It is a good indicator of the degree to which the channel is open or closed. It is also an indicator of the degree of bonding and the level of attention in the listening mode. Of the three main variables considered, the speak-listen mode is by far the most indicative of the relation of ocular contact to conversational action. Therefore the effects of sex structure and content half should be considered holding the speak-listen mode constant. The two modes are essentially complementary and must be combined in a reciprocal process in order to produce successful conversational exchange. Eye contact is primarily characteristic of the listening and contributes to the quality of information intake. This is an integral part of bonding and also contributes to the effectiveness of response in the speaking mode.

FACIAL BEHAVIOR

Facial behavior is not communicative to the person who emits the facial behavior, and he is often unaware of what his facial behavior is revealing to the other partner. Particularly when he is in the speaking mode, he has little opportunity to take account of all that is transpiring on his face. In the listening mode, although he is less loaded, he is probably more concerned with what he sees and hears from the other person than with what he is revealing. It is possible for those who perform in public to rehearse and stage their facial expressions. However, in informal conversation, it is more typical for persons to respond spontaneously with a variety of facial expressions. The facial expression conveys the actor's state to the observer. It therefore transmits more general information and for the most part does not transmit any specific information in the form of signals. The emitter is for the most part not aware of the detailed changes in his facial expression and it is therefore impossible for him to convey intended information by this means. The information which he does convey is limited to that which the observer can infer. To the extent that the partner takes notice of the other's facial expressions, the interpretation is largely subjective. For example, there is no difinitive meaning for a smile or a facial contortion. The smile is generally taken to indicate satisfaction, amusement, or pleasure. The facial contortion generally indicates at least a momentary state of discomfort, and frequent or continuing facial contortion indicates confusion, consternation, or rejection. The communicative value of these facial expressions is that they either sustain or tend to redirect the conversational stream. It also allows the emitter to inject himself physically into the conversational engagement. Through this means he tends to heighten and accentuate the feeling tone of the verbal stream. Thus the prime carrier of the signal sequence in conversation is the verbal stream, and the somatic behaviors provide auxiliary signals which highlight and modify the primary verbal message. This creates considerably more interest for the other partner through the dynamics of facial animation.

In conversational exchange the speaker is the pilot of the action. Since he plans and organizes the verbal emission stream, he is in a position to anticipate the positive or negative qualities of what is coming and should therefore initiate the first facial reaction in response to the verbal stream. Also since he is investing the greater degree of energy he may be expected to have a stronger and longer enduring reaction. The partner who is in the listening mode will get the full impact somewhat later and with somewhat less intensity. Therefore, we would expect the actor in the speaking mode to have a greater frequency and duration of smiling and facial contortion than in his listening mode.

The findings confirm the expectation of a greater frequency of both smiling and contorting behavior in the speaking mode. The frequencies indicated in Table 5 consistently show a proportionately great difference for both actors and for both halves of the dyads and for all sex structures. On the average, including the pooled frequency data for the 52 dyads, as shown in Table 3, 62 percent of all the contortion behavior occurs in the speaking mode as contrasted to 38 percent in the listening mode. The relationship is similar with regard to the frequency of smiling. In the speaking mode, 58 percent of the initiation of smiling occurs, as compared to 42 percent in the listening mode. This data incorporates a total of 853 contortions and 1737 smiles. The difference in frequency for contortion between the speaking and listening mode is statistically significant at the .001 level (chi² = 21.4). The difference in frequency for smiling between the speaking and listening mode is also statistically significant (Chi² = 99.6; $p <$ .001).

The hypothesis that the speaking mode will manifest a greater duration of smiling and contorting is contradicted by the data. Of the total duration of smiling in the 52 dyads, 58 percent occurs in the listening mode, as contrasted to 42 percent of the smiling in the speaking mode. This pattern is consistent by content halves and for all sex structures. The relationship is similar although somewhat less consistent for contortion. Of the duration of contortion, 55 percent is manifested in the listening mode and 45 percent is in the speaking mode. Since the frequencies of these acts are the same as those which have been presented immediately above, the differences are statistically significant.

The fact that the speaker has a shorter duration of each facial posture indicates that some condition is overriding the influence of the speaker's anticipation of his verbal action. A likely explanation is that the speaker is busily occupied in creating the varying details of the verbal action stream and therefore must immediately move on to the requirements of the next action. There is also some mechanical interference between the muscular movements required to maintain the smile and those muscular movements required for the lips and mouth in speech. This does lead to the conclusion that frequency of initiation is more closely associated to the action elements or the speaker mode and that duration of facial behavior is more closely associated with the more passive elements of the listening mode. With this reasoning the actor during his listening mode is at greater leisure to maintain any given facial posture.

On the assumption that smiling and contortion are functions of expression, we would expect females to initiate smiling and contortion more frequently and to maintain these postures for longer duration. The basis for this is that females are more expressive, more skilled, and are thought to be more deeply involved in social relations. An increase in the frequency or duration of smiling and contortion would indicate a greater readiness to show feelings and to become personally involved. The greater readiness to reveal one's feelings should contribute to the conversational bond by giving faster and more veridical information between partners. This suggests that it is easier to talk to a person who is more open and expressive than to one who is more restrained. Here we assume that the contortion contributes positively to the bond because it facilitates the appropriate response in those areas where there has been confusion or doubt.

In comparing the data by sex structure, as indicated in Table 5, there is no consistent difference between males and females on the frequency of smiling in the heterogeneous dyad structure or between the male and female homogeneous structures. The frequency of

TABLE 5

The effect of speaking and listening mode on the frequency of somatic acts during conversation by sex structure
(Mean duration in syllables)

	Speak	Half 1	Listen	Speak	Half 2	Listen		
	Actor 1	Actor 2	Actor 1	Actor 2	Actor 1	Actor 2	Actor 1	Actor 2
Male-Female — 26 Dyads								
Contort	3.5	2.3	1.8	1.5	3.3	2.1	1.8	1.5
Eye	8.4	9.1	5.6	3.6	9.0	7.4	4.6	3.8
Nod	5.2	5.4	3.5	4.0	4.4	6.6	3.1	4.4
Smile	4.8	5.3	3.7	3.5	5.0	4.9	3.7	3.4
Female-Female — 13 Dyads								
Contort	2.0	1.5	1.3	1.1	1.8	1.6	1.3	1.2
Eye	9.7	10.5	5.3	5.5	7.7	8.6	2.3	4.3
Nod	5.7	7.6	5.6	6.3	6.6	7.2	5.1	5.3
Smile	4.8	5.6	3.6	4.6	4.0	3.6	2.6	3.5
Male-Male — 13 Dyads								
Contort	3.6	1.8	1.4	1.4	3.6	2.3	1.3	2.0
Eye	7.1	8.9	5.9	6.3	6.2	9.3	4.3	6.3
Nod	5.3	4.8	5.0	2.9	7.6	4.0	4.0	4.4
Smile	4.6	5.3	3.8	3.3	4.2	4.6	2.6	3.7

TABLE 6

*Effect of speaking and listening mode
on the frequency of head tossing*
(Mean frequencies)

	Half 1				Half 2			
	Speak		Listen		Speak		Listen	
	Actor 1	Actor 2	Actor 1	Actor 2	Actor 1	Actor 2	Actor 1	Actor 2
Total	20	23	11	12	19	21	11	10
M-F	20	20	12	12	20	19	12	12
M-M	19	27	9	12	17	24	13	10
F-F	23	24	10	10	18	22	10	9

smiling appears to be about the same in all sets and on the average each actor smiles about 17 times in the five minute contact. There is a difference of frequency of contortion by sex structure in the opposite direction of that predicted, which is statistically significant at the .001 level (Chi^2 = 19.9). In general, the average number of contortions for females per five minute contact is about seven, and the frequency for males is about nine. If we assume that contortion is an indicator of strain, then the fact that males manifest a greater frequency of contortion might indicate that they are under greater strain in the conversational contact than are females. At the same time this would make the males somewhat more expressive with regard to contortion and somewhat better bonded in the conversational relation than they would be if they were less expressive.

Females maintain smiles longer in both the heterogeneous dyad structure and, in comparison to males, in the homogeneous dyad structure. In general females maintain the smile about three syllables longer which is slightly more than .5 seconds. The average length of the duration of a smile for females is 20 syllables (4 seconds) and seventeen syllables for males (3.5 seconds). The duration of the contortion in the heterogeneous sex structure is the same for males and females (about 11 syllables). In the homogeneous sex structure the duration of the female facial contortion is twenty syllables (4 seconds) as compared to ten syllables duration for the male (2 seconds). Since facial contortions last twice as long when females are talking to females this suggests that females are more expressive when talking to each other and more willing to reveal strain. The net effect on communication is probably positive. For the female, the duration of the smile is equal to the duration of the contortion in the homogeneous dyad. In the heterogeneous dyad, the duration of the smile is about twice as great as the duration of the contortion. Similarly, in the male homogeneous dyad the duration of the smile is 60 percent longer than the contortion.

In evaluating the incidence and duration of facial behavior by content half, there should be a general increase in communication after the first minute and this should include those somatic behaviors which are connected with expressiveness. As the conversational contact progresses there should be an improvement in the organization of verbal delivery and in the level of interpersonal involvement. If this is the case, then the facial behavior of smiling and contortion should become greater in the second half of the contact. Since these facial behaviors are affected by the speech stream, we would expect to find this relationship primarily in the speaking mode but not necessarily in the listening mode. Our findings give little support to this expectation. There is no consistent difference between halves in the frequency of smiling or contorting (Table 5). The differences which can be identified in duration relate only to contorting and in this the pattern is reversed within sex structures. In the heterogeneous sex structure, both males and females maintain contortion longer in the second half. The males also maintain contortion longer in the second half when talking to males, but females maintain contortion longer in the first half when talking to females and the duration in the first half is twice as long. This suggests that there are factors operating in the female-female structure which have not been considered.

Facial behavior serves an ancillary function to verbal communication. It is primarily connected with the emitting phase of the actor's engagement in conversation and serves to highlight his verbal action. Through facial behavior there is a rapid succession of events through which each actor reveals his reaction to the varying elements in the verbal stream when it originates both from himself and from the other person. Females maintain smiling and contortion for longer duration than males, particularly when talking to each other. Aside from this there is a tendency for smiles to be much longer than contortions. In general the frequency of smiling is twice as great as the frequency of contortion. Smiling is indicative of pleasure and satisfaction and it tends to increase both for the two partners. It is likely that the sustaining of the conversational contact requires a favorable reaction and that the contact would more quickly tend to fail if the verbal and somatic actions were predominantly painful. Conversation is believed to be inherently pleasant although it may include difficult and painful episodes.

HEAD MOVEMENT

A continuing sequence of movements of the head is virtually universal to the conduct of conversation. Since the head represents a fairly substantial portion of body weight, the continued tossing, turning, and bobbling of the head requires as much energy investment as any activity normally included in speech. Therefore the part that head movement plays is not neglible. For the most part head movement represents a limited source of communication potential. Various cultural conventions of nodding and shaking the head represent agreement and disagreement and certainly function to sustain the flow of conversation. The tossing, tilting, repositioning and drifting movements of the head have no well recognized signal value. It may have a function of affording some exercise and movement and a reaction to the restraints of staying in the same place to maintain the conversation. It is also a concomitant to action and should be more frequent in the speaking mode than in the listening mode. When head tossing is communicative, it derives its meaning from previous assignment in verbal action, and constitutes a tiny fraction of the vast number of head movements. The head can be used as a pointer for direction by an appropriate tilt from the vertical. Occasionally a toss of the head either back or downward can mark an emotional reaction. The majority of these slight movements, however, could not be assigned any definitive meaning.

Nodding is measured by the frequency of the initiation of nods and by the duration of the nodding sequence by syllable count. For the purposes of this research, we have not discriminated shaking the head from nodding. Our logic is that both movements are simply supportive of the verbal stream and are incorporated so as to parallel affirmative and negative elements therein. It does not necessarily indicate affirmation or denial but seems to function more as a signal to add further elements to the verbal action stream. Like other forms of action we expect nodding to be initiated more frequently in the speaking mode, and at the same time we would expect duration to be greater in the listening mode since the individual when listening has more leisure to continue his mode than he does when he is under the complex load of speaking.

The data with respect to nods in Table 5 show a consistent preponderance of frequency of nodding in the speaking mode, and this is stable over all sex structures. During the average five minute contact, there are 24 nods from both actors, or one nodding sequence approximately every 12 seconds. Since there is a greater frequency of the initiation of nodding by the speaker, and if we assume nodding is a form of support for the verbal stream, then the speaker is providing more support for his own verbal outputs than he is receiving from his partner in the listening mode. From Table 4 the duration of nodding is consistently greater in the listening mode with a duration of somewhat over two seconds and there is a fairly consistent tendency for the duration of nodding to be greater in the second half. There is little difference in the frequency of the initialization of nodding by sex structure. Although there are differences in duration of nodding between males and females, the pattern is not consistent (Table 4). The frequency of head toss is strongly associated with the speaking mode (Chi^2 = 806) as indicated in Table 6. There are approximately 120 head tosses arising from the two actors in the five minute contact (approximately every 2.5 seconds). The frequency is approximately twice as great in the speaking mode as it is in the listening mode. In general the head tossing is a consistent part of the action pattern in the speaking mode. There is variation in the frequency of head movement by actor but the standard deviation tends to be low. There is little association between the frequency of head tossing and sex structure with all correlations well within chance variation and about equally distributed above and below zero correlation. There is also little difference by content half in the frequency of head tossing.

RELATION AMONG SOMATIC ACTS

In general the somatic acts tend to be integrated into the verbal stream in variable order. There are no simple mechanical regularities in the occurrence of somatic acts in either the speaking or listening mode. We will use the term cluster under two distinct concepts. The first of these is the temporal clustering of two or more somatic acts simultaneously at various points in the verbal stream. The second is the mathematical concept of clustering which is derived from the degree of shared variance among correlated variables. Since the correlations among the four somatic acts — contort, eye, nod, and smile — are generally low and within chance variation, the content of the somatic clusters is quite variable. The somatic acts do not correlate with each other and neither do they correlate with the various verbal acts. Clustering occurs about 50 percent of the time and the average frequency is fourteen times per five minute dyad with either the initiation or termination of three acts per cluster. For the most part the two actors are making some somatic change simultaneously.

Factor analysis has been applied to a collection of 96 variables incorporating the actor, mode, half, and frequency and duration of words and syllables for contort, eyes, nod, and smile. The objective was to determine the degree of association between somatic acts. Forty-seven of the variables were heavily loaded on seven factors (Table 7), and accounted for 55 percent of the variance.

TABLE 7

Factor loadings for somatic acts in 26 male-female Dyads

Factor 1	Male Nodding With Female Smiling				
Measure	Actor	Half	Mode	Act	Loading
Syllables	Male	2	Speak	Nod	.86
Words	Male	1	Speak	Nod	.84
Syllables	Male	2	Listen	Nod	.88
Words	Male	2	Listen	Nod	.87
Syllables	Female	2	Speak	Smile	.77
Words	Female	2	Speak	Smile	.75
Syllables	Female	2	Listen	Smile	.77
Words	Female	2	Listen	Smile	.76

Factor 2	Female Facial Contortion				
Measure	Actor	Half	Mode	Act	Loading
Syllables	Female	2	Speak	Contort	.83
Words	Female	2	Speak	Contort	.83
Frequency	Female	2	Speak	Contort	.82
Syllables	Female	2	Listen	Contort	.68
Words	Female	2	Listen	Contort	.67
Frequency	Female	2	Listen	Contort	.78
Frequency	Female	2	Speak	Contort	.83

Factor 3	Male Facial Contortion				
Measure	Actor	Half	Mode	Act	Loading
Syllables	Male	2	Speak	Contort	.90
Words	Male	2	Speak	Contort	.91
Syllables	Male	2	Listen	Contort	.87
Words	Male	2	Listen	Contort	.88
Syllables	Female	2	Listen	Nod	.61
Words	Male	1	Speak	Smile	.60

Factor 4	Ocular Contact				
Measure	Actor	Half	Mode	Act	Loading
Syllables	Male	1	Speak	Eye	.79
Words	Male	1	Speak	Eye	.79
Syllables	Female	2	Listen	Eye	.60
Words	Female	2	Listen	Eye	.60
Syllables	Male	1	Speak	Eye	.82
Words	Male	1	Speak	Eye	.83
Syllables	Female	2	Listen	Eye	.77
Words	Female	2	Listen	Eye	.76

On only one of the seven factors did two somatic acts appear to be strongly related through shared variance. This analysis involved the heterogeneous dyads. The first factor incorporated nodding by the male actor and smiling by the female actor. All of the other six factors represented separate somatic acts of contortion, eyes, and smiling. This suggests that the somatic acts tend to occur independently and to vary in no consistent pattern.

The correlations between somatic acts from which the factor analysis was derived were generally low and account for no more than sixteen percent of the shared variance between any two act types. Correlations in this range are found between eye break and contort and between eye break and nod. There is also some correlation between nodding and contorting (Table 8). There is

TABLE 8

Relations between four somatic acts

	Contort	Eye	Nod	Smile
Means	10.7	35.2	24.1	19.5
Sigmas	10.3	14.0	13.2	10.2
Correlation				
Contort	1.00			
Eye	.42	1.00		
Nod	.36	.42	1.00	
Smile	−.09	−.06	.23	1.00
	$r.05 = .27$			

no significant correlation between any of these three acts and smiling. We would expect either no correlation or a negative correlation between smiling, contorting, and eye break. The somatic acts are not consistently tied in a mechanical way to the process of communication and they are not tied to each other. Although taken together they have a rather frequent occurrence, for the most part they appear to be episodic and to be woven into more or less unique sequence patterns. This suggests a creative and spontaneous element which is generally recognized in conversational exchange.

CONCLUSIONS

There is an infinite variety of somatic movements of all parts of the body which may be and have been conceived to be centrally involved in the communication process. For example, Hewes identified over 1000 different body postures many of which had some communicative potential which was largely culturally determined (Hewes 1957). Mehrabian has identified relevant body postures which are indicative of relations between communicators. He studied the relationship between body posture and degree of affect for both sexes. He found that subjects tended to orient the body away from persons that they disliked and oriented their bodies more directly toward persons that they liked (Mehrabian 1969: 359-72). Krout has identified more than 5000 hand gestures to which he has attributed unintended communicative significance (Krout 1954: 121-52). Scheflen notes that certain body orientations are used to include some and to exclude others in constituting a communicative group (Scheflen 1965: 245-57). Meerloo writes that the body continually expresses inner emotional activity in a somatic way through sudden precipitate motions of approach or withdrawal (Meerloo 1964: 37). Birdwhistell has developed an exhaustive lexicon with descriptive symbols of the movements of all parts of the head, face, trunk and shoulders, arm and wrist, hand, fingers, thighs, legs, and feet, and some variations of standing, sitting, and walking (Birdwhistell 1970: Appendix 1). Birdwhistell assumes that various detailed somatic motions have social meaning. He believes that no more than 35 percent of the meaning of a conversation is carried by the words (Birdwhistell 1970: 158). This means that 65 percent must be carried by some sequence of somatic movements. This must be a difficult assignment for somatic communications since the same author emphasizes that no position, expression, or movement ever carries meaning in and of itself (Birdwhistell 1970: 44-45). He also notes that there is no universal nonverbal language and no single gesture which has the same meaning in all socieities. We are more inclined to believe that detailed and definitive communication is carried by the verbal stream and that nonverbal communication is incorporated with the verbal stream in a supplementary capacity.

Taken together, all movements and their small variations make up an infinite flood of somatic action which defies decoding in detail. If a nonverbal act cannot be readily discriminated and interpreted by at least one of the two actors then it has only doubtful implications for the verbal action. In precise research on body motions where the action has been slowed down by a slow motion film or studied frame by frame, the researchers themselves have been hard put to sort out and classify all the minute details of movement. In the flow of natural conversation, the actors are able only to make broad and approximate interpretations of somatic movements simultaneously with the intricate stream of detailed verbal cues. If the observer is interested in describing the relation of somatic behavior to the verbal stream he must use the same conventions of decoding as those that would be applied by the participants. This implies that it is possible to become overly precise to the extent that meaning is sacrificed for minute details of mechanical movement.

There is a considerable range of modifications which somatic behavior can impose on the verbal stream. Knapp cites modifications such as repeating, contradicting, substituting, complementing, accenting, relating, and regulating (Knapp 1972: 8-11). A somatic act can repeat the idea of a verbal message if physical movements can simulate the verbal motion. For example, beckoning by a hand motion toward self accompanying a verbal message "Come here" repeats the implied verbal action. Contradiction is illustrated by stifling a yawn while saying "I'm not tired". Holding up the hand with the palm outward can be substituted for the verbal message "Wait". Combining the verbal message "Yes" with with continued nodding serves to complement the agreement. The child who screws up his face vigorously while saying "I don't like spinach" is accenting his verbal message, perhaps involuntarily. Manual gestures are often used to illustrate the relation between physical objects along with a verbal description of their arrangement. Nonverbal acts may also be used to regulate the flow of communication by signaling the end of a verbal act or the desire to begin speaking.

Of all the somatic behavior associated with communication, those of the head and face are the most immediately associated with the verbal stream. In modern society, the head and face are most closely monitored in conversation. Action sequences of the head and face make up a major part of the somatic action stream, and thus presumably account for most of the effect of nonverbal cues in conversation. In order to optimize the record of facial behavior on video tape it is necessary to enlarge the facial image in a head and shoulders closeup of each of the two actors, using two television cameras recording on a split screen. This procedure is particularly necessary for an accurate observation of ocular behavior. The advantage of the video tape record is that each somatic action can be isolated and carefully rechecked individually for each actor to assure a veridical record of the somatic behavior in relation to the verbal sequence.

We now wish to review the role of ocular contact as a communicative element in two person conversation. Kendon's four functions of ocular contact include: (1) cognition, (2) monitoring, (3) regulation, and (4) expression of internal state (Kendon 1967). These categories are not entirely exclusive since monitoring may have a cognitive function and expression may operate as a regulatory function. Ocular contact is the most regular and consistent of the nonverbal behaviors. We find that it is primarily a modal phenomenon of speaking and listening. Eye contact is relatively constant for actors in the listening mode. The breaking of eye contact is mainly associated with the speaking mode and, as Kendon noted, tends to occur after the beginning of a statement. The cognitive function of the eyes is to recognize the stream of events arising from the conversational partner, the peripheral environment, and the self. These events include gestures which may be taken as signals, a recognition of the level of animation of the partner, and external events which could facilitate topical change. The relation of sex to ocular contact is dependent upon the modal structure. Females maintain eye contact approximately twice as long as males in the listening mode, but there is no difference between males and females in the speaking mode. Insofar as Kendon's functions of ocular behavior influence the contact, females are monitoring, regulating, and expressing themselves more effectively than males. The minimum requirement for ocular monitoring is periodic looking to note changes in the partner to verify the continuity of interest. Since the speaker already has the channel and is rather fully occupied with expressing himself verbally, he can reduce his stimulus load by breaking his eye contact periodically and still keep sufficiently informed about his partner. The listener, since he does not have the channel, must maintain a more constant gaze in order to find a point at which he can enter the verbal stream. The regulatory function concerns the exchange of the channel between partners through nonverbal cues and the modification of the verbal stream where a topical change, or clarification, or a change in approach is desired. The expressive function operates in both directions. The pattern of scrutiny, the intensity of gaze, and changes in pupilary dilation are expressive of the degree of interest and involvement. At the same time the eyes pick up or note other somatic expressions which indicate the state of the actor including emotional posture, physical tension, and the effect of existing social pressures.

The exact function of facial behavior for verbal communication is difficult to assess. The main categories of facial behavior, smiling, and contortion may be either reactive or contrived. A reactive smile may be related to an internal event such as a pleasant sensation or a humorous thought. It may also be related to an external event such as a burst of laughter from the partner or a funny statement. The reactive smile is essentially spontaneous and involuntary. It constitutes what we would call natural behavior. The contrived smile is deliberately created to meet the requirements of the social situation and may mask the actual feelings of the actor. Under this category we may list the artificial smile, the frozen smile, polite smile, and the posed smile. The reactive contortion may arise spontaneously from a physically painful or socially embarrassing event, or from an unpleasant verbal message. It may be contrived to simulate sympathy or to feign a negative reaction when the situation seems to call for it. As Argyle says, smiles and frowns do not necessarily indicate emotional states, but may be parts of greetings or social reactions not withstanding the emotion being experienced (Argyle 1967: 36). Therefore, it is necessary to study facial behavior as a communicative element in the social setting if we are to understand the ranges of meaning which humans of a given society convey to each other when they display facial activity (Birdwhistell 1970: 35).

Facial behavior appears to be a consistent element which accompanies communicative behavior in virtually all conversational contacts. The initiation of facial behavior occurs more frequently in the speaking mode and it endures longer in the listening mode for all actors. Sex differences which do exist have to be considered within the context of the modal phenomenon. We find no difference in the frequency of initiating smiles in either the speaking or listening mode with respect to sex. However, females tend to maintain the smile longer than males. The duration of contortion is the same for males and females in the heterogeneous structure although males initiate contortion more frequently. In comparing the homogeneous dyad structures, females maintain contortion about twice as long as males. In general, in all dyads there is about twice as much smiling as contorting. Facial behavior is basically a vehicle of expression and conveys either the spontaneous or contrived actions of each partner. It adds animation to the contact and heightens the impression of interest. It therefore contributes positively to the bonding process and reinforces the effects of verbal communication.

Nodding and head shaking is that part of the head movement which is clearly a part of the communication pattern. Head tossing and repositioning is virtually continuous for most actors during conversation, but only rarely do these head movements have a communicative function. Dittman observed that the listener tended to insert a nod at the end of rhythmic segments in the sentence. He believes that this is often used as a signal that the listener is ready to speak or that the speaker is ready to listen

(Dittman 1969: 79-84). Nodding and shaking the head is helpful to the flow of communication because it does not interfere with verbal communication. After eye movements, nodding is the most frequent somatic behavior during conversation. We find that nodding is initiated much more frequenntly in the speaking mode and that it endures longer in the listening mode. We also find that there is an increase in nodding behavior after the first two minutes of contact. Head tossing is more a function of the speaking mode than of the listening mode and may simply be a part of a generalized body activity pattern.

In an attempt to study conversational behavior as a system of social action, it is necessary to recognize somatic cues and other body movements as an integral part of the action flow along with the verbal stream. Knapp states that the future of research in human communication will also require an analysis of verbal and nonverbal behavior as an inseparable unit (Knapp 1972: 11). We will try to deal with some additional aspects of this issue at the end of the chapter on verbal communication. The components of nonverbal behavior must be isolated and measured separately. But the analysis can be complete only when the various components have been reintegrated into a total pattern of actions in which the interrelations and mutual dependencies are well understood.

The discussion to this point might give the impression that somatic cues are an indispensable component of the conversation process. This particularly becomes evident in Birdwhistell's claim that body motions carry 65 percent of the social meaning in conversation. Such a claim is contraindicated by the fact that successful conversation can be carried on by telephone. It is possible that the conversational bond can be improved when it is established between intimate friends in darkness or in reduced light. The reader can probably recall various occasions when he has shared in an extended intimate chat with some close friend in which the intellectual content was exceptionally satisfying and complete in reduced light. It is not essential that the conversational partner be an intimate friend before the chat occurs. In fact, the feeling of intimacy often arises as a result of the intimate chat.

Restaurants and bars, for example, often deliberately reduce the light level in order to encourage conversational intimacy. The effect of this can only be to reduce the impact of somatic cues. In most conversational experience, however, normal light levels are maintained and somatic behaviors do in fact constitute a vital element of the action.

6

SELECTED PROPERTIES OF THE VERBAL EXCHANGE

Of all the components of conversational interaction, the verbal stream is the most difficult to analyze. First, it has an extremely broad capacity for variability in the potential use of specific words. We have dealt with this to some degree in our earlier chapter on vocabulary. All languages offer the choice of tens of thousands of words to be used in the formation of sentences. Second, further variability arises from the infinite number of potential orderings and combinations of the available lexicon. Symbol substitution provides the foundation for organized thought and rational preparation to cope with a changing world. Without symbol substitution for the elements of experience, the environment is confined and limited to the unique present population of components. The array of environmental elements of the here and now is not simply the only reality; it stands isolated and unrelated to antecedent and succedent environmental sets. When an arbitrary symbol can be substituted for any object, a new flexibility is generated because the symbol, as an idea, can be freely juxtaposed and combined with other symbols, whether for artistic, whimsical, or pratical purposes. The generation of successive symbol sets permits the substitution of symbols for sets of symbols. It now becomes possible to recognize generalized classes, classes of classes, and classes of classes of classes to the nth order, simply by assigning well-defined symbols to them. Through exploration of the indefinitely extended alternatives of combination and discrimination of classes represented by symbols, it becomes possible to reorder the world of experience both in imagination and in fact.

In view of the complexity of the verbal process in conversation, we have chosen to disregard the problems of syntactical analysis of the grammatical construction of assertions. We shall concentrate on the somewhat broader phenomena of the interrelations among verbal acts and the order in which they are likely to occur.

The verbal act is defined as a word or group of words which functions as a separate element in the verbal stream. Assertions and questions are verbal acts which convey meaning through the interrelation of a series of words. Their length can vary from one to thirty words or more. The support is defined as a simple agreement or disagreement of one word. The interjection is a verbal act consisting of a single word usually of indeterminate meaning which may indicate exclamation, emotion, or noncommital. Laughter is a verbal act consisting of a variable series of explosive syllables which vary in form by individuals. Fragmentation includes parts of words and parts of sentences which are never completed, and various forms of vocalization such as "uh", "ah", "er", and "eh".

It is through the variation and combination of verbal acts that a conversational exchange manifests a dynamic character. We are less interested in the static properties of actors as a psychological dimension than we are in the variable properties of the action itself, which we see as a social dimension. What is the nature of the ongoing social contact? Does it manifest variation in degrees of intensity, involvement, and amplitude of information exchange? Do these characteristics seem to remain constant for the duration of contact, or do they give evidence of a modal conversion from rapid to slow, from shallow to deep, from fragmented to integrated?

Variation in the expressive change reflects variation in the nature of the social contact. We do not picture any given property of the expressive chain as a fixed characteristic of an actor. Rather, the sequence of actions cumulatively builds up the character of the social contact between actors. Moreover, we would not expect to characterize any one actor by a specific type of action, but would expect each actor to manifest varying action patterns which limit and describe the quality and characteristics of the interaction.

With the same two partners the exchange ratio might be high early in the contact, and much lower after a short probing period when a topic is found. Then the cycle might lengthen, amplitude might increase, and the intracycle equilibrium might decline as the action enters the narrative mode.

ELEMENTS OF VERBAL INTERACTION

The assertion is the most frequently occurring act in the verbal stream. In natural direct conversation the assertion may vary in length from a single word to a long grammatically complex and complete sentence. The assertion, regardless of length, carries a complete thought. It communicates successfully without requiring other verbal elements which the grammarian might wish to regard as implicit. The assertion is coded in natural conversation as a word or group of words uttered separately:

The girls all end up just going to the drive-in. The Universal. With the girls or dates? Dates. Do? That's what the dates do mostly around here. Where's there a drive-in around here? The Tower. Wait a minute. Funland. The cheap one. The what? Skyway. It's thirty-five cents. Heard of it. Thirty-five cents.

This example represents two actors in a rather rapid exchange. Few of the assertions are grammatically complete, and for the purposes of effective communication need no elaboration. It carries information through a rapid probing of alternatives. Errors are corrected by simple substitution and without comment or other recognition that there was an error. There is often a tendency for these assertive elements to be streamlined to the minimum number of words needed to convey desired meaning.

The assertion is the primary carrier of detailed and highly defined information. Although there is much redundancy in a series of assertions, in a typical natural conversation, each new assertion generally carries some novel element which adds cumulatively to the mass of information transferred and shared between partners. Assertions are generally nonrepetitive in that one assertion is rarely identical to the assertion which preceded it. Thus, the indefinitely extended series of assertions is the vehicle by which significant cognitive transfers are accomplished. Each participant comes to know more about himself, his partner, and the objects of discussion through the exchange of assertion chains. Much of the informative power of assertions arises from the external relations among assertions in the series. Earlier assertions may modify assertions which come later and assertions coming later may create important modifications of those made earlier. It is a primary task in tne course of conversation for each partner to integrate both his own and his partner's assertion sequences into a complex whole. It is the assertion which is more or less imperfectly retained in memory and which constitutes the basis for later reference, for modification of social action and other behavior, for extending the intellectual experience of the actors, and for increasing the corpus of knowledge. Try to imagine how much you could communicate if you were deprived of grammatically organized assertions. This situation occurs when you are hearing one end of a phone conversation in which the speaker utters only nonassertive elements such as "yes", "no", "oh", "really", and the like. The person overhearing the conversation can develop no idea from this of what is being said, although he may infer the emotional tone. However, when he begins to overhear assertions, he can begin to piece the conversation together and to infer the nature of the assertion which he does not hear. An attempt to communicate solely with facial or somatic movements would be equally impoverished as a carrier of detailed informations.

The question is a syntactically and grammatically organized series of words and is essentially assertive. Like the assertion, the question has informative content. This informative content may be contained in a single word such as an interrogative adverb or in a group of words in the basic format of an assertion. At least four discrete functions can be identified for the question. First, the question may be so constituted as to demand an assertive response which is concentrated and focused on the information content of the question. For example, a student, repeating a dormitory supervisor said, "And he says what have you got in the bag?" demands an assertive answer with organized information. A second form of the question is an assertion in interrogative form which seeks agreement, consent, acceptance, or confirmation. For example, two students were discussing the effect of attending college. One said, "And haven't you found that it kind of sharpens your mind a little bit?" This could be answered with a simple affirmation. A third form of the question directs or redirects the topical flow and calls for a change in subject matter.

... I'd like to see him in a football game. I've never seen (Florida) A and M team play. Heard a lot about their band, too. A real nice band. You a major here in sociology?

This illustrates the use of an unrelated question to bring about a drastic shift in the direction of the conversation. A fourth function of the question in conversation is to call for clarification, repeating, verification, or more detailed information. Essentially this type of question helps to carry or support the continuity of the conversational stream. These functions can be illustrated by the following conversational excerpts:

Clarification: (two females discussing contact lenses)

It floats. There's some sort of vacuum. You don't feel it as you apply it to your eye? Don't feel it? But not on your eyeball. You probably think you do. But it's actually your eyelid.

Repetition: (a male and a female student)

My daddy said I never used to do it when I went to the academy. Went where? The Academy of the Holy Name on Bayshore.

Verification: (two males)

I just dropped psych. Did you?

More Information: (two males discussing the Vietnam involvement)

I really don't think we belong over there. Somebody has to be there. Why does somebody have to be there?

The interrogative assertions in their various forms have an important function of directing and sustaining the flow of conversation. They tighten the relationship between successive assertions, introduce fresh elements, and improve the congruence in the conversational stream between the two partners, thus contributing to the quality of the communication contact and to the bonding process. Support is defined in functional terms as a short verbal element which sustains the sequence of assertions, or more generally, the flow of verbal action. Whether in the form of affirmation or negation, it has a primary relation to the assertion and question. It may or may not indicate acceptance in some broader sense, but it does indicate acceptance of the preceding assertion or assertion series. The support element often appears as the listener's acknowledgment of receipt and understanding of the speaker's last output sequence. It may constitute the listener's only verbal contribution to the conversational chain over a relatively extended series of verbal acts by the speaker. At the same time, the speaker may more or less regularly insert support elements among his own assertions, providing a kind of verbal punctuation which indicates his own acceptance of a precedent sequence together with readiness for further assertions by himself or by his partner.

A problem arises concerning the recognition of support elements, because consistency requires that any element so designated must always be counted as support behavior if the element occurs separately among a series of other verbal acts. We believe that the verbal support classification can properly be confined to direct affirmations and negations of one or two syllables which do not include verbs or verbs forms. Free standing occurrences of "yes", "yeah", "uhhuh", "okay", "right", "sure", "no", and "huhuh" represent the support forms. Expressions containing verbs such as "I see", "I agree", and "that's right" are excluded from the verbal support classification because they include a verb and are sufficiently information bearing to be classified as assertions. The expression "you know" standing alone when habitually injected in the conversational stream without specific reference is classed as an interjection because it appears to fall short of the support function and is not used by the listener to signal acceptance of what has been said or readiness to hear sequent outputs. The listening partner frequently gives one and two syllable supports simultaneously with the continuing stream of speech of his partner. These supportive elements are usually inserted in a softer voice and appear to have no interfering effect on the other speaker. Periodic injection of short supports increases the participation level of the listener and improves his relation to the speaker.

Like supports, interjections have no grammatical organization and they do not convey detailed information through definitive symbols. They tend to be simple and repetitive and are often idiosyncratic of the actor. They are frequently used as verbal fillers where a participant is not ready to give a more indicative response. Words such as "well", "oh", "really", and "indeed" when standing alone are examples of interjections. Tonal variations of interjections also serve to indicate the level of emotional reaction, which can range from noncommittal to elated, surprised, or hurt. Such interjections may manifest changes in the state of one or both actors but they convey information in a crude and general sense as contrasted to the refined and delicately modified information which emerges in assertions and questions. It is quite common for meaningless interjections to be affixed habitually to nearly all assertions in a way which is both irritating to the partner and contracommunicative. For example, the person who habitually begins sentences with "well" or "you know" is wasting channel time and is detracting somewhat from every assertion he utters. Interjections which are used functionally to convey emotional changes can serve to create a greater variety of interest and response and to lend animation to the exchange. In this use, interjections contribute positively to the success of the communication.

Laughter has a convulsive quality which is for the most part involuntary. The basic unit of laughter consists of a single expulsion of air beginning with an initial "H" sound and followed by one of several vowel sounds: "ha", "ho", "he", "haw", "huh", "hih". Natural laughter, a serial combination of identical syllables of varying and indeterminant length, is primarily the actor's reaction to a set of cognitive elements which are in incongruous and ludicrous relation to each other. The actor does not laugh deliberately or with any known purpose of communicating. In the natural situation the actor is overcome by the humor of the situation and he breaks down in laughter. This creates a momentary break in the communicative symbol stream and requires some effort later to reconstitute it. The communicative function of laughter is auxiliary to the vocal stream in that it reveals the emotional state of the actor to his partner. Thus laughter is basically a vocal somatic act. Laughter has a contagious quality in that one person tends to join the laughter of another provided he is not discomfited and is not himself the object of laughter. We can suggest two reasons for the contagion of laughter. First, the person joining in the laughter also sees the humor of situations which precipitated the laughter. Second, a person may not see the humor of the situation but may be amused by the sight of another person laughing. These two causes of contagious laughter can and do work either separately or together. Darwin (1872) took a special interest in the physiological nature of laughter.

The sound of laughter is produced by a deep inspiration followed by short, interrupted, spasmodic contractions of the chest, and especially the diaphragm...the mouth is open more or less widely, with the corners drawn much backwards, as well as a little upwards; and the upper lip is somewhat raised.

He recognized that laughter in response to a humorous situation is unique to human beings but he did not attempt to explain its social function. Berlyne has identified three basic theoretical approaches to the origin of laughter (Berlyne 1969: ch. 27). These are the relief theory, superiority theory, and conflict theory. Descartes (1649) thought that laughter originated from a sense of relief on the realization of escape from some evil. Spencer (1891) had a similar explanation when he described laughter as a device for discharging nervous energy. Hobbes (1651) is the earliest of the modern thinkers to propose that laughter arises from a feeling of superiority over the degradation of others. Beattie (1776) is perhaps the earliest exponent of the conflict theory.

Laughter arises from the view of two or more inconsistent, unsuitable, or incongruous parts or circumstances, considered as united in one complex object or assemblage, or as acquiring a sort of mutual relation from the peculiar manner in which the mind takes notice of them.

Various other theorists have described the source of laughter in similar terms (Schopenhauer 1819; Kant 1790; Koestler 1964). These three theoretical approaches need not be contradictory to each other or mutually exclusive. Although they can operate separately, they can also operate in combination. One might view a conflicting situation and feel both superior and relieved because he is not trapped in the situation; viewed in this sense, he senses superiority and relief on extricating himself. None of the approaches to laughter discussed above have recognized the temporal and dramatic element in real life laughter situations. The humorous situation typically develops in a temporally linked series of elements among which the conflict gradually becomes apparent. The climax is reached when the conflict is suddenly resolved, generating a feeling of superiority and relief. No one knows better than the professional comic the importance of sequence and timing in the successful presentation of humor. The expression of superiority and relief is vocalized in the outburst of laughter. Thus humor and laughter results from the emotional readjustment of a conflict situation. Thus it seems that these three approaches are complementary to one another and constitute portions of a single system of action.

Fragmentation is one of the more complex phenomena in natural conversation because it appears in so many forms and has at least three conceptually different functions. Mishler and Waxler (1968: 37-38) assign five separate codes to verbal fragmentation. These include: (1) incomplete sentences or sentences having an incomplete idea; (2) repetition in which words or phrases are exactly repeated; (3) incomplete phrases including acts containing a word or words having unclear meaning; (4) laughter; and (5) number of fragments in one act where an act is defined as a complete sentence or a complete idea. Coding of the fifth category becomes somewhat ambiguous since the authors note that the complete idea may include more than one act. Here they have used the Bales' system of act coding (1950) used in Interaction Process Analysis. We have attempted to define coding for the different kinds of fragmentation somewhat more rigorously because we are concentrating more narrowly on the properties of the conversational action stream. We identify four kinds of fragmentation, all of which are primarily associated with assertive acts. It is only the assertive act, whether declarative or interrogative, which we assume to be fragmented. First, we code as fragmentation a word or group of words which clearly manifests an incomplete thought as presented to the partner. This requires prima facie evidence that the thought was too incomplete to be understandable. Examples are "I just/I think you miss a lot on college campus life when you commute." The slash is the code for the fragment "I just". The two words "I just" clearly demand something more and constitute an incomplete thought. This type of fragmentation is also evidenced when a longer partially formed sentence is abandoned and replaced by a completely reorganized statement. For example, "When I was a/ There was a girl across the hall from me." The second coding category is the incomplete word or phrase. Examples are "with just a/ Just a B A degree". The phrase "just a B A degree" does convey a thought while the partial phrase "with just a" calls for something more. Fragmentation in words occurs as in the following; "I've had ano/ a sma/ a lower course in small groups." It is often unclear as to what the word would have been if completed but in this case the words "another" and "small" seem to be indicated. This example illustrates the frequent phenomenon in natural speech to edit and reconstitute parts of the sentence in the process of delivery. Stuttering which is much more rare among college students appears in the following: "wha/wha/wha/wha/What did you do for your study for social investigation?" The third category of fragmentation is repetition of words or groups of words which are incorporated in assertions. For example: "That's/that's/I'm doing an attitude study on that." In this case the speaker evidently intended a statement which he twice initiated only to abandon it for an assertion of a completely different form. The fourth category of fragmentation includes vocalizations which are not words or parts of words and therefore could not be an integral part of the word stream in the assertion. They include most variants of vocalizations which are conventionally spelled "ah", "eh", "er", "aw", and "uh". This is a frequent and nearly universal practice of speakers in natural conversation. In our transcript, we have conventionalized all of these vocalizations as "ah", regardless of their original form, for purposes of cataloging. Unlike the other syllables encountered in the speech stream, these vocalizations are extremely elastic and in practice are held for a variable length of time ranging from stacato to tenuto. This is illustrated as follows: "They'll pretty well ah/ have to be accepted in the main by the/ by the/ah/org/ah/ administration."

The functions of fragmentation in natural conversation include the filler function, channel management, and verbal catharsis. From observing a person who is trying to maintain a conversational output, one gets the impression that the speaker is striving to sustain a uniform, regular, and well-controlled stream of vocalization. When he encounters difficulty in phrasing or finding the exact word, the even flow of vocalization is interrupted, and he feels compelled to insert some sound to repair the breach. As we have noted this sound is of variable duration, continuing until he has found the necessary words to complete his output. The speaker is usually unaware of the extent of these vocal insertions, although if they are excessive they usually become a source of irritation to the listener. If they do not occur excessively, the listener also tends to overlook them and to be relatively unaware of them. This almost universal tendency to employ nonverbal vocalizations to cover temporal gaps in speech leads to the second function of channel management. Here we restrict the term "verbal" to the use of conventional words and the term "vocal" to the uttering of sound. Continued use of these vocalizations has led to the convention of them to signal either the desire to retain the channel or to transfer it to the other partner. A signal to retain the channel consists of a strong continuation of the vocalization. The signal of readiness to relinquish the channel consists of a series of weak or faltering vocalizations. As the speaker continues, the listener feels some pressure to assume the channel and to express his ideas verbally. If this pressure is extreme, the listener will seize upon a strong continued vocalization as a suitable gap to capture the channel. If the pressure is low, the listener may allow the speaker to struggle and falter for some time before he assumes his share of the verbal exchange.

The function of verbal catharsis is to repair and restore portions of the verbal stream which are erroneous, misleading, or undesired in relation to the intent of the speaker. Natural speech has a novel and creative element in that the speakers are formulating new statements on the spot. The speaker does not know beforehand exactly how he will word his output. As he goes he organizes and edits it in a piecemeal fashion, formulating first a phrase, then a clause, then a modifier and then a new sentence which hopefully is well related to what has gone before. In practice he often finds that he has already uttered words and sentence elements which do not fit grammatically or which are entirely contrary to his intention. Consequently he is forced to abandon these incongruent elements and start anew. The result is the bypassing of an irregular series of odd verbal elements which constitutes one form of verbal fragmentation. The detailed components of this verbal debris are for the most part overlooked and mentally edited out by both speaker and listener. However, they do cause some embarrassment and discomfort, and sometimes an unintended word or phrase may seriously damage the impression the speaker is trying to create. In natural conversation, the effects of fragmentation are not entirely negative. A moderate incidence of normal slips and slight difficulty in verbalizing an expression give evidence of the genuineness and sincerity of the speaker and make him seem "human". Mishler and Waxler (1968: 37) note that speech fragmentation, if it occurs at moderate rates, is highly functional for group interaction. They found that there was less verbal fragmentation in families in which there was a schizophrenic child and that speech in these families tended to be rigid, formal, hostile, and unheeding. In the normal family there was frequent interruption among family members, an animated level of speech, moderate fragmentation, and a readiness of each family member to listen to other family members regardless of the age relation. The verbal communication in the normal families, although more fragmented, was judged to be eminently successful in contrast to the failure in communication in the families with a schizophrenic member.

Self-interruption is defined as the intrusion of nonassertive acts or elements within an assertive sequence such as an assertion or a question. The speaker often interrupts his own assertions by including supportive acts (affirmations or negations) as a means of reinforcing his own verbal output. Interjections may emerge within the assertions to indicate an emotional overtone. As indicated earlier, the assertion is often in need of internal repairs and amendments which are evidenced by fragmentation and reformulation. Laughter may erupt within the assertion and interfere with its execution to the extent that it is not understandable to the listener. The speaker may also be interrupted by the listener which we have coded as simultaneous speech. The interruption is usually not so complete as to stop the speech flow of the speaker but simply runs parallel to it in time. These elements of simultaneous speech are usually short and generally consist of simple supports of one or two syllables, laughter, or short two or three word assertions. It indicates active participation on the part of both partners, and the listener provides a periodic support to the speaker which improves the quality of the interaction. It may also serve as a means of channel exchange.

PROBLEMS OF MEASUREMENT

At this point we are concerned with the measurement of the conversational stream as it appears in the unedited transcript of the audio record. Two distinct methods of analysis are applicable. The first is stream analysis which concentrates on the dynamic properties of the sequence of action. The examination of the action stream is of far greater interest to sociologists who wish to determine the basic characteristics of social action. Unfortunately little is known about the details of this process. The second method is aggregate analysis which is concerned with identification and description of components in a collection of data arising from verbal interaction. This analysis typically involves establishing the relationship between components of the data set and properties of elements in the social environment which are relevant to the interest of the investigator. Such findings are of value and of interest but they tend to develop a patchwork of information and isolated facts which cannot be immediately integrated into the explanation of social process. Each method admits of a large number of alternative measuring techniques. We have selected just a few of these many alternatives to apply on an exploratory basis with the anticipation that they can be refined in future research and that more suitable alternatives will be developed.

In stream analysis we are dealing with the manifest properties of the record as they appear to the external observer and in general we avoid the attempt to infer the internal state of the actor or his motivational orientation. Sequences in the verbal stream can be approached in a hierarchy of levels beginning with syllables, words, verbal action, actors, topics, and molar social action. Studies of the patterns in which one syllable follows another could be of interest to those investigating the development of language habits in children at various age levels. A second level involves the study of the development of word sequences in dyadic interaction. In the word analysis we see the different patterns which emerge in the verbal flux as assertions are generated for communication. The word string varies widely in length from a single word to more than thirty words. In this research we have identified the minimum word string which in context could convey a complete thought. We have included no compound sentences but have separated them out into their simple sentence components as separate assertions. The pattern and order in which words actually follow each other, building up the internal structure of the assertion, offers a basis to understand the genesis and organization of the single communicative act as it appears in live conversation. The assertion and the process of its construction illustrates one form of the simple elementary social act. The third level of stream analysis concerns the verbal action sequence. This sequence emerges in the ordering of such verbal actions as assertions, questions, supports, interjections, fragmentation, and laughter. Measurement of these elements presents a greater problem due to major differences in variation in the length of different kinds of acts. The finest unit of counting is the single identifiable act. Affirmations and interjections consist almost universally of one or two syllable elements. The continuation of a syllable sequence in laughter varies considerably but tends to be confined to relatively short bursts of laughter of two to four syllables. Fragmentation emerges largely in the form of single syllable vocalizations and, if it is an incomplete assertion, it is usually abandoned within three or four syllables. The potential value of studying the action sequence is that it could illuminate the dynamic relation between assertion length and auxiliary acts such as supports, interjections, fragmentation, and laughter. This would lead to an appreciation for the need for variety and the need to control assertion length for successful communication. The fourth level of stream analysis is the actor sequence which determines the regularity or irregularity of the shifting of verbal emissions between partners. A string of verbal output from a single actor constitutes a half cycle in the dyadic interchange and a half cycle from each of the two actors in sequence constitutes a full cycle of verbal interaction. Each half cycle contains one or more verbal acts. Half cycles may vary by kind depending on whether they contain one or more assertions or are confined only to auxiliary verbal acts. Because verbal acts are more highly variable because of their potential composition, they can be subject to a greater variety of measures. These include syllable counts, word counts, action counts, the clustering of assertions, and the pattern of increase or decrease in assertion length. Variations in cycle characteristics include length and the composition of cycles in terms of assertive and nonassertive half cycles. The pattern and characteristic of cycling between actors has immediate implications for the quality of sharing and the characteristics of bonding for the conversational relation. The manner of building up a well-integrated exchange is highly significant for determining the quality of social interaction in real time. The fifth level of analysis is a topical sequence in which the investigator could determine the macro characteristics of the development of the total exchange. It is at this level that we get at the area of conversation and the generalized outcomes. Here we can study the dynamics of topical development, topical conversion, and the social implications of a series of topics. It is at this level that we identify the social processes of informing, teaching, persuading, and influencing between partners through the effective sequencing of varying kinds of topics. The sixth level of the verbal action stream involves the method and effects of putting together and evaluating the temporally separate segments of verbal interaction between the same partners. These socially vital processes occur in an extended succession of contacts between two friends, two family members, two colleagues, the professional and his client, or the manager and his subordinate. The success or deterioration of these relationships is determined and indicated by the verbal content of these repeated encounters.

The same six levels of analysis of verbal action are applicable with the use of aggregate data. Measures applicable to aggregate data are much more familiar in current sociological research. The frequency count is an excellent measure for assessing the properties of conversational data because the source is generic to the social action and does not include the input of the researcher as a primary component. In aggregate analysis the syllable is a relatively stable and uniform unit of measure which permits refined comparisons between kinds of verbal action. The components of conversation are sufficiently standardized to permit the application of uniform measurement across samples. A wealth of data which is readily assessible for complete and detailed recording permits exhaustive analysis through the application of precise measures. The fact that conversational data has not been extensively exploited should not detract from recognition of this area as a rich source of sociologically relevant information. The content and format of conversational data could be examined to determine skill in sociability, role adequacy, the substance of communication, the spontaneously expressed opinions of the participants, and the quality of the social relation. At present it is conventional to adduce these measures on an ad hoc basis, but they could be determined by rigorous analysis through precise measurement. Other mathematical measures dependent upon the frequency count include simple ratios, coefficients, variability, and linear and curvilinear relations. Variations in the lengths of verbal segments can be measured and comparison of cycle lengths for different kinds of dyadic contacts can be made.

PROPERTIES OF VERBAL FLUX

The stream of speech generated between two persons in conversation has four properties which vary in fairly orderly patterns. First, the speech stream appears in a sequence of cycles. The first cycle begins when the first partner starts emitting one series of verbal acts and ends when the second partner completes his verbal response. The verbal acts which a speaker may emit include assertions, questions, supports in the form of simple affirmation or negation, interjections, laughs, and fragmentation. Assertions and questions are verbal information carriers by virtue of the order and relations among the syllables which they contain. Supports seem to help the flow of conversation although they make up a rather small portion of the output. Laughter, fragmentation, and interjections appear to have fairly low value for transporting detailed information, but they, like the supports, may have a positive function in maintaining the flow of speech.

A cycle in which each of the two partners have injected assertions and/or questions is called a responsive cycle. A cycle in which only one partner emits assertive material and the other emits only nonassertive material, such as supports, laughter, or fragmentation, is called a narrative cycle. A cycle in which both partners emit only nonassertive materials is called a null cycle. The responsive cycle is more balanced and is effective in maintaining a tighter bond of verbal action between partners. Each is active in developing the sequence of speech and each must edit and integrate his own and his partner's outputs in a somewhat unpredictable and uncertain sequence of action. Responsive cycles require close coordination of thought and action between actors. The narrative cycle is of greater value in transferring extensive and complex information from the one who has it to the one who lacks it.

Both assertions and questions vary in amplitude or length of syllable string. They also vary in the extent to which an unbroken series of assertions are banded together without other kinds of verbal acts intervening between them. Variation in the amplitude of assertions and questions is suggestive of the quality of the verbal contact, as when we contrast extremely short assertions of one or two syllables to elaborate grammatically developed sentences of 20 to 30 syllables. The sequence of assertions in an unbroken series is referred to as clustering. The clustering measure permits identification of the pattern of single assertions preceded and followed by a low information bearing element, and sets of two, three, or more assertions in uninterrupted sequence. The extent of clustering of assertions indicates the degree of organization of the verbal output and is probably related to the density of information emitted, provided the amplitude is not too low.

A consistent pattern of increase or decrease in the amplitude of a series of assertions is called crescence. It indicates the speaker's tendency to invest increasing energy in a series of outputs within his half-cycle, or the opposite tendency — to decrease the length of successive assertions. We will define crescence as a continuing increase of three or more syllables from one assertion to the next in a series of at least three assertions within a half cycle, or alternatively, a decrease of at least three syllables per assertion over a series of at least three assertions. Nonassertive acts may be interspersed among the assertions without affecting the crescive property, as we treat it here.

Finally, there is the property of fluency, which we define as the proportion of assertions and questions to the total number of acts within the half cycle. Fluency is at a maximum when a half cycle contains only a series of assertions. Fluency is at a minimum

when a single assertion is accompanied in a half cycle by an extended series of nonassertive verbal acts. It is believed that a higher
degree of fluency facilitates the transfer of information, and that
it denotes a more effective use of time.

HYPOTHESES ON THE PROPERTIES OF CONVERSATION

Lacking a rigorous theoretical basis for generating hypotheses,
we have developed a series of hypotheses based on assumptions
about the developing nature of the conversational contact. The
conversational episode is generally marked by short exploratory
assertions in the beginning and near the end. We have predicted
that (1) the mean amplitude of assertions measured in syllable
length will be less in the initial and end portions and greater in
the middle portion of the contact; (2) males will manifest greater
mean amplitude than females in male-female pairs in conversation;
(3) greater amplitude will be manifested in male-male conversing
pairs than in female-female conversing pairs; (4) males conversing
with males will not have higher amplitude than males conversing
with females, that is, the sex structure of the dyad will not affect
assertion amplitude in the male; and (5) females conversing with
males will have a lower mean amplitude than females conversing
with female partners — the sex structure of the dyad will affect the
assertion amplitude by the female.

We expect (1) that the crescive property of the half cycle will
be predominantly positive, based on the tendency of an assertion
of a given length to contain information elements which will
require elaboration in the following assertion. The ensuing elaboration is therefore likely to be longer than the assertion which gave
rise to it. (2) Since crescence is more evident if amplitude is greater,
we expect that the positive crescence will be greater in males
participating in male-female dyads, than in the females. However,
(3) we expect that positive crescence will predominate over negative
crescence in all sex structures, and in the middle portions of the
conversation.

The clustering property depends on the ability of the speaker to generate uninterrupted sequences of assertions and questions, and we expect a strong inverse relation between the extent of the cluster and its frequency. Clustering could afford an index of the level of concentration of the speaker on what he is saying.

An inspection of the large scale flux vector (Figure 1) indicates the cycling process where the first actor emissions are plotted above the origin and the second actor is plotted below. The contrast between narrative and response cycles is evident. The narrative cycle is marked by a well-developed profile only on one side of the origin and a short abbreviated output on the other side. The response cycle is marked by well-developed profiles on both sides of the origin. The large scale plot (.04 inches per act on the horizontal axis and .04 inches per two syllables on the vertical) is more informative regarding action sequence, the distribution of fragmentation, assertion, support, and interjection. The small scale plot (Figure 2: .01 inches per act and per syllable), represents a lower level of magnification and better indicates cycling regularity, balance, and narrative and response exchange patterns. It provides an economical signature of the pattern of verbal intercourse between any two actors.

The results of the analysis of amplitude (Table 1) show support for the hypothesis that amplitude is greater in the inner portion of the conversational contact. The absolute difference is about .5 syllables, and the standard deviation is relatively high, which indicates a broad distribution of assertion lengths. Male pairs show somewhat greater amplitude than female pairs and a greater variability of assertion amplitude. In the male-female dyad, males average higher amplitude on about the same scale, but variability of assertion length for both males and females is reduced. The male amplitude mean is not significantly different when the male-male mean is compared to the male amplitude mean in the mixed dyad, and the null hypothesis is tenable. Females talking to other females manifest a higher amplitude in assertions than do females talking to males, and hence, the fifth hypothesis on amplitude is supported.

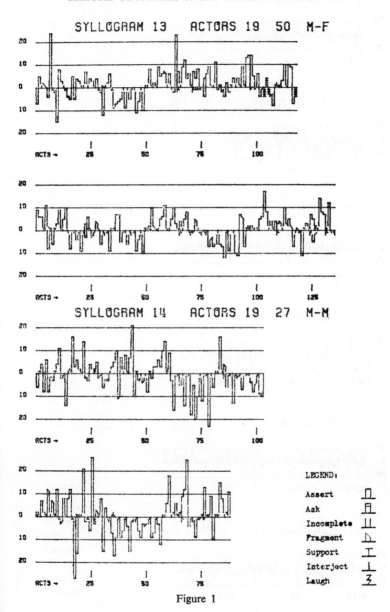

Figure 1

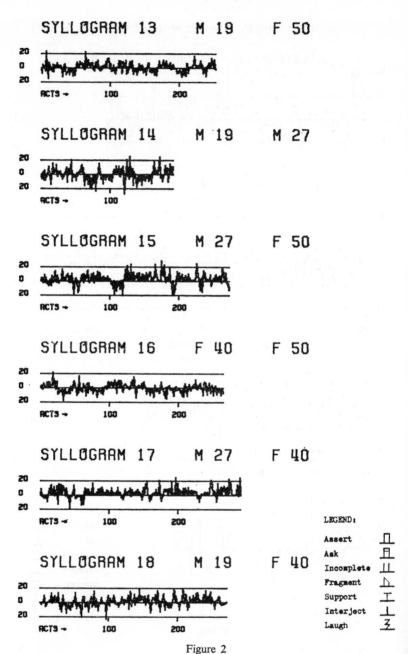

Figure 2

TABLE 1

Syllabic amplitude of assertions

Category	Dyads	Half Cycles	Mean Amplitude	S.D.	t	p^*
Ends	74	3690	7.9	4.8	−3.32	.001
Middle	74	5234	8.3	5.0		
Male-Male	18	2119	8.4	5.2	2.36	.008
Female-Female	17	2139	8.0	4.6		
Male	39	2567	8.3	5.0	3.48	.001
Female	39	2099	7.8	4.8		
Male-Male	18	2119	8.4	5.2	.74	.266
Male	39	2567	8.3	5/0		
Female-Female	17	2139	8.0	4.6	1.78	.035
Female	39	2099	7.8	4.8		
Narrative	74	1898	8.0	4.7	−2.34	.009
Response	74	2381	8.3	5.0		

* One-tail test.

The crescive property (Table 2) is predominantly positive in all comparisons, and the hypothesis is well supported. There is no support for the proposition that males manifest positive crescence or the crescive property in general more than the females. We also fail to find support for the proposition that crescence is greater in the midportions of the conversational contact than in the beginning and end. The extent of clustering demonstrates a consistent inverse function of frequency in all comparisons, a finding which is virtually implicit in the concept (Table 3). It does not appear to vary consistently according to the sex structure of the dyad, or according to the temporal portions of the conversational episode.

Amplitude appears to vary systematically in relation to dyad structure and temporal regions. It has the advantage of simplicity both conceptually and empirically. There is good reason to believe that assertion amplitude has a significant fundamental relation to the verbal communication process. It is probably one of the most useful measures of verbal flux. Amplitude is a substrate

TABLE 2

Crescence standardized by Dyad

Category	Dyads	Half cycles	Proportion of half cycles	Irregular	Positive +	Negative −	+−
Ends	74	1368	.37	29.9	2.6	1.4	.8
Middle	74	1882	.36	36.7	2.8	1.7	1.2
Male-Male	18	749	.35	35.5	3.2	1.7	1.3
Female-Female	17	781	.38	39.8	3.1	1.9	1.1
Male	39	942	.37	36.7	2.6	1.3	1.0
Female	39	779	.37	40.1	3.1	2.0	1.0
Male-Male	18	749	.35	35.5	3.2	1.7	1.3
Male	39	942	.37	37.2	2.6	1.3	1.0
Female-Female	17	781	.38	39.8	3.1	1.9	1.1
Female	39	779	.37	40.1	3.1	2.0	1.0
Narrative	74	1345	.34	39.5	3.0	1.7	.9
Response	74	1903	.49	36.8	3.1	1.8	1.3

TABLE 3

Assertion clusters per minute

Category	Dyads	Minutes	Assertions per Cluster					
			1	2	3	4	5	6+
Ends	74	148	7.3	3.5	2.0	1.2	.7	1.5
Middle	74	222	6.5	3.2	1.9	1.1	.7	1.9
Male-Male	18	90	6.4	3.4	1.9	1.1	.6	2.0
Female-Female	17	85	7.2	3.1	2.3	1.4	.9	1.6
Male	39	111	6.5	3.2	1.7	1.1	.7	1.8
Female	39	84	7.2	3.8	2.0	1.1	.7	1.5
Male-Male	18	90	6.4	3.4	1.9	1.1	.6	2.0
Male	39	111	6.5	3.8	1.7	1.1	.7	1.8
Female-Female	17	85	7.2	3.1	2.3	1.4	.9	1.6
Female	39	84	7.2	3.8	2.0	1.1	.7	1.5
Narrative	74	149	6.5	3.4	2.1.	1.2	.7	1.5
Response	74	221	6.9	3.3	1.9	1.1	.7	1.9

variable for the crescence property and it is probably operating within rather definite limits. Factors affecting these limits remain to be examined. Amplitude is potentially a suitable measure for the amount of information exchanged between conversing partners.

The property of crescence, which appears in about 6 percent of the half cycles, suggests a measure of elaboration in the assertion sequence. There is probably a generic difference between crescive cycles and cycles which contain assertions of relatively uniform length. The crescive property may indicate an expansion of interest as well as an expansion in the degree detail conveyed. The crescive cycles are predominantly positive, and they appear to enliven the stream of verbal outputs.

Assertions appear about 50 percent of the time in clusters. The clustering is a potential measure of speech integration and of efficiency in delivery. The degree of clustering is probably inversely related to the speaker's familiarity with what he is trying to convey. A person anticipating a verbal confrontation will sometimes rehearse what he plans to say in order to increase his familiarity with the syllable strings he will emit. This should improve his delivery, reduce fragmentation, and should be indicated by an increase in the clustering of assertions.

Fluency may be measured most efficiently in terms of assertions and questions. Maximum fluency, defined as 1.00, would be illustrated by well-edited prose. A zero index of fluency could be illustrated by a series of unorganized fragments. In normal conversation, it is probable that some admixture of supports, laughter fragmentation, simultaneous speech, and interjection lends impetus to the flow of speech and serves to highlight the assertive content. In this case, the optimal ratio for fluency would probably be around .5, indicating a substantial mix of various auxiliary verbal acts with assertions. It is this mix which helps to give the impression of spontaneity and a human quality to the conversational exchange. Our data yields a fluency ratio varying between .48 and .51.

PERIODICITY ASSESSMENT FOR AUXILIARY VERBAL ACTS

It is germane to the understanding of the speech process to determine whether or not the auxiliary verbal acts tend to occur with uniform regularity. If there is a high degree of regularity in the reoccurrence of auxiliary verbal acts, this would tend to indicate that speech is mechanical and that the auxiliary forms are required by social or rhetorical convention. Moreover, this regularity would have to occur in spite of the irregularity in the syllabic length of assertions. This would degrade the auxiliary function of these acts. Irregularity in the occurrence of the auxiliary verbal acts would indicate greater spontaneity in the formulation of the ongoing stream of speech and a higher degree of creativity in self-expression. If the speaker were creating and organizing new material, he would be expected to have greater difficulty and hesitation in resolving the various problems of composing his own verbal output. It is something of a struggle to formulate new speech.

Periodicity is defined as the regular reoccurrence of a particular auxiliary verbal act measured in terms of the number of intervening syllables or acts. We have measured periodicity by a coefficient which depends on the relationship of the mean to the standard deviation of the period.

$$C_p = 1. - \frac{\sigma}{\hat{u} + \hat{\sigma}}$$

where: C_p = coefficient of periodicity estimated
$\hat{\sigma}$ = standard deviation of the population of all periods for the verbal act
$\hat{u}$ = estimated mean length of all periods

As the standard deviation approaches zero, the length of the period becomes invariant and we have perfect periodicity indicated by a coefficient of 1.00. As the standard deviation increases to the point where it equals the mean, the coefficient of periodicity declines to .5 which indicates a widely variant period. As the standard deviation exceeds the mean, the coefficient of periodicity approaches zero, indicating virtually no regularity.

The assumptions that these periods are highly irregular in natural conversational exchange is supported by our findings. For the four auxiliary verbal acts — fragmentation, interjection, support, and laughter — the coefficient of periodicity ranges from .39 to .54.

Of these four auxiliary acts, laughter is the most widely variant in occurrence and should be termed episodic, rather than periodic, as indicated by the coefficient of approximately .4 (Table 5). The same may be said of fragmentation, interjection, and support.

TABLE 4

Assertion fluency coefficients

Categories	Dyads	Clusters	Acts	C	S.D.	t	p*
Ends	74	4527	6896	.40	.45	−1.10	.135
Middle	74	7008	10114	.42	.48		
Male-Male	18	2903	4132	.42	.45	−.47	.323
Female-Female	17	2748	3886	.43	.50		
Male	39	3360	4984	.41	.46	.19	.423
Female	39	2524	4008	.40	.45		
Male-Male	18	2903	4132	.42	.46	.42	.337
Male	39	3360	4984	.41	.46		
Female-Female	17	2748	3886	.43	.50	1.04	.149
Female	39	2524	4008	.40	.45		
Narrative	74	2022	3086	.43	.48	1.65	.047
Response	74	3390	4884	.40	.46		

* One-tail test.

Although these acts are more episodic than periodic, there are significant differences between the mean length of the interval between occurrences in the conversational stream. With regard to the intervals of laughter, males laugh twice as frequently as females when conversing with females. Males also laugh twice as much in the heterogeneous structure than they do in the homogeneous structure. Females laugh more frequently in the homogeneous structure than in the heterogeneous structure though the difference between mean intervals is less (Table 5). A similar pattern exists by sex structure for supports and interjections. The pattern by sex structure for fragmentation is generally reversed. Females fragment more than males when talking to males. Females fragment more in the heterogeneous sex structure than in the homogeneous sex structure. Males fragment less in the heteroge-

TABLE 5

Periodicity by verbal acts

	Fragmentation				Interjection			
	Period	SD	N	C	Period	SD	N	C
Half 1	6.5	6.2	1654	0.51	7.9	7.8	1387	0.50
Half 2	6.4	6.2	1606	0.51	7.8	7.7	1310	0.50
z, p	0.5	0.3623			0.3	0.2443		
Male	7.1	7.0	747	0.51	7.2	6.7	750	0.52
Female	5.8	4.9	1026	0.54	8.5	8.4	707	0.50
z, p	4.6	0.0001			−3.2	0.0018		
Male-Male	6.1	5.5	817	0.53	816	9.1	560	0.49
Female-Female	7.3	7.5	670	0.49	7.2	6.9	680	0.51
z, p	−3.3	0.0013			3.0	0.0029		
Male	6.1	5.5	817	0.53	8.6	9.1	560	0.49
Male	7.1	7.0	747	0.51	7.2	6.7	750	0.52
z, p	−3,1	0.0022			3.0	0.0033		
Female-Female	7.3	7.5	670	0.49	7.2	6.9	680	0.51
Female	5.8	4.9	1026	0.54	8.5	8.4	707	0.50
z, p	4.6	0.0000			−3.2	0.0017		
High	6.1	5.2	2015	0.54	8.3	8.0	1449	0.51
Low	7.2	7.4	1245	0.49	7.3	7.5	1248	0.50
z, p	−4.8	0.0000			3.1	0.0024		
	Support				Laugh			
Half 1	10.6	13.7	1023	0.44	25.3	37.7	430	0.40
Half 2	10.0	12.1	1033	0.45	20.7	32.2	497	0.39
z, p	1.1	0.2574			2.0	0.0456		
Male	9.1	11.4	599	0.44	16.0	24.5	350	0.39
Female	13.0	16.5	447	0.44	30.6	42.7	173	0.42
z, p	−4.4	0.0001			−4.2	0.0001		
Male-Male	11.8	12.9	408	0.48	29.6	40.5	148	0.42
Female-Female	8.6	10.7	602	0.44	23.1	35.8	256	0.39
z, p	4.1	0.0002			1.6	0.0991		
Male-Male	11.8	12.9	408	0.48	29.6	40.5	148	0.42
Male	9.1	11.4	599	0.44	16.0	24.5	350	0.39
z, p	3.4	0.0010			3.8	0.0004		
Female-Female	8.6	10.7	602	0.44	23.1	35.8	256	0.39
Female	13.0	16.5	447	0.44	30.6	42.7	173	0.42
z, p	−5.0	0.0000			−1.9	0.0556		
High	12.7	15.2	931	0.46	25.0	37.4	458	0.40
Low	8.3	10.3	1125	0.45	20.7	32.2	469	0.39
z, p	7.4	0.0000			1.9	0.0565		

neous sex structure than in the homogeneous sex structure. When we aggregate the periodicity intervals for all actors having the higher number of verbal outputs in each dyad and compare them to the corresponding aggregate of actors having the lower number of outputs, there are highly significant differences. The more talkative actors have a higher frequency of fragmentation and lower frequencies of interjection, support, and laughter as indicated by the lengths of the intervals. This indicates that fragmentation is a positive function of talking.

THE SEQUENCE PROBABILITY OF VERBAL ACTS

Sequence probability refers to the likelihood that any given kind of verbal act will be followed by any kind of verbal act. For example, what is the probability that an assertion would be followed by another assertion? What is the probability that an assertion would be followed by a question or a fragment or a support? Knowledge of the probability of the sequence among verbal acts affords a basis for a dynamic analysis of the characteristics of the stream. Such analysis would foster a better understanding of the basic function of the assertion in conjunction with other kinds of verbal acts. It is commonly assumed that the verbal action sequence within the speech segment constituting the output of one actor is predominantly made up of assertive acts which are well connected. The better the connection among assertions in the sequence, the greater the extent to which each assertion determines the direction and content of the assertion which follows it. As the assertion chain is more tightly linked, there is less freedom for innovation and range of subject matter. As the proportion of nonassertive acts in the speech stream increases, a greater mix will result with nonassertive acts being inserted more frequently between assertive acts which results in a looser relation between assertions and the reduction of influence of one assertion on the next. This would increase the latitude of the speaker, permit more rapid change of subject, and give the speaker greater freedom to modify his speech stream in the very process of formulating it.

The assessment of the sequence of all adjacent verbal acts was based on a frequency count of all such sequences within half cycles, separating out all male and female actors which for the eight acts yielded a sixty-four cell matrix. Dividing each of these cells by the grand total of all paired act sequences produced the proportion of the occurrence of every possible combination. These proportions were then summed by row and column where row totals represent the aggregate of all acts following a given act and column totals represent the total proportion of each act in the follower position. Table 6 represents the distribution of total sequence probability under the assumption of aggregate equilibrium (Coleman 1964: 161). For the total set, 41 percent of all acts were statements and 4 percent were questions. Thus 45 percent of all verbal acts were assertive acts and 55 percent were auxiliary acts. Since more than half of the acts are nonassertive, this means that for the most part assertions will be followed by something other than an assertion. In fact, an assertion is followed by an assertion only about 16 percent of the time. Fragments make up 24 percent of all acts so that for every two assertions we have one fragmentation. Moreover the distribution of fragmentation indicates that about 9 percent of all verbal acts are fragmentation following a break. The break is defined as the intrusion of some nonassertive act within an assertion. The summation of break (Column 5 in the Total, Table 6) indicates that 8.6 percent of all verbal acts are breaks, suggesting that slightly more than one-fifth of all assertions contain internal breaks. Interjections make up 13 percent of all verbal acts and they are primarily associated with statements. Of the times when an interjection occurs, about 50 percent of the time the interjection precedes the statement, and about 40 percent of the time the interjection follows the statement. Supports and laughter are about equal in incidence, each accounting for about 4 percent of all verbal acts. Insofar as laughter has a role, it precedes or follows a statement more than 50 percent of the time. Supports are followed by statements about 50 percent of the time and they are preceded by statements, interjections, or other supports. The verbal act labeled as interruptions in Table 6

TABLE 6

Verbal flux. Periodicity
sequence probability within half cycles

	All flux	1	2	3	4	5	6	7	8	Total
1	Statement	.1614	.0546	.0501	.0106	.0427	.236	.0091	.0037	.3557
2	Fragment	.1104	.0532	.0282	.0035	.0225	.0032	.0117	.0013	.2338
3	Interject	.0817	.0281	.0196	.0109	.0139	.0038	.0091	.0008	.1679
4	Support	.0343	.0103	.0086	.0093	.0046	.0038	.0023	.0015	.0749
5	Break	.0005	.0850	.0155	.0002	.0001	.0052	.0001	.0001	.1067
6	Laugh	.0157	.0031	.0055	.0032	.0020	.0005	.0015	.0007	.0321
7	Question	.0046	.0038	.0039	.0019	.0004	.0026	.0080	.0006	.0259
8	Interrupt	.0002	.0001	.0004	.0008	.0	.0001	.0	.0015	.0030
	Total	.4089	.2381	.1318	.0403	.0862	.0428	.0419	.0102	14561

	Male flux	1	2	3	4	5	6	7	8	Total
1	Statement	.1530	.0564	.0514	.0087	.0423	.0256	.0094	.0035	.3502
2	Fragment	.1085	.0497	.0266	.0035	.0235	.0042	.0136	.0013	.2308
3	Interject	.0822	.0253	.0192	.0118	.0162	.0041	.0099	.0008	.1695
4	Support	.0339	.0102	.0088	.0083	.0041	.0038	.0024	.0014	.0728
5	Break	.0004	.0850	.0167	.0	.0001	.0064	.0003	.0	.1089
6	Laugh	.0183	.0031	.0046	.0036	.0027	.0007	.0014	.0011	.0355
7	Question	.0049	.0050	.0050	.0017	.0003	.0020	.0094	.0010	.0293
8	Interrupt	.0003	.0	.0	.0011	.0	.0001	.0	.0015	.0031
	Total	.4014	.2347	.1323	.0386	.0892	.0469	.0463	.0106	7145

	Female flux	1	2	3	4	5	6	7	8	Total
1	Statement	.1695	.0529	.0489	.0124	.0431	.0216	.0088	.0039	.3611
2	Fragment	.1122	.0565	.0297	.0035	.0214	.0022	.0098	.0013	.2367
3	Interject	.0812	.0307	.0201	.0101	.0117	.0035	.0084	.0007	.1664
4	Support	.0348	.0104	.0084	.0104	.0051	.0039	.0023	.0016	.0769
5	Break	.0007	.0850	.0143	.0004	.0	.0040	.0	.0001	.1045
6	Laugh	.0131	.0031	.0063	.0027	.0013	.0004	.0016	.0003	.0289
7	Question	.0043	.0027	.0028	.0020	.0005	.0032	.0067	.0003	.0227
8	Interrupt	.0001	.0001	.0008	.0004	.0	.0	.0	.0015	.0030
	Total	.4159	.2414	.1313	.0419	.0833	.0388	.0376	.0097	7416

	High flux	1	2	3	4	5	6	7	8	Total
1	Statement	.1731	.0583	.0515	.0106	.0477	.0203	.0080	.0033	.3727
2	Fragment	.1214	.0550	.0278	.0036	.0247	.0025	.0083	.0010	.2443
3	Interject	.0786	.0266	.0170	.0076	.0151	.0033	.0058	.0002	.1543
4	Support	.0316	.0097	.0059	.0070	.0055	.0031	.0015	.0005	.0647
5	Break	.0007	.0930	.0162	.0002	.0	.0053	.0002	.0	.1157
6	Laugh	.0141	.0025	.0045	.0027	.0012	.0003	.0015	.0006	.0275
7	Question	.0039	.0020	.0027	.0015	.0006	.0030	.0048	.0003	.0187
8	Interrupt	.0001	.0001	.0001	.0006	.0	.0001	.0	.0010	.0020
	Total	.4234	.2472	.1259	.0339	.0948	.0380	.0300	.0069	8800

Low flux	1	2	3	4	5	6	7	8	Total
1 Statement	.1436	.0489	.0481	.0106	.0351	.0285	.0108	.0043	.3298
2 Fragment	.0936	.0503	.0286	.0033	.0191	.0042	.0168	.0017	.2177
3 Interject	.0863	.0304	.0236	.0160	.0122	.0045	.0142	.0016	.1887
4 Support	.0385	.0113	.0127	.0128	.0033	.0050	.0036	.0031	.0904
5 Break	.0003	.0727	.0142	.0002	.0002	.0050	.0	.0002	.0929
6 Laugh	0181	.0040	.0069	.0038	.0031	.0009	.0016	.0009	.0392
7 Question	.0057	.0066	.0057	.0024	.0002	.0021	.130	.0010	.0368
8 Interrupt	.0003	.0	.0009	.0010	.0	.0	.0	.0023	.0045
Total	.3864	.2243	.1408	.0502	.0731	.0502	.0601	.0151	5761

TABLE 7

Verbal flux. Periodicity
sequence probability between half cycles

All flux	1	2	3	4	5	6	7	8	Total
1 Statement	.0922	.0280	.0685	.1108	.0115	.0196	.0350	.0556	.4216
2 Fragment	.0352	.0082	.0158	.0178	.0035	.0029	.0089	.0180	.1103
3 Interject	.0340	.0096	.0106	.0151	.0049	.0034	.0043	.0160	.0979
4 Support	.1024	.0224	.0156	.0057	.0185	.0042	.0082	.0066	.1837
5 Break	.0002	.0001	.0002	.0011	.0	.0001	.0	.0018	.0037
6 Laugh	.322	.0048	.0092	.0056	.0038	.0162	.0049	.0070	.0837
7 Question	.0300	.0090	.0150	.0315	.0025	.0014	.0027	.0030	.0951
8 Interrupt	.0006	.0	.0003	.0011	.0	.0	.0	.0021	.0041
Total	.3268	.0821	.1353	.1888	.0447	.0478	.0644	.1100	8760

Male flux	1	2	3	4	5	6	7	8	Total
1 Statement	.1044	.0317	.0773	.1282	.0139	.0246	.0413	.0598	.4810
2 Fragment	.0367	.0096	.0170	.0198	.0048	.0046	.0094	.0182	.1201
3 Interject	.0223	.0073	.0109	.0157	.0051	.0041	.0035	.0142	.0831
4 Support	.0785	.0157	.0124	.0071	.0180	.0035	.0079	.0061	.1492
5 Break	.0005	.0003	.0003	.0008	.0	.0	.0	.0018	.0035
6 Laugh	.0243	.0038	.0061	.0038	.0033	.0167	.0035	.0051	.0666
7 Question	.0306	.0086	.0175	.0309	.0023	.0018	.0013	.0020	.0950
8 Interrupt	.0003	.0	.0	.0005	.0	.0	.0	.0008	.0015
Total	.2976	.0770	.1413	.2067	.0474	.0552	.0669	.1079	3948

Female flux	1	2	3	4	5	6	7	8	Total
1 Statement	.0823	.0249	.0613	.0966	.0096	.0156	.0303	.0522	.3728
2 Fragment	.0339	.0071	.0148	.0162	.0025	.0015	.0085	.0179	.1022
3 Interject	.0436	.0114	.0104	.0145	.0048	.0029	.0050	.0175	.1101
4 Support	.1220	.0278	.0183	.0046	.0189	.0048	.0085	.0071	.2120

5 Break	.0	.0	.0002	.0015	.0	.0002	.0	.0019	.0037
6 Laugh	.0387	.0056	.0118	.0071	.0042	.0158	.0060	.0085	.0977
7 Question	.0295	.0094	.0129	.0320	.0027	.0010	.0039	.0037	.0952
8 Interrupt	.0008	.0	.0006	.0017	.0	.0	.0	.0031	.0062
Total	.3508	.0862	.1303	.1741	.0426	.0418	.0623	.1118	4812

High flux	1	2	3	4	5	6	7	8	Total
1 Statement	.0979	.0281	.0545	.0867	.0125	.0146	.0278	.0411	.3632
2 Fragment	.0376	.0080	.0157	.0141	.0043	.0025	.0068	.0128	.1020
3 Interject	.0422	.0132	.0103	.0137	.0046	.0023	.0043	.0125	.1031
4 Support	.1310	.0276	.0187	.0050	.0242	.0039	.0096	.0066	.2266
5 Break	.0002	.0	.0002	.0059	.0062	.0185	.0027	.0043	.0865
6 Laugh	.0335	.0052	.0100	.0059	.0062	.0185	.0027	.0043	.0865
7 Question	.0338	.0119	.0176	.0367	.0030	.0016	.0027	.0041	.1113
8 Interrupt	.0007	.0	.0007	.0007	.0	.0	.0	.0021	.0041
Total	.3769	.0940	.1278	.1638	.0548	.0436	.0541	.0851	4383

Low flux	1	2	3	4	5	6	7	8	Total
1 Statement	.866	.0279	.0825	.1350	.0105	.0247	.0427	.0701	.4800
2 Fragment	.0327	0085	0158	0215	0027	0032	0110	0233	.1186
3 Interject	.0258	.0059	.0110	.0164	.0053	.0046	.0043	.0194	.0928
4 Support	.0738	.0171	.0126	.0064	.0128	.0046	.0069	.0066	.1407
5 Break	.0002	.0002	.0002	.0014	.0	.0	.0	.0021	.0041
6 Laugh	.0308	.0043	.0085	.0053	.0014	.0139	.0071	.0096	.0809
7 Question	.0263	.0062	.0123	.0263	.0021	.0011	.0027	.0018	.0788
8 Interrupt	.0005	.0	.0	.0016	.0	.0	.0	.0021	.0041
Total	.2767	.0701	.1428	.2138	.0347	.0521	.0747	.1350	4377

actually refer to simultaneous speech usually consisting of two or three words uttered by the listener while the speaker continues. It constitutes a small part of the nonassertive acts. We may conclude, first, that auxiliary acts are primarily associated with assertions and, second, there is a substantial mix of nonassertive acts among and within assertions.

A comparison of the distribution of sequences of verbal acts (within half cycle) between the male flux and the female flux (Table 6) reveals virtually identical patterns between the two and a close approximation to the total pattern. The male flux and the female flux do constitute two independent replications of the verbal sequence patterning. Therefore, we can tentatively conclude that there is considerable stability and regularity to this pattern. When we compare the general characteristics of high flux and low flux to the male or female distribution of verbal sequence, the general pattern is also similar. The high flux refers to the aggregated output of all actors who do more talking within the five minute contact. Low flux refers to the actors who did less talking. The more productive actors produced 60.5 percent of the talking. The high talkers had considerably more of their output in assertions, fragmentation, and breaks. For high talkers, 23 percent of the assertions contained breaks as contrasted to 19 percent of the assertions for low talkers. The main difference between the high and low talkers is the higher frequency of assertions for the high talker. The low talker has proportionately more fragmentation, support, laughter, and proportionately twice as many questions as the high talker. This tends to indicate that they are essentially cooperating to maintain the conversational flux.

We would expect a major difference in the verbal sequence when we compare the pattern within half cycles for the individual actor to the pattern between half cycles when the action shifts from one actor to the other. The first pattern refers to the internal organization of speech by a single emitter. The second pattern refers to the integral organization of the two speakers in linking their outputs together. At this point we are ready to examine the process of interactor linkage. Comparison of the total frequencies between (8760) and within (14561) half cycles indicates an average of three acts per half cycle before there is a between-actor exchange. This characterizes a rapid pattern of interchange and suggests close bonding. Comparison of the between and within half cycle sequence patterns shows a number of major differences. First there is a marked decline in the proportion of assertions as the first verbal act by the new actor and a decline of more than 60 percent in the proportion of fragmentation as the initial act. The proportion of supports increases from 4 percent within half cycles to 19 percent between half cycles. There is a marked decline in the proportion of breaks within the first assertion and a tenfold increase in the proportion of interrupts. There is a markedly higher probability that a support will either precede or follow an assertion. In general there is a much greater proportion of auxiliary verbal acts between half cycles than within half cycles. Fragmentation is primarily associated with the construction of assertions and the linking of assertions into an organized unit of speech. Support is primarily employed as a means of separating from the preceding half cycle in order to initiate a new one.

NARRATION AND RESPONSE

The profile of the assertive content of the conversational exchange has two clearly contrasted forms. In the narrative profile, one speaker emits verbal sequences which include one or more assertions while his partner's verbal sequences contain only auxiliary verbal acts. In the responsive profile, both speakers alternately include assertions in their verbal output. The narrative form has the advantage of the rapid and economic delivery of large blocks of information. It manifests itself in the telling of a story, the giving of detailed instructions, or developing an elaborate explanation. The narrative form may become so extended as to assume the format of a lecture. It has the advantage of allowing one actor to deliver his oration fully without the distractive influence of assertive inputs of his partner. The profile of the narrative form is well illustrated by Syllogram 15 (Figure 2). In the corresponding five minute dyad, the proportion of syllables in narrative cycles was .73 and .66 for the two actors. Since the narrative cycle by definition is dominated by one actor, it is imbalanced and this reduces the quality of the bond between actors. The responsive cycle permits a more uniform exchange between the two partners and leads to a progressive interlocking of assertions and ideas in a closely cooperating and reciprocating process. This presumably contributes positively to the quality of the conversational bond. The responsive cycle has the important social function of creating a close temporary union between pairs of actors which leads to understanding, agreement, and consensus. It also develops the socially essential skill whereby one actor can closely coordinate his behavior with that of another. The response pattern is illustrated in Syllogram 18 (Figure 2). In the corresponding dyad, the proportion of syllables in the response cycle was .95 and .65 for the two actors. About 90 percent of the 74 dyads were predominantly in the responsive pattern and this appears to be the primary mode of ordinary conversation. In general, about 60 percent of all cycles were in the responsive form.

Males talking to males are more responsive than females talking to females since 66 percent of the males' cycles are responsive as contrasted to 55 percent of the females' cycles (Table 8). When males talk to females, the male manifests a precipitous drop from 66 percent to 55 percent responsive cycles, while the female has a smaller but significant increase from 55 percent to 59 percent responsive cycles. Thus the male when talking to a male is much more responsive than when he is talking to a female, and the female when talking to a female is less responsive than when she talks to a male. Thus both sexes are more responsive toward males and less responsive toward females. This relationship may be indicative

TABLE 8

Narrative and responsive patterns
(By proportion of syllables)

Category	Narrative	Responsive	Cycles
Male-Male	.34	.66	500
Female-Female	.45	.55	666
Male	.45	.55	665
Female	.41	.59	665
Male-Male	.34	.66	500
Male	.45	.55	665
Female-Female	.45	.55	666
Female	.41	.59	665
Ends	.41	.59	978
Middle	.41	.59	1518
High	.45	.55	1248
Low	.36	.64	1248

of the socially subordinate position of the female and the power advantage of the male. A firm conclusion should await further replication of this comparison.

Contrasting the proportion of narrative and response cycles in the temporal portions of the dyad, it appears that there is no difference between the end portions and the middle portions. There is a major difference in the proportion of narration and response between the aggregates of high speakers and low speakers. Both speakers have more responsive cycles but high speakers have a much higher proportion of narrative cycles than low speakers (45 percent versus 36 percent). Low speakers have a proportionately higher number of response cycles than high speakers (64 percent versus 55 percent). This suggests that the low speaker is being cooperative and is supporting the higher output rate of the high speaker.

THE LAST LAUGH

Laughter is the consequence or outcome of verbal exchange and therefore should tend to arise later in the sequence of verbal acts. It is generally assumed that there is a positive relationship between the degree of amusement and the number of syllables of laughter (termed "ha's" in this text). It is likely that a single "ha" represents a low degree of amusement and may indicate sarcasm or surprise. Two or three "ha's" typically indicates rather mild amusement. If the number of "ha's" extends beyond ten, this indicates extreme amusement, intensive expenditure of energy, and often a breakdown in the verbal stream. There is an inverse relation between the extent of the laughter and the frequency of its occurrence (Table 9). The two syllable laugh is by far the most frequent although laughter of three, four, and five syllables are not uncommon. There are only six out of 1464 cases of laughter extending between 15 and 18 syllables. This distribution suggests that there is an inhibitor to the continuation of laughter. Females tend to have about one more syllable of laughter per act which would tend to give them

TABLE 9

Patterns of laughter

Number of "ha's"	Male-Female (39 Dyads)				Male-Male (18 Dyads)				Female-Female (17 Dyads)			
	Half 1		Half 2		Half 1		Half 2		Half 1		Half 2	
	A1	A2	A1	A2	A1	A2	A1	A2	A1	A2	A1	A2
1	16	31	30	50	8	10	18	16	10	6	17	14
2	41	57	83	143	17	18	35	29	22	28	48	58
3	20	41	44	90	7	8	12	19	14	19	35	47
4	8	21	18	40	2	4	6	8	9	9	15	16
5	2	8	7	19	2	3	4	5	3	2	8	7
6	1	8	2	17	1	3	1	3		3		6
7	1	2	1	6								1
8		1		2					1			
9				1					1	1		
10	1		1	1								
11		1	1	1								
12				1								
13												
14								1				
15										1		1
16												
17	1		1									
18										1		1
Mean "ha's"	2.6	2.8	2.6	2.9	2.4	2.6	2.3	2.7	2.5	3.1	2.7	3.0
Sigma	2.0	1.6	1.7	1.6	1.2	1.4	1.1	1.8	1.1	2.6	1.3	2.0
Laughs	91	170	188	371	37	46	76	81	58	69	125	152
Laughs/Dyad	2.3	4.3	4.8	9.5	2.1	2.6	4.2	4.5	3.4	4.1	7.3	8.9

the last laugh. The frequency of laughter is about twice as great in the second half suggesting that the level of amusement has built up to a greater degree and may indicate greater bonding in the second half through the pleasure of shared humor and amusement.

SENTENCE-CONCEPT ANALYSIS

The highest level of analysis which we shall undertake is the identification of concepts reflected in sentence units as indicated by the General Inquirer program for content analysis. The General Inquirer is a computer program which reviews the verbal content of each sentence and attempts to match each word in the listing of a specialized dictionary which is loaded with words indicative of certain preselected themes. We used the Harvard III dictionary which includes the themes of objects (social realm, cultural realm, natural realm, processes, psychological processes, behavioral processes), qualifiers, institutional contexts, psychological themes, and status connotations (Stone, Dunphy, Smith, and Ogilvie 1966: 172). The dictionary includes word listings under 113 specific concepts as listed in Table 10. Concepts are not mutually exclusive since the same word may be listed under more than one concept, and, therefore, the index percentages are not additive. Input for the General Inquirer program is conventionalized English with normal punctuation. The conversational record was edited so as

TABLE 10

Differential concept distribution by sex structure

(Index = sentences with listed concept/all sentences with any concept X100)

Concept	Male-Male (18 Dyads)	Female-Female (17 Dyads)	Male-Female (18 Dyads)
Male Role	10 (High)	6	7
Sign Accept	17 (High)	13	14
Impersonal Action	28	27	23 (Low)
Quantity	28 (High)	26	25
Over-under	29 (High)	25	25
Cultural Patterns	41	36 (Low)	40
Group	9	6 (Low)	10
Thought	36	32 (Low)	35
Cultural Realm	50 (High)	47	48
Institutional Context	41 (High)	37	38
Psychological Process	53 (High)	46	49
Behavior Process	46 (High)	44	42
Social Realm	53	48 (Low)	54
Evaluation	14 (High)	9	10
Concept Sentences	2025	2060	1889
Total Sentences	2127	2145	1978
Concepts/Dyad	112	121	105
Sentences/Dyad	118	126	110

to retain only assertions and questions eliminating all nonassertive verbal acts in preparation for content analysis. The dyads were sorted by sex structure to determine basic topical differences between structures. We randomly selected 18 of the male-female dyads (1968 sentences) for comparison. We retained the 18 male-male dyads (2127 sentences) and the 17 female-female dyads (2145 sentences). Comparison of the three sets of data indicated major differences in only 14 of the 113 concepts. This suggests a high degree of similarity across sex structures in the application of the basic concepts. This is of special interest since the conversations were spontaneously directed as to subject matter. The male-male dyads consistently produce higher sentence-concept indices for nine of the fourteen concepts which show major differences (Table 11). There is some indication that the males more frequently employ concepts referring to processes, the strength of assertion, the male role, and cultural and institutional context. Females are consistently lowest of the three structures on these heavily loaded items and are relatively low on concepts relating to the society such as cultural patterns, the social realm, and the group.

Content analysis has been used all too sparingly by sociologists in view of the fact that the expression of the topics constitutes social action and often indicates the direction of social orientation. Stone believes that sociology could use content analysis in research on opinions and attitudes and on the details of the "dramaturgical script" of an individual role performance (Stone, Dunphy, Smith, and Ogilvie 1966: 56). Content analysis is effective in producing a topical profile to permit assessment of social components and referents of social action. Since it is precise and detailed, content analysis would readily show major shifts in social orientation or topical interest in comparing groups over time. Sentence-by-sentence tabbing could be useful for intensive analysis of short passages of texts. At its present stage of development, content analysis of verbal material on the computer has several limitations. First, content analysis is presently limited by the size of the dictionary although additions may be made to the dictionary as desired by the researcher. The Harvard III dictionary includes 3,564 words

TABLE 11

Similar concept distribution by sex structure
(Index = sentences with listed concept/all sentences, with any concept X100)

Concept	Male-Male (18 Dyads)	Female-Female (17 Dyads)	Male-Female (18 Dyads)
Sex Role	12	12	13
First Person	11	9	11
Other	25	26	26
Nonspecific Object	25	23	27
Think	13	13	13
Logic Thought	20	17	19
Get	10	11	10
Overstate	25	23	23
Understate	18	16	16
Sign Strong	11	11	9
Sign Reject	15	15	16
Time	28	27	29
Space	30	29	28
Academic	13	12	14
Emotion	13	12	12
Role	19	18	20
Sign Potency	14	14	13
Person	34	34	35
Sign Relation	29	26	28
Sign Emotional	25	23	25
Social Place	11	12	12
Sign Ascend	11	11	10
Ascend Theme	11	11	10
Psychological Theme	68	67	66
Qualifier	63	63	62
If	13	12	12

which are oriented toward social and psychological themes. A second problem is ambiguity since many words have multiple meanings in the same contextual setting. This is illustrated in the sentence, "They were always kind of *gross*" where the word "kind" is correctly tagged as sign-relation, and incorrectly tagged as values, ideal-value, cultural realm, sign-accept, and psychological theme. These errors occur less frequently in analyzing well-edited prose and pose special problems in processing conversational data where specialized references and colloquial usage can be misleading.

The researcher particularly interested in conversational relations could prepare a special dictionary for analysis of such material. Short documents or short samples of verbal material are better suited to content analysis. Documents of excessive length are demanding of time and memory. For example, processing 13,000 words on the IBM 360, Model 65, required 32 minutes of time on the central processor unit and 225,000 bytes of core storage. However, the computer permits a level of efficiency and accuracy which makes possible definitive analysis of verbal material.

RELATION BETWEEN VERBAL AND NONVERBAL CUES

The somatic acts were coded into the verbal stream to the nearest whole word to permit analysis of the relationship between the two. This permits a determination of whether the somatic acts seem to be more closely associated with the assertion process or are more closely tied to one or more auxiliary verbal acts. If they were more closely associated with the assertion process, we would be inclined to think that they are auxiliary to the communicative process within the assertions and serve an expressive function. If they were more closely associated with fragmentation and interjection, then they would seem to be evidence of strain, hesitation, and uncertainty. If they were primarily associated with supports and laughter, then they would simply be equivalent to the auxiliary verbal acts. We can also attach some significance to the points in the verbal stream where the somatic acts are initiated and terminated. One might also assume some consistent differences in the positioning of the somatic acts in the verbal stream and the listener who follows it.

For the person in the speaking mode, there is a clear and invariant tendency for somatic acts to be positioned within an assertion or immediately at the end of an assertion. For all four somatic acts — contortion, eye contact, nod, and smile — approximately 55 percent of them begin or end within an assertion. Approximately 25 percent of these somatic acts begin or end immediately following an assertion or question. Since 80 percent of these acts are associat-

ed with verbal assertions, they are clearly auxiliary to and supportive of the primary communicative elements in the verbal stream
— the assertions. This would suggest that these somatic acts serve
an expressive function. About 10 percent of the somatic acts begin
or end with about equal frequency with fragmentation and interjection. The remaining 10 percent of the somatic elements are
variously distributed among the other verbal acts. The only exception is that about 13 percent of the termination of nodding is
associated with supports in the form of affirmation and negation
(Table 12). When a somatic act starts or ends within an assertion,
it is consistently more likely to be the start of the somatic act.
When a somatic act starts or ends immediately following an assertion, it is consistently more likely to be the end of the somatic act
(Table 12). This entire pattern of the association of somatic and
verbal acts is closely replicated in the male-male dyads and in the
female-female dyads, giving clear evidence that the pattern is
stable.

The patterning of the correspondence of the somatic acts of the
listener to the verbal acts of the speaker is so nearly identical with
that of the speaker as to constitute a mirroring process. The only
marked difference is that the frequency of the somatic acts of the
listener is about 75 percent of that of the speaker. Like the speaker,
the listener begins and ends about 55 percent of his somatic acts
within the speaker's assertions and about 25 percent immediately
following the speaker's assertions and questions. Also like the
speaker, the listener begins or ends somatic acts in conjunction
with fragmentation and interjection by the speaker. Thus 80 percent
of his acts are associated with the speaker's assertions. This would
suggest that the listener in rehearsing the speaker's verbal emissions
is supporting them to a reduced degree with this same pattern of
somatic acts. Therefore, in the listening process, the listener is
mirroring the speaker's action stream, both in its verbal and somatic components. The listener's somatic behavior also has a response
function which provides a sequence of supports to the speaker's
action. This close intermeshing of action constitutes a part of the
bonding of the action between the two partners.

CONCLUSIONS

The basic nature of the verbal action stream is that of a non-periodic and irregular communication carrier. The verbal stream has a spontaneous and natural quality of being newly created as it grows. The examination of sequence probability of verbal acts indicates a constant mix which is irregular in that an act of any given type is more likely to be followed by an act of some other type than by its own type. The central element of the verbal action stream is the assertive act consisting of the assertion and the question. The assertion is the only element which carries detailed and elaborately specified information which can be remembered or repeated with reasonable fidelity. The nonassertive verbal acts have been shown to be auxiliary to the assertion stream and to have relatively little consistent association with each other. The function of the somatic acts appears to be similar to that of the nonassertive verbal acts. Somatic acts are also auxiliary to the assertions and are strongly associated with them. They function primarily in an expressive capacity for the speaker. For the listener they have mirroring function at a slightly reduced level. The listener tends to repeat most of the somatic acts at approximately the same point in the speaker's verbal stream as does the speaker. We feel that he is not copying the speaker's behavior but is reconstituting it in conjunction with the assertion stream as he takes it in and recreates it mentally in the listening process. We do not believe that either the nonassertive verbal acts or the somatic acts could successfully stand alone to carry any respectable portion of a communication exchange.

In contrasting the narrative and response cycles, the former is better suited and more efficient, carrying large blocks of information in minimum time. It seems to have some function in all of the dyads and is used about 40 percent of the time. The response cycle produces a much better level of participation and hence better bonding between partners. The response cycle is probably more efficient in creating a close integration of action and a feeling of community through the close meshing of responsive outputs.

A broader level of analysis is available through content analysis. When the assertion is the unit of analysis, this allows us to get at the meaning and the direction and general import of the exchange. For purposes of understanding social action, the level of content analysis constitutes an advanced step which can reach its full potential only if it is based upon a rigorous investigation of conversation at the more microscopic levels.

7

THEORETICAL ASPECTS OF THE CONVERSATIONAL PROCESS

An attempt to develop a workable theory on the conversational process in the dyadic form, if in some measure successful, could be most useful for developing insight into the complexities and the problems of the process. Moreover, at the present, we need theoretical efforts aimed at natural conversation as it occurs in everyday life if we are to become aware of the basic requirements of the relation. It is necessary to direct the theoretical effort at the conversational relation as a whole. Homans (1961: 114) brings out this point as follows:

It is really intolerable that we can say only one thing at a time: for social behavior displays many features at the same time, and so in taking them up one by one we necessarily do outrage to its rich dark organic unity.

Thus it will be necessary to recognize the full range of basic elements within live conversation with sufficiently precise objective definitions and then to begin the complex task of establishing the limits of their integration. The final outcome of a successful theory would lead from an integration of these microscopic elements to the various macroscopic social alternatives which emerge in conversation between men.

Operational theory must incorporate a mix of both abstract and empirical elements if it is to be useful for explanation or experimentation. Sorokin has said that no significant theory can be purely abstract nor can it consist of a mere collection of empirical facts. He notes that sociology has accumulated a mountain of empirical data with only a modest part resulting in significant conclusions or the discovery of uniformities of middle range generality (Sorokin 1965: 481). The conversational process is ideally suited to this two-pronged attack which relates empirically oriented abstract generalizations to the detailed behavioral and verbal elements in the conversation in the sequence in which they naturally arise. The problem then arises of selecting an adequate conceptual base for the theory. The well-established psychological concept of stimulus-response is not adequate for a balanced sociological theory of this relation. For example, Ruesch describes the two person interaction as a set of stimuli composed of a statement of the first person and a set of responses which are the reply of the second person (Ruesch 1957: 189). This is a simple bipolar model which conceptually isolates a segment consisting of only two acts, the first of which is arbitrarily termed stimulus and the second response. This is unrealistic in the ongoing stream of statements and in fact constitutes a static excerpt from it. Every act operates as a consequence of preceding acts and to some extent as a cause of following acts. The conversational behavior consists of a directional chain of acts which become progressively less dependent upon one another as they are farther removed from each other in the stream. Moreover there is the generalized relation between partners in the conversational dyad which develops and becomes manifest in the course of interaction. Polya believes this can be interesting only if there is some difference of opinion (Polya 1954: 109). There is some truth in this idea but it might be more appropriate to broaden the scope to state that successful conversation requires some difference in information level for two actors regarding some specific subject. We might define this as the requirement for an information differential. Chomsky specifies three levels for the study of language: phonological, syntactical, and sematic (Chomsky as interviewed by Mehta 1971: 58). The phonological level refers to the identification and distribution of phonemes and morphemes as they conventionally appear in the language. These Chomsky believes are well understood, and he has dedicated his effort to the rigorous explanation and description of the many varieties of the syntactical relations within assertions.

The sematic level which is not well understood refers to the difficult phenomenon of the transfer of manifest meaning. We will not attempt to struggle with the difficult philosophical interpretations of meaning (see Brown 1958; Carnap 1959; Ogden and Richards 1923; Vygotsky 1962; Whorf 1956). Manifest meaning refers to the interpretation which the listener would place on a verbal message which he had accurately heard. The difficulty of being explicit regarding meaning arises in large part from the fact that meaning is accretive and can be variably assigned to individual words, parts of assertions, complete assertions, and collections of assertions. The subjective element of meaning enters twice, first in the verbal approximation of the speaker of what he wants to say and second in the election of the listener of some one of the alternative meanings which he could reasonably assign. Of course, the words used have a constraining effect on the meaning which could be assigned. The attempt to describe language at the three levels of phonological, syntactical, and semantic does not account for the nonassertive verbal elements, intensity variation, and somatic behaviors which accompany live language exchange between persons. Therefore, it would be opportune to orient an operational theory toward the makeup and functioning of the conversational stream incorporating assertions and the auxiliary acts.

Communicative behavior may be somewhat mysterious as regards its true source or its ultimate repository in the memories of the actors, but it is emitted as an external reality which we can jointly observe and discuss and sometimes agree about (Pittenger, Hockett, and Danehy 1960: 246). The focus of this discussion can be viewed in two dimensions: static and dynamic. Rapoport defines static theory as concerned with the structure of the system, the description of the relation among the variables without regard to time. Dynamic theory studies the behavior of a system as it progresses from state to state (Rapoport 1969: 18). Static theories often tend to be partial and to deal with isolated aspects of a system. They can be helpful in preparing the groundwork for the dynamic theories and for developing a more rigorous understanding of a specific property. The first advantage of the dynamic theory is that it is likely to take the system as a whole and to identify and interpret sequencing patterns among the elements in the moving stream. Dynamic theory thus reaches a position where it can evaluate direction, velocity, and terminus of verbal interaction. The second advantage of dynamic theory is that it permits recognition of the concept of the channel in which the communication flows. Lennard notes that category systems used in static research are limited to only one channel, usually the verbal one. He feels that a still more serious objection is that the parameters selected for study and amenable to measurement are not the significant ones (Lennard and Bernstein 1969: 54). A dynamic theory permits one to see the functional relation between the auditory and visual channels and the bidirectionality of each. This picture becomes even more complex if the conversing group consists of more than two people.

A final and fully satisfactory explanatory theory does not usually emerge in an early attempt to organize a complex of data. More typically there is a series of gradually improved formulations which may extend over a considerable period of years or decades. The best that we can hope for here is to make some usable contribution to this series of formulations. Homans sets forth some conditions for a theory:

A theory of a phenomenon consists of a series of propositions each stating a relationship between properties of nature.... Propositions do not consist of definitions of properties...nor may a proposition merely say that there is some relationship between the properties. Instead, if there is some change in one of the properties, it must at least begin to specify what the change in the other property will be. To constitute a theory the propositions must form a deductive system (Homans 1964: 811).

Thus a theory of dyadic conversation should incorporate a description of the relevant properties followed by definitive propositions concerning the interrelationships among properties, ending with a statement which integrates these properties into a system which is temporally variant and developmental. This falls within the purview of social interaction which, as Blumer has noted, has been taken for granted and has been treated as having little if any significance within its own right (Blumer 1969: 7). Furthermore, it is not sufficient to treat social interaction in global terms as an abstract concept. It is essential to make a careful and detailed breakdown of the components of interaction and to discover the principles which govern their integration into an action system. The usual structural approach in sociology tends to neglect microscopic analysis of interaction and also inhibits attention to its developmental character (Glaser and Strauss 1964:678). These same authors point out the value of discovering theory from data systematically obtained and analyzed in social research which they call *grounded theory* (Glaser and Strauss 1967: 1). We must also consider the question of the various forms of language. Much of the early research in the area of language has dealt with written forms or with a generalized concept of the whole body of the language illustrated with supposedly typical usage. Thus Whorf gives the Hopi Indian statement *hari rita* which he translates "it lies in a meandering line, making successive rounded angles" (Whorf 1956: 52). This ignores the basic task of determining how language in use relates to and defines social action. One authority notes that a problem which always arises when language is to be defined is whether the vocal nature of speech should or should not be included in the definition, although it is a fact that the languages linguists deal with are or were primarily spoken (Martinet 1962: 25). The natural form of language is the vocal form and therefore it is the most direct approach to the study of social interchange. The reciditative form of vocal language, such as sayings, slogans, and set speeches, constitutes an initial step in formalization. The second step in formalization is the written form with its elaborate reworking, editing, and careful improvemnt of passages to attain some kind of compositional ideal. These latter forms are derived both directly and indirectly from the original vocal form.

There are certain universal characteristics which can be analyzed with any spoken language. Each language has an extended standardized vocabulary usually referred to as the lexicon, which provides consistent elements which the speaker may assemble in making assertions. The large vocabulary offers virtually infinite latitude in the specifics of what the speaker may say. Each language also has certain auxiliary verbal elements, which may or may not be standardized, which accompany the assertion sequence. In theorizing about assertions, a problem arises precisely because assertions have such wide latitude. They are not standardized. Thus assertions are nonuniform and unpredictable. They are constantly incorporating some novel element which in the mass lead to some unique outcome. The task of theory then becomes one of discerning the principles whereby assertions are assembled into strings which lead to an accumulation of shared knowledge between speakers. Theory should point to the specific social outcomes of the series of assertions exchanged between persons.

The essential problem for theory is to determine the make up of the elements governing the formulation and sequencing of messages emerging between conversing partners. This in turn is one of the core problems in studying the nature of social process which ultimately roots in dyadic interaction. Cherry calls conversation — the two person interaction — the fundamental unit of human communication (Cherry 1971: 12). All verbal communication, both written and oral, has a dyadic property in that it requires both a source and a receiver isolated in a private interaction sequence even though the source may be something recorded or something written years before. Successful communication with a prerecorded source requires the exclusion or ignoring of potentially distracting stimuli, a condition which we refer to as concentration. Our concern, however, is with face to face verbal interaction. Miller claims that communication, if it is anything at all, is a social event, and that the spread of information among a group of people is one of the most important events that can occur (Miller 1951: p.v.). It is not sufficient to center attention merely on the source or the receiver and their related properties. As Blau has noted, an alternative approach which has not yet been sufficiently explored is to treat not the individual but the interpersonal relationship as the unit of analysis (Blau 1962: 42). This means that analysis must be concentrated on the interaction stream itself and that theory must strive to set forth the principles governing the make up and flux of the stream.

The analysis of the process of interpersonal communication leads directly to more general implications. Rapoport identifies the task of a general system theory as the deduction of equilibrium states and/or the short term and long term changes that classes of systems undergo, and to deduce or postulate laws that govern the existence, the behavior, or the evaluation of classes of systems (Rapoport 1969: 18). Bertalanffy, the modern father of general system theory, recognizes the sociological import for such analysis (Bertalanffy 1968: 196).

Present sociological theory largely consists in attempts to define the sociocultural "system", and in discussion of functionalism, i.e. consideration of social phenomena with respect to the "whole" they serve.... Concepts and theories provided by the modern systems approach are being increasingly introduced into sociology, such as the concept of general system, of feedback, information, communication, etc.

As Bertalanffy implies, a general theory of communications would have some application and some consequences throughout the discipline of sociology insofar as it is concerned with active social systems. Therefore, it is desirable to suggest some limits for the application of a general theory relating to the two person conversation process. We suggest that a reasonable limit might be the inclusion of the immediate outcomes of the conversational encounter. The first kind of outcome is the action effect of the conversation as it affects agreement, disagreement, or joint action. These effects are attained through processes which we identify as persuasion, argument, discussion, and information. Persuasion may include coercive or reward pressures verbally defined or the various levels of threat or entreaty. The second kind of outcome would be a partially entailed contact of a verbal nature growing out of a preceding verbal contact. For example, the next contact with the same partner has some relation to the verbal content of the earlier contact and a sequence of verbal contacts progressively modifies the social nature of the relationship of which it is a basic constituent element. There is also a progressive branching in conversational contacts from one partner to another. In these contacts, the individual builds up contagious verbal resources which affect what he passes on to another as the dyadic chaining extends on through time.

SOME THEORETICAL CONTRIBUTIONS RELATED TO VERBAL COMMUNICATION

Although there is no organized body of theory which bears precisely on face-to-face conversational process, a number of scientists in sociology, anthropology, psychology, medicine, speech, and engineering have set forth propositions which are relevant to the theory of conversation. Most of the propositions are static in that they relate properties or set forth generic descriptions of properties. Theories which recognize the dynamic aspect of the conversation tend to remain vague and abstract without any obvious carryover to the empirical level. Space permits reference only to a select few of the hundreds of authors who have commented on the conversational process. Mead indicated that what language seems to carry is a certain content which is measurably identical in the experience of certain individuals so that the symbol has to mean the same thing to all individuals involved (Mead 1934: 54). In another context, he noted that the process of communication cannot be set up as something that exists by itself, or as a presupposition of the social process since the social process must be presupposed in order to render thought and communication possible (Mead 1934: 260). Here Mead's primary contribution appears to be in his recognition of the symbol as an agency for exchanging meaning between persons. Vygotsky was concerned with the origin of the speech process and referred to what he called "egocentric speech" as a phenomenon of the transition from inter-psychic to intrapsychic functioning, i.e. from the social collective activity of the child to his more individualized activity. He thought that speech for oneself originates through the differentiation from speech for others (Vygotsky 1962: 133). He also pointed out that the child went through numerous vocal exercises as a precursor of dyadic speech. He was primarily concerned with the relation of language to the development of concepts and the expression of thought.

The concept of immediacy has been used as a theoretical base for referring to a dimension within language which indicates an attitudinal state. Wiener and Mehrabian define immediacy as the degree of directness or intensity of interaction between the communicator and his referents. Nonimmediacy is any variation in word usage which indicates differences in the degrees of separation or nonidentity among the communicator or the addressee. They find a positive correlation between positive affect and verbal immediacy and also a positive correlation between negative affect and nonimmediacy (Wiener and Mehrabian 1968: 4, 31). The literal meaning of verbal communications is the basic for an analysis of immediacy. For example, use of the present tense is more immediate than use of the past or future tense. Reference to objects physically near is more immediate than reference to objects more remote. Rapoport suggests a mathematico-hypothetical theory construction based on the semantic structure. Once corpuses of verbal output become visible as systems, Rapoport believes that hypotheses to be tested will likely suggest themselves. He stresses that the important thing is to have hypotheses suggested by system properties rather than chosen on an ad hoc basis (Rapoport 1969: 35). Whorf introduces a sociocultural dimension which constitutes an important theoretical contribution to the study of the social functioning of language. According to Whoff, speech is culture bound. The illusory appearance of spontaneous speech results from the fact that the obligatory phenomena within the apparently free flow of talk are so completely autocratic that speaker and listener are bound unconsciously as though in the grips of a law of nature (Whorf 1956: 221). Whorf points out that the words and the referents used are in many cases uniquely determined by specific cultures so that it is impossible to fully equate the thought processes of two persons from different cultures even though they appear to be saying the same thing. Such differences arise from pronounced cultural biases such as the militaristic society with its elaborate terminology for weapons, tactics, and martial exercises; the religious society stressing God, prayer, salvation, and miracles; the commercial society concentrating on money, trade, production, and industry; or the agrarian society which talks in terms of soil, crops, tillage, and seeds. With obsessive differences in so many directions, it will be difficult for these people to talk in a cross-cultural relation and maintain full congruence of terms and referents.

A dynamic theory of conversation could lead to a far more adequate model for integrating the phenomena which are involved in the exchange process. Various theorists have set forth theoretical propositions which incorporate a dynamic component. Among sociological theorists, Erving Goffman is perhaps the most energetic in developing a theoretical framework to accommodate the many ramifications of face-to-face interaction. First, he defined the state of talk as a process of reciprocal ratification where two persons have declared themselves officially open to one another for purposes of spoken communication and guarantee together to maintain a flow of words. This state of talk also includes a set of significant gestures which can be employed when a new participant officially joins the talk or when one officially withdraws or when the state of talk is terminated (Goffman 1967: 34). A prerequisite for sustaining the state of talk Goffman refers to as facework. Face is defined as the positive social value a person effectively claims for himself by the line others assume he is talking during a particular contact (Goffman 1967: 5). During active social confrontation face can be gained or lost. When the actor emits actions which are appropriate to the spate of communication and are approved by his associates he gains face. When the actor fails to emit appropriate actions or when his behavior is disapproved by his associates, he loses face. Through ritual, the individual is taught to be perceptive, to have feelings attached to self, have pride, honor, dignity, considerateness, tact, and a certain amount of poise (Goffman 1967: 44). In opening up talk to the other, the individual exposes himself to pleadings, commands, threats, insults, and false information; the mutual considerateness characteristic of face engagements reinforces these dangers, subjecting the individual to the possibility of having his sympathy and tactfulness exploited (Goffman 1963: 105). Goffman identifies the ultimate behavioral materials as glances, gestures, positionings, and verbal statements that people continuously feed into the situation whether intentionally or not (Goffman 1967: 1). Thus the proper study of interaction is not the individual and his psychology but rather the syntactical relations among the acts of different persons mutually present.

The conversational process must be described as a system of action in which highly variable components are composed an element at a time. Meerloo states that the play of conversation must be a collective action, spoken in such a way that the listener is able to receive the words and know what to do with them in a mutual experience if it is to be real communication (Meerloo 1967: 146). There are two basic models of interaction according to Lennard and Bernstein (1969: 34-35). The first they term the reactive model which involves long interaction chains rather than immediate action-reaction sequences. The second model takes account of cumulative effects and these authors suggest that the stochastic process is applicable. The stochastic process can be applicable at a generalized level of interaction such as assessing the probability of the occurrence or nonoccurrence of a discrete event. For example, such an event would be responding or not responding or the probability that a given actor would respond. The stochastic model is not useful in predicting the form or content of the next assertive act since speech is potentially so variable in content and is more typically something of a unique event. Convergence is one of the consequences that interaction in social systems may be expected to accomplish because interaction between individuals tends to decrease dissimilarites in their expectations, goals, and behavior (Lennard and Bernstein 1969: 14). As dissimilarites are decreased, a trend toward consensus, shared information, and shared beliefs develops. Theoretically this process could be specified between pairs of persons and groups of persons. In the two person relation, Cherry notes that conversations are not just signals passing back and forth between people but are to some degree or other matters of personal involvement. What you say cannot be unsaid and this affects the relationship to some extent, changing it either for better or worse (Cherry 1971: 11). Conversation has its full impact in the present moment while it is being delivered and received. If gaps or excessive hesitation occurs, much of the effect is lost and some assertions may be ignored altogether. Keltner believes that we speak as a result of certain conditions and feelings and responses that are current at the moment and are of such multiplicity that we can never recapture them in exactly the same intensity or in the same extent or degree (Keltner 1970: 188). There is no simple basis for synthesizing these particular aspects of the conversational relation and they represent only a limited portion of the wide variety of propositions which may be found in the literature. Their primary value for our purposes is to indicate the rather fragmentary and ill-coordinated character of theory regarding the flux of conversation.

DIMENSIONS OF THE WORKING MODEL

A coded excerpt of live convesation will be useful to illustrate the central requirements of an explanatory theoretical model for conversation. The following excerpt represents approximately 94 seconds in the latter part of a conversation of 300 seconds in length between a male and a female. The coding legend is as follows:

Category	Code	Category	Code	Category	Code
1. Male Actor	1	8. Fragmentation	/	15. Eyes Off	F
2. Female Actor	2	9. Assert Break	+	16. Start Nod	N
3. Assert	.	10. Simultaneous	(12)	17. Stop Nod	P
4. Question	?	11. Syllable	—	18. Start Smile	S
5. Support	*	12. Start Contort	C	19. Stop Smile	T
6. Interject	=	13. End Contort	D	20. Head Toss 1	@
7. Laugh	&	14. Eyes On	E	21. Head Toss 2	%

The coded conversational specimen (Figure 1) is followed by an edited version (Figure 2) which includes only the assertive acts

CODED CONVERSATIONAL SPECIMEN

2,I WAS TALK-ING TO%SUE A-BOUT SOME-THING A LIT-TL
E WHILE A-GO ABOUT HER FI-AN-CE.1T,ARE YOU GO-ING
TO%GET MAR-RIED AND MAKE YOUR MILLION.OR MAKE YOUR
MIL-LION AND THEN GET%MAR-RIED.AND MAKE YOUR MIL-L
ION AND THEN GET MAR-RIED?2F,1,1S,AH/2E,I DONAT K
NOW.1C,IAM EN-GAGED.1D,HA-HA-HA-HA&(12,HA-HA-HA
&)2S,2,1F,WELL=THAT',S%2N,A GOOD START.2P,(21,HA
-HA-HA&)HA-HA-HA&1E,2T,1,I'VE LOST∂HALF,2S,OF MY
∂MIL-LION AL-REA-DY.1T,2,HA-HA-HA-HA&1,AH/2%SHE
∂MUST%BE WEAR-ING THE ROCK OF,2N%GI-BRAL-TAR.2P,H
A-HA-HA-HA&1,WELL=IF YOU'LL USE A∂MAG-NI-FY-ING G
LASS,1S,IT LOOK S∂HUGE.1T,2,HA-HA-HA&1S,1,1C,0-T
HER-WISE∂IT'S,1D,NOT THAT∂BIG.2F,1T,2,OH=I THINK
MY CON-TACT'S GO-ING,2C,TO FALL OUT.2D,AND IT'S G
O-ING TO BE BEAU-TI-FUL.HA-HA&1,1S,OH=NO*IF YOUR
CON-TACT FALLS OUT THEN WE'LL HAVE TO∂DIS-CON-TI
N-UE(12,TO%STOP.)THIS TALK.WE'LL,1C∂SQUINT DO SO
ME-THING.2;I'M%TRY-ING.HA-HA-HA-HA&1,GET IT%BAC
K IN.1T,1D,2,OH=DO YOU∂HAVE A-NY CLASS-ES WITH%JE
R-RY?HE JUST%FAS-CI-NATES ME.1,AH/∂YEAH I HAVE+A
H/PER-SON-NEL∂MA-NA-GEMENT.

2,OH=%RE-AL-LY=1,WITH JER-RY.2,HE VE-RY SEL-DO
M%GOES.HA-HA&I'M SUR-PRISED YOU KNOW HIM.HA-HA&1
F,1,YEAH*AH/NO*IT IS A TUES-DAY∂THURS-DAY+AH/THR
EE-THIR-TY CLASS.2,2N%UH-HUH*2P,1,1N,AND HE, 1E,
TRIES TO MAKE THOSE.HE'S(12,OH=DOES%HE?RE-AL-LY=
)1P,U-SU-AL-LY∂A-WAKE BY THAT TIME.2%OH=FINE*WEL
L=I KNOW HE U-SU-AL-LY DOES-N'T GET UP UN-TIL ABOUT
(21,1N,YEAH*1P)TWELVE.2T,HE'S,2N%DAT-ING ONE OF
THE GIRLS O-VER 2P,AT THE HOUSE.1,OH=YOU'RE IN THE
SAME HOUSE THAT/I THOUGHT HE HAD JUST LOST∂THAT,2S,
LO-VER.1S,2,HA-HA-HA&1,I DON'T KNOW WHY WE'RE TAL
K-ING A-BOUT POOR∂JER-RY.2,HA-HA-HA-HA&I THINK(2
1,JER-RY IS/)HE'S,2N,FUN-NY.2P,1,I HOPE HE NE-VER
HEARS THIS.2%HA-HA-HA-HA-HA&I,2N,GUESS=HE WOULD
-NAT.2P,SURE-LY HE/HAS HE BEEN TELL-ING YOU ALL OF
HIS PROB-LEMS?1,1T,OH=1F,YES*JER-RY/JER-RY'S∂LH
E,1E,LAST RO-ME-O OF,1C∂O-S-U.1D,AND/AH/HE/2,THA
T'S%RIGHT.1,HE IS IN LOVE ONE WEEK.AND GET-TING MA
R-RIED THE NEXT WEEK.AND2T,DI-VORCED THE WEEK AF-T

ER.1C,AND+YOU∂KNOW=HIS THREE WEEK,1D,STINTS∂ARE+
THEY'RE/,1C,1S∂AW-FUL.1D,IT,2S,I MEAN=WE FEEL SO
SOR-RY FOR∂HIM,2T,PLAY-ING OUR,2S,SMALL VI-O-LIN
S.2,HA-HA&IT WAS-N*T SO%FUN-NY+ACT-U-AL-LY=BECAU
SE I WAS THE LAST ONE.HA-HA&AND IT ON-LY LAS-TED TW
D WEEKS.HA-HA&1%YOU∂ON-LY∂LAS-TED TWO WEEKS?2,2N,
YES*2P,(21,THAT AS∂AW-FUL.)BUT WE HAD%BETS ON IT.J
ER-RY DID.WE FIG-URED WE,2T,NEE-DED THE MO-NEY.AN
D E-VER-Y-ONE SAID WE%COULD-N'T MAKE A MONTH.AND W
E%THOUGHT WE COULD WITH SPRING BREAK IN BE-TWEEN.H
A-HA&1F,AND WE DID-N'T%E-VEN DO THAT.1E,1S,1N,1,
SON,1P,OF∂A GUN=WA/WAS-N'T,1T,THERE A∂BLONDE IN B
E-TWEEN?2,2N,YES*2P,1,IS THAT ONE NOW?2%NO*2N,NO
*NO 2P,2S%THAT'S/2N%THERE'S A/(21,THE∂BLONDE WAS
BE-FORE YOU?)THERE'S A BRU-NETTE%NOW.THE BLONDE,2
P,(21,OH=D-KAY=)WAS BE-FORE%ME KIND OF WEDGED%IN.
IS,HA-HA-HA-HA&

Figure 1

EDITED CONVERSATIONAL SPECIMEN

2 I WAS TALKING TO SUE ABOUT SOMETHING A LITTLE WHI
LE AGO ABOUT HER FIANCE. ARE YOU GOING TO GET MARRIE
D AND MAKE YOUR MILLION. OR MAKE YOUR MILLION AND TH
EN GET MARRIED. AND MAKE YOUR MILLION AND THEN GET M
ARRIED?1 I DONAT KNOW. IAM ENGAGED. 2 THAT S A GOOD S
TART. 1 I VE LOST HALF OF MY MILLION ALREADY. 2 SHE M
UST BE WEARING THE ROCK OF GIBRALTAR. 1 IF YOU LL USE
A MAGNIFYING GLASS IT LOOKS HUGE. OTHERWISE IT S NOT
THAT BIG. 2 I THINK MY CONTACT S GOING TO FALL OUT. A
ND IT S GOING TO BE BEAUTIFUL. 1 THIS TALK. WE LL SQUI
NT DO SOMETHING. 2 I M TRYING. 1 GET IT BACK IN. 2 DO
YOU HAVE ANY CLASSES WITH JERRY?HE JUST FASCINATE
S ME. 1 I HAVE PERSONNEL MANAGEMENT. WITH JERRY. 2 HE
VERY SELDOM GOES. I M SURPRISED YOU KNOW HIM. 1 IT IS
A TUESDAY THURSDAY THREETHIRTY CLASS. AND HE TRIES
TO MAKE THOSE. USUALLY AWAKE BY THAT TIME. 2 TWELVE.
HE S DATING ONE OF THE GIRLS OVER AT THE HOUSE. 1 I TH
OUGHT HE HAD JUST LOST THAT LOVER. I DONT KNOW WHY
WE RE TALKING ABOUT POOR JERRY. 2 HE S FUNNY. 1 I HO
PE HE NEVER HEARS THIS. 2 HE WOULDNAT. HAS HE BEEN TE
LLING YOU ALL OF HIS PROBLEMS?1 JERRY S THE LAST RO
MEO OF OSU. 2 THAT S RIGHT. 1 HE IS IN LOVE ONE WEEK. A
ND GETTING MARRIED THE NEXT WEEK. AND DIVORCED THE
WEEK AFTER. AND HIS THREE WEEK STINTS ARE AWFUL. WE
FEEL SO SORRY FOR HIM PLAYING OUR SMALL VIOLINS. 2
IT WASN T SO FUNNY BECAUSE I WAS THE LAST ONE. AND IT
ONLY LASTED TWO WEEKS?2 BUT WE HAD BETS ON IT. JERRY
DID. WE FIGURED WE NEEDED THE MONEY. AND EVERYONE SA
ID WE COULD N T MAKE A MONTH. AND WE THOUGHT WE COULD
WITH SPRING BREAK IN BETWEEN. AND WE DIDN T EVEN DO
THAT. 1 WASN T THERE A BLONDE IN BETWEEN?IS THAT O
NE NOW?2 THERE S A BRUNETTE NOW. WAS BEFORE ME KIND
OF WEDGED IN.

Figure 2

with actors codes; the intensity profile (Figure 3) of the same passage is included to demonstrate the typical variability of loudness
in conversation.

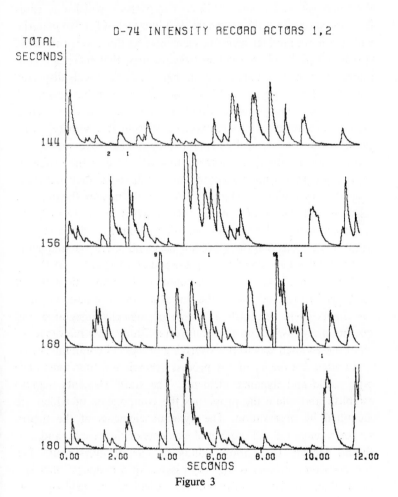

Figure 3

As this discussion is read, the reader should check back to the coded conversational specimen through which we plan to make manifest some of the essential requirements for the theory of the conversational relation. The first impression which one gains from the specimen is the considerable admixture of foreign material with the more familiar assertive elements. As this foreign material is scanned in detail, it becomes evident, first, that there is a considerable amount of it and, second, that it is rather evenly dispersed throughout the specimen. It contains a considerable sprinkling of supports, interjections, laughter, fragmentation, assertion breaks, and instances of simultaneous speech. It is apparent that the assertions are typically separated by nonassertive verbal acts and are not usually linked directly together. One of the problems of theory is that it must accommodate itself to the fact that these assertions are not directly linked. Added to the mix are the frequent comings and goings of somatic acts of which we have included facial contortion, eye contact, nodding, smiling, and tossing the head. It is curious that these somatic acts tend to emerge frequently in the middle of an assertion or at the end of an assertion. A theory of conversation needs to take account of these somatic acts and the basis for their location in the verbal stream. The basic problem for theory is to set forth a system of logically integrated and operationally useful propositions establishing the relevance of all of these varied acts to this overlying process of communication.

An adequate theory of any process occurring in time must have both static and dynamic elements. The static elements help to establish and relate the properties the components of which are identified by observation. The dynamic elements of the theory set forth temporal and sequential elements of the process and also should include the various kinds of energy investment. The conversational process is the very essence of a temporal phenomenon which consists of an impressive variety of relatively vigorous acts. A vital task of theory is to describe and explain the principles which govern periodic, semiperiodic, and nonperiodic characteristics of the total action stream which is manifest in live conversation. In view of the remarkable dearth of relevant ratio measures in sociology, the use of time as a measure of analysis in communicative behavior affords an exquisitely precise tool. A dynamic theory should also seek to develop the rules of ordering between and among all kinds of verbal and somatic acts. Above the molecular level of the separate verbal and somatic acts, the dynamic theory of conversation then has to concern itself with the cumulative effects of longer act sequences, topical sequence, and the social outcomes of communication.

Theory must attempt to explain the elastic property of communicative behavior. Elasticity varies from inelastic to indefinitely extended. Many nonassertive verbal acts, such as supports, interjections, and syllables of stuttering, are either monosyllabic or dissyllabic. Laughter, theoretically one of the more intriguing elements in conversation, varies in length from a single syllable to a miximum of eighteen syllables in our sample. Assertions may vary from a single word to 30 words or more in live conversation and fluctuate rather widely around an average of eight words per assertion. The somatic acts are much more elastic in duration than any of the verbal acts except for head tossing which we define as a single act when head motion stops. By far the most rapid and fluctuating of the somatic acts is the making of eye contact, which may endure for only a small fraction of a second or for the entire duration of the contact. This wide fluctuation complicates the theoretical problem of relating somatic behavior to verbal behavior in particular and communicative behavior in general. The other somatic acts tend to be less variable in duration than eye contact, with nodding being the least variable. Elasticity also applies to intensity and gaps which can be identified in the conversation stream. The energy investments which are the analog of loudness are highly variable and have major implications for the success of oral communication. The speaker maintains the interest of his partner through modulution and articulation varying from soft to loud and pointing up and stressing key words. The theoretical problem is to determine and explain the minimum requirements for variation in intensity as it relates to the conversational bond.

The problem of meshing concerns the integration of nonassertive verbal acts and somatic acts in and around assertive acts. In the conventional grammatical sense, these other acts are extraneous to the well-formulated assertive act. But it appears that these other acts are fruitfully embedded with the assertive acts and apparently make a positive contribution to the conversation process. The combination and mixture of the verbal and somatic acts in addition to their relation to assertive acts also calls for appropriate theoretical formulation.

The actor as a part of a two person social relation manages to sustain a highly variable stream of assertive and other potentially communicative acts. He does this under some combination of social and environmental pressures. The most immediate pressure comes from the partner with whom he is interacting, but considerable effect can arise from the presence of third parties and from environmental noise. The problem of theory is to explain how the action is sustained and how it relates to the external pressures of the system. A second factor of theoretical importance in sustaining the action is the internal verbal action system of each actor. This is not directly accessible for operational theory but it can be inferentially related to the social history, and to the social and cognitive resources of the actor.

One of the most constant and dynamic processes of conversation is the turning about and changing of the source of verbal emission. The channel must be transferred periodically between the two partners and a theory of conversation must take account of limits and modes which characterize the transfer period. Since the channel transfer is an inherent and generic element in conversation, it is essential to develop a theoretical base for determing the rules of exchange. Such a theory should be able to account for both the one-sided and balanced conversations since both forms appear in natural social action. The word "converse" comes from two Latin elements: *con* and *vertere* which mean to turn together in a continuing process of reversal.

It soon becomes manifest in the reading of any transcript of live conversation that any given topic has a limited life. Although this life is admittedly variable in the number of assertions which it includes, it apparently has a natural termination which is readily recognized by both partners. The information which is exchanged in conversation between partners is developed in organized packets of assertions which in themselves have a limited reach. The two partners together taking turns add elements which build up the topic. Within a clearly limited time this accretion process reaches a point of saturation beyond which further additions would degrade the topic. One partner is then forced to change the subject. At this point there may be some hesitation unless one of the partners has beginnings of a new topic in readiness. An adequate operational theory of conversation should attempt to account for the dynamics of topical development as an emergent outcome of the bipolar assertion chain and the theoretical restraining factors which control its reach. When we consider theorizing about the sequence of topics, the problem becomes much more complex. Within topics there is a reasonable determinancy from one assertive element to the next and this relationship arises from the need to satisfy the requirements of the topic by adding relevant increments. Between topics this relevancy is no longer required. We therefore often observe a broad topical jump which has no apparent relation to the preceding topic and strongly suggests a principle of indeterminancy. Introduction of something novel through topical leaps can operate as a sustaining factor in maintaining the interest and stimulus level of both partners. The next problem for an operational theory of conversation is the integration of the elements which we have just enumerated into a middle range theory. The middle range theory must incorporate all the elements and show their interrelation through a unified and comprehensive statement. Ideally, it is necessary that this statement be capable of transformation into mathematical form. Finally, the intermediate theory should provide a basis for developing a general theory of conversation. This general theory should consist of a single simplified statement expressible in mathematical terms which defines the generic reality process of the conversational bond.

A GENERAL MODEL OF THE CONVERSATIONAL PROCESS

The task of developing a fully adequate general theory of conversation will have to await the formulation and testing of a set of integrated propositions which fully identify the primary components of the conversational process. Our task at this point is to formulate a logical and minimal set of propositions which are sufficiently well knit to describe the conversational process at the theoretical level. We will attempt to satisfy this requirement with a set of ten propositions.

Proposition 1:
Because assertions in natural conversation are spontaneously generated, it is highly probable that a nonassertive act will either follow the assertion or occur within the assertion.

In natural conversation, a spontaneously developed assertion is fraught with uncertainties. A subject of an assertion may be selected and uttered before a final decision has been made regarding the verb and its modifiers. One of these modifiers may be uttered and then rejected and replaced by another. Finally, there may be one or more false starts concerning the utterance of the object, its modifiers, and the various possibilities for grammatically dependent sentence elements. A second source of nonassertive insertions includes supports, interjections, or laughter coming from either the speaker or the listener.

Proposition 2:
The nonassertive particles in and among the assertions constitute a required auxiliary function in which the speaker reorganizes and the listener catches up and so contributes to the conversational process.

When a conversation is edited so as to retain only the grammatically formulated assertion content, a false impression is created of the actual series of events. In the edited text, each speaker appears to have been fully fluent, logical, and well-organized, when in fact this was never the case. Everything emerging in the action stream from both partners is genuinely a part of the communicative relation. The full record makes each actor appear more natural and sincere and this in itself helps to carry conviction.

Proposition 3:
Somatic acts emerge in conjunction with assertions in varying combinations to add stress, animation, and strength.

The nonassertive acts, both verbal and somatic, serve in the same basic capacity of enriching and facilitating the assertion stream. The degree of enrichment accessible to the somatic acts could be approximated by comparing the total dyadic interaction in a telephone communication with that in a face-to-face relation under conditions of equal permissiveness for equal contacts. Somatic behavior has the function of communicating feeling tones and of allowing close mutual surveillance through ocular contact. Somatic behavior can supplement the verbal channel without interfering with it. It has the advantage of allowing the listener to emit a sequence of actions relevant to the bond because it keeps the emitter informed of the listener's continuing response sequence. The somatic behavior arising from both partners constitutes a second channel which operates primarily to support the assertion string.

Proposition 4:
Because natural conversation is spontaneously generated, it is essentially nonperiodic for all acts, assertive and nonassertive.

We believe that this may rest in the uncertainty which seems to be inherent in the generation of assertions. If these acts are functional, then they are called for at varying points in the stream which is probably somewhat dependent on the topic being discussed. This point is obvious in the case of laughter and facial contortions but it works with equal effect in all nonassertive auxiliary acts. Although the nonassertive acts vary in incidence, they all have particular conversational functions and are therefore used as required and not in a mechanical way after a constant number of syllables has elapsed.

Proposition 5:
Through the property of elasticity the main components of conversational action are varied in conformity to the variable requirements of the communicative task.

The central value of the elastic property is that it gives the emitter the necessary latitude to constrain or to extend his assertions. The degree of complexity which is desirable for the assertions varies a great deal according to the nature of the action. Imperatives and warnings must be short. Explanations of unknown materials must necessarily be elaborated until it seems sufficient for the under- standing of the listener. While the actor has the channel, the elastic property gives him a great deal of freedom to develop his line in his own individual way. We can also illustrate the value of the elastic property with laughter because the actor can closely satisfy his need for laugh release by varying the syllabic amplitude of his laugh. The same advantages are operative with the somatic acts of eye contact, facial contortion, nodding, and smiling. Both emitter and receiver can restrain or prolong these behaviors as they are called forth by the development of the assertion sequence and the development of the interaction sequence between partners.

Proposition 6:
Intensity is an energy analog which through loudness variation permits the stressing of selected words and phrases, facilitating recognition of assertion elements and attentiveness through dramatization.

There is a consistent inverse relationship between the intensity difference between adjacent syllables and the frequency of its occurrence. The larger differences between adjacent syllables thus seem to be reserved for the more important stress points in the assertion stream. If this were not the case, they would lose their stress value and they would also require excessive amounts of energy. If there were no intensity differences between adjacent syllables, the result would be a monotonic syllable stream which would be featureless and inanimate. The monotonic stream would be indiscriminate and would make difficult the recognition and grouping of acts. Intensity variation contributes in great measure to the intelligibility of the verbal action stream.

Proposition 7:
The sustaining of conversational action is dependent on a combination of pressures arising from the presence of the expectant partner, the immediate goal of the emerging assertion, and the communicative acts which have preceded it.

Sustaining the action operates at two levels: (1) the half cycle (within actor), and (2) the cycle (between actors). The actor must organize, muster energy, and then articulate the verbal output. In generating these pieces which at last make up an assertion, he inserts the nonassertive verbal elements and somatic acts to help sustain the action flow. As long as the actors can maintain the links between half cycles, the generation of cycles will continue and the dyadic contact goes on. Sustaining the cycle depends upon the readiness of the listening partner to assume the verbal channel. If he is not ready then there may be a large gap, a faltering, and a delay in the action. This would mark a strained contact which is vulnerable to failure. If the listening partner is eager to assume the channel he may overlap with the emitter and cut off the tail of an assertion.

Proposition 8:
Channel change gives the dyadic contact its bipolar dynamics and recognizes some law of limitation on channel retention.

The conversational relation demands a fairly rapid sequence of interaction and a fairly good mix of participation of both actors. The time frame within which the assertions occur is generally between one and thirty seconds and more typically is less than ten seconds. Channel retention by a single actor rarely lasts as long as thirty seconds. There are dyadic contacts in which the channel shift is rapid, usually characterized by a high degree of responsiveness between actors. Deceleration of the channel change rate is caused by incorporating longer strings of assertions within the half cycle. If it becomes too sluggish, there may be reduced participation and termination of the contact. For operational purposes, we can measure the total dyadic contact in terms of the rate of channel change.

Proposition 9:
The topic is characterized by an additive property originating from the accretion of related assertions which rapidly increases the constraints on the selection and addition of further assertions related to that topic.

The introduction and establishment of a topic immediately creates approximate bounds of the conceptual region from which assertions may be developed. The topic, of course, may be jointly developed by the two partners in a succession of cycles. But as they do so there is a practical limit in that as assertions are added, the speakers exhaust their highly relevant information and feel constrained to terminate the topic. Initial assertions clarify and build up the topic and this is followed by a condition where added words obfuscate the topic. This means that there is a convenient limit beyond which the topic cannot be successfully extended. The topic is both a focus and a basic unit in the communication process. Since there is a finite body of knowledge which could contribute to assertions, maximum latitude of choice exists only with the first assertion and predictability is at its lowest level. As the source region becomes exhausted, the predictability for any given assertion yet to be added becomes higher. If the next statement of the speaker becomes fully predictable, there is little point in making it.

Proposition 10:
As a topic is more completely exhausted, there is a sharper transition to a logically more remote topic, and the effect is to drive the discussion into a highly contrasted topical region.

There is an infinitude of topics potentially available to the interactants, and their continued interaction is likely to impel them to a fuller utilization of this reservoir of topics. Since there is a negative drive away from the exhausted topic, there is a low predictability as to which new topic will become established. Frequently neither partner is aware of what the next topic will be, and both may experience considerable surprise at the variety and nature of the topics which leap to mind. This results in an uncertainty principle in the topical development of spontaneous dyadic conversation. This is what gives the social contact its high stimulus quality, and constitutes a significant part of the enjoyment of the social relation.

Middle range theory must attempt to integrate all ten of these propositions into a single operational model. This integrated model centers on a core of assertive segments made up of word strings and within and between assertions by nonassertive verbal acts which facilitate the generation of the core. The assertive acts are elastic in that they vary in length and contribute a longitudinal fluctuation to the stream. The intensity property constitutes a transverse fluctuation in loudness which highlights certain syllables and improves the receivability of the stream through contrast. Somatic behavior parallels and figuratively envelops the verbal stream. It is coherent with the verbal stream because it does not interfere with it and serves to supplement the flow of verbal information.

Assertion sequences with the accompanying nonassertive behavior are constituted in a segment of assertions which together make up a topic. Topical shift could be represented by an offset of the conversational flow as indicated in Figure 4. The dyadic conversational relation is a dynamic bipolar system of alternating and integrated inputs which is nonperiodic and imperfect as a communication system. Fundamentally it represents a conversational endeavor which is only partially carried out. However, from the viewpoint of social action, it is predominantly effective in accomplishing its goals. It successfully transfers some information although it usually leaves some doubts. These are more often resolved in subsequent encounters between the partners.

A general theory of conversation should assert the relationship between topical rangeability, encounter sequences, and bonding. These are both the outcomes and the basic dimensions of conversation in the larger sense. Minimal topical rangeability restricts future encounters and thus the potential for bonding is reduced. Encounter sequences provide new opportunities for interaction and for a gain in the informational pool through sharing. The exercise of conversation enhances the actor's communication skills. If a workable general theory of conversation could be developed, it would be extremely useful as an analytical tool for evaluating the conversational process regardless of cultural level and for all actually functioning dyadic sets. A truly general theory of conversation would be applicable in all cultures and would therefore permit reliable transformations in the analysis of conversational outcomes

*A schematic operational model of conversation
showing relation of topical segments*

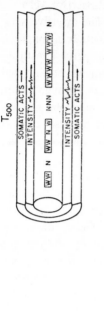

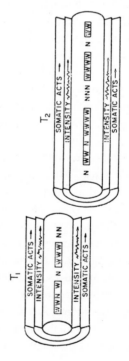

TIME ⟶

LEGEND: ASSERTION WORD   W
         NONASSERTION WORD   N
         ASSERTION   WWWN WW
         TOPICAL SEGMENT   T
         VERTICAL DISPLACEMENT OF TOPICAL SEGMENTS
         DENOTES DEGREE OF DISCONTINUITY.

Figure 4

in crosscultural comparisons. Basically a general theory must enable us to set forth the quality of the conversational bond based on precise quantifiable properties of the action stream.

CRITICAL EVALUATION OF THE MODEL

The set of ten basic propositions concerning the conversational process was confined to verbal action, intensity, and somatic behavior of the head and face. The advantage of so confining the propositional set is that it allows more penetrating analysis of the immediate source in content of communicative behavior between persons. These propositions do seem suitable to get at the core of the conversational process as it occurs in real time and it avoids excessive elaboration of the infinite number of distinctions which could be made in the process. At the same time we have omitted a number of properties which could be used in developing a theoretical base and it is to be expected that the exploitation of some of these could add important dimensions to the understanding of what goes on in live conversation. Phonemes would be useful in the analysis of dialectical variation in conversational usage. Phonemes could also be useful for developing a precise history for language development in the child. Tonal variations are closely related to intensity variations and fruitful research could be directed at determining the degree of correlation between them. Tonal variations could also be a significant indicator of sex differences, power differences, and social differences. Tonal differences would also be an important consideration in crosscultural comparisons. In some languages tonal variations are employed to indicate differences in word meanings (Chinese), tonal differences are commonly used with different conventions to indicate the declarative, imperative, and interrogative modes and to indicate termination or continuation. Special tonal variations are sometimes characteristic of formatistic and ritualistic speech as it appears in introductions, in official intercourse in public places, and in religious and judicial settings.

There is a well-acknowledged communicative function which is carried out in movements and positionings of the limbs and torso. Movements of the arms and hands and fingers are perhaps the most universally used accompaniment to the communication process. Fingers are directly communicative in indicating counts, direction, and various conventional signs and motions, such as beckoning, waving off, and waving a greeting. The legs and feet are sometimes used in stamping to communicate anger or insistance, and kicking another person is sometimes used for the same message. The torso is not a versatile signal sending device although the lifting of the shoulders is used to convey lack of knowledge or indifference. Inferences could be made from the positioning or repositioning of various parts of the body and these inferences have a communicative function but the communication is not based upon the direct use of a conventional symbol. It is germane to the communication process to recognize, catalog, and measure the action sequences which are used by this means of communication. This whole area of communication should be related to verbal communication which often accompanies it and this should be done on both a theoretical and operational basis. It then would be possible to put all of the somatic means of communication into the proper perspective in relation to verbal communication.

We have dealt with the phenomenon of topical development and topical sequencing only to a minimal degree. Yet the completion of a topic is the first level where communication can be said to have been achieved. The composition, variability, and content of the topic could in itself furnish a major independent field of study because a completed topic constitutes a finished segment of social action. Because the development of a topic is a joint action between participants, it also constitutes the elementary unit of social cooperation. A second phenomenon which requires further research and theoretical treatment is the transition between topics. There is always some discontinuity when there is a shift from one topic to the next but the magnitude of discontinuity is variable. The primary advantage of studying topical transition is that it gives a dynamic dimension to topical analysis. If there is a close relation and good continuity between topics, there results a system-ized corpus of information shared between two partners. This would lead to a higher quality adjustment between the participants and to the social environment. When the discontinuity between topics is extreme, it results in poorly integrated conversation in which the final outcome may be quite doubtful but it does have the advantage of encouraging innovation and of expanding the potential area of contact.

We recognize the complexity of studying the conversational process and our efforts have been focused primarily on the micro-scopic level of conversation. This is an area which has heretofore received little definitive research and it is to be hoped that such research could be greatly expanded in the future. Our effort to select and incorporate certain properties has resulted in an approach which appears to promise an effective start. This level of research has deliberately focused on the manifest operational properties of conversation with a constant effort to minimize arbitrary, con-ceptual, and inferential aspects. We have necessarily omitted certain properties which are admittedly functional in the conversational relation and we hope that other researchers will become interested in these areas. We also hope that other researchers will be suffi-ciently interested to replicate, modify, or refute our findings and propositions. However, it is essential that such replication be grounded in meticulous observation, coding, and measurement of representative live conversation in suitably extended samples. In short, any refutation must be based upon sound empirical evidence. It is also hoped that the microscopic properties of conversation can be assimilated and integrated to a macroscopic level resulting in a more general theory of the conversational process.

8

THE APPLICATION OF CONVERSATION RESEARCH

It would be useful to illustrate the relevance and potential application of research to a broad variety of interpersonal relations, social relations, and crucial encounters which are critically dependent upon conversation. In this illustration, space demands that we be selective and therefore we must slight many important applications which the reader may call to mind. Conversation is the elementary social relation in all situations where a group of men come together to review, discuss, and agree on a course of action. Action carried out through conversation concerns all matters from the gravest to most trivial, and all levels from the conference rooms of government and industry to the family home. To suggest the possible extent of research applications we will offer a few examples of analytical potential in the area of basic social processes, certain kinds of social actions, some important interpersonal differentials, and some typical role-relevant conversation functions. Disciplines to which the effects of conversation are immediately relevant include sociology, social psychology, psychology, language, speech, speech therapy, psychiatry, anthropology, and social work.

The practical problem of precision research on conversation records can be readily resolved today by using modern audio recording equipment, supplemented if desired with video recording and with the use of high capacity electronic computers for analysis. All of this equipment is commonly found at the larger modern universities; it could easily be assembled at a specialized laboratory with appropriate fundings. One of the more time-consuming requirements for processing conversational data is that of literal transcription from the audio record to typed scripts and computer cards, verification, and accurate coding of verbal acts. The intensity record can be entirely machine processed except for the entry of actor codes. The intensity can be accepted as a veridical analog of loudness variation in the original specimen of conversation. Access for suitable conversational data is no more difficult than for other kinds of research. The primary problems in obtaining conversational samples include making a good quality verbal record with minimal incident noise, providing a suitable and sufficiently insulated social environment for dyadic interaction, and providing adequate instruction for the partners once their consent is obtained. It is also desirable to have one of the participants assist in the transcription of the verbal record to assure accurate interpretation of all passages. It is practical and desirable to integrate the full set of computer programs so that the desired analytical parameters can be processed in a single pass on the computer.

THE CONVERSATIONAL DIMENSION IN SOCIAL PROCESS

Socialization, a subject much treated in a general way in sociology, is actually accomplished moment by moment through direct conversational interaction. When two persons talk together, both are experiencing some social growth. If one party has less experience or fewer resources than the other, he would tend to receive the greater socializing effect. Although socialization is a primary process in society, there is no genuine agreement among sociologists as to its definition, content, or operation. Since the only place socialization could occur is in the direct conversational contact, it is imperative to make a rigorous search for the roots of socialization in the conversational history. Socialization progresses incrementally throughout the series of conversational contacts for every member of society. The socialization process should be investigated by a careful analysis of a properly selected time series sample of conversational contacts between specific pairs of people.

Such time series are relevant to the various age levels of childhood and adult life. Socialization progresses rapidly through the first ten years of life and should be studied for every year from birth. In the later stages of life, it should be studied for every five year interval. The socialization process may also be identified with the induction and training of a new member into a new social system such as a commercial company. In this case, such characteristics as vocabulary and speed of response to technical questions mark the progress and extent of socialization in the system. One of the more intensive socialization periods occurs in the child's preschool years at home with his mother. Interaction rates for daylong observation periods have averaged as high as one of every two minutes. In other cases the rate may be much too low for the successful socialization of the child. Since the mother is the child's primary source, it is important to determine just how the conversational process affects this outcome and what measures of improvement might be possible. Individuals vary tremendously in their ability to convey information, feeling, and instructions to others; the precise analysis of the conversational output would allow quantitative evaluation of their socialization ability. Friendship pairs of both boys and girls age 12 to 13 have been observed to reach a high level of conversational interchange as measured by tempo and loudness. This would be a particularly good time to record a time series sample for selected pairs of actors and to relate various conversational dimensions to various external measures of socialization.

Cooperation. Cooperation, as Kropotkin noted, is one of the most universal social processes (Kropotkin 1902). The act of dyadic interaction, even in its shortest interchanges, demands cooperation. Variations in the degree of cooperation are immediately apparent in the conversational record in the form of channel sharing, response delays, coherence of response, extreme intensity shifts, and the degree of topical continuity. We are treating the concept of cooperation at three levels. First, there is a working agreement which must be developed between two partners in order to sustain the conversational interchange. This, of course, is internal to the conversational process. A second level of cooperation is identified as topical agreement in which the partners attain a common understanding and some degree of shared belief. Through diffusion the development of shared belief leads to consensus in a community. A third level of cooperation is identified as the accomplishment of a joint task involving coordination, manipulation, and purposeful reordering of materials which is dependent on discussion, instruction, and decision in a conversational interchange. When two men are working together they converse in order to coordinate their efforts and to get the job done. Success in completing the job is often dependent on their ability to discuss, explain, listen, and agree and to accept each other as a conversational partner. The analysis of the conversational ability of the prospective employee may be just as important as the evaluation of his technical knowledge and manual skills. The ability to converse is the core of the general ability to cooperate with a wide variety of people.

Conflict. Conflict is a universal social process but is far less frequent than cooperation. Conflict generally marks the failure of social relations. It frequently arises from a misunderstanding of what has been said or intended, or from a conflicting claim to the same resource, or from a refusal to enter expected role relations. We can get at the dynamics of conflict by analysis of the verbal interaction in which it arises. By this means it is often possible to identify the deficient element in the conversational stream and to more effectively direct the search for corrective measures. When a social pathology arises between two people who are bound together in continuing role relations, it often becomes evident in the hostile verbal exchange and the verbal exchange may well contain the clue to the basis of the pathology. An analysis of an observational record should also afford indices of the severity of the pathology. A time series analysis of the verbal record in the case of continuing conflict could lead to a better understanding of the profile, dynamics, and the composition of the conflict situation. Verbal parameters which are likely to relate to conflict include sentence length, topical sequence, intensity variation, and somatic behavior, particularly facial contortion. For example, conflict in a working situation can create further misunderstanding, loss of time and productivity, and the waste of materials. Conflict, as widespread as it is, is a little understood process. It has not had the benefit of direct, detailed, quantitative analysis. Yet such analysis is readily possible with careful observation and recording of verbal action in the conflict situation. If knowledge of the conflict situation were sufficient, then corrective measures would be known and could be readily applied.

Assimilation. The conversational process is closely related to assimilation on the level of direct face-to-face relations in the social group, the work group, and the play group. By assimilation we mean the process whereby the new member comes to be a fully effective and accepted member of the group. This status he attains progressively over time, and it is evident in the quality of his exchanges with other members. One evidence of this is the adoption of speech patterns peculiar to the group. Through topical analysis one could measure the degree of relevance of a conversational sample to the central interest peculiar to the group. The rate of speech flow would probably accelerate somewhat with increased assimilation of each member. We would also expect a consistent reduction in temporal gap between verbal acts and actor speeches. And we would expect a decrease in nonassertive verbal elements and an increase in the number and length of assertions. Assimilation is an ongoing process which never reaches an absolute state and the members of the real life group fall somewhere along a spectrum from very low to very high assimilation. The preservation of the group requires some minimal efficiency in assimilating. Well-established quantitative indices would provide a useful tool for identifying this minimum and the appearance of trends of increasing or decreasing assimilation efficiency.

Information Transfer. Information transfer is a simple essential of all social operations regardless of language or culture. It is the essential outcome of every conversational relation. The information content is one of the more apparent and accessible elements in the conversational stream. Applicable indices for measuring information content include number of assertions, length of assertions, vocabulary range, and the ratio of nonassertive syllables to total syllables in the record. These are measures which have been treated in earlier chapters. For a rigorous measurement and analysis of information content, it is also necessary to develop indices at the molar level which involve topics, topic sequences, and their immediate mutual implications. Every dyadic contact which contains assertions effects a transfer of information which contributes in some measure to the sharing of knowledge and the development of consensus in the community. The rate of flow of information to the individual is a determinant of the extent of his knowledge and the rate of his social development. The assessment of information flow would make a primary diagnostic tool for evaluating the relative success of all other social processes. This tool would be equally valuable for diagnosing the developmental state and the needs of the individual as regards educational adequacy, social adjustment, and role proficiency. The evidence of the quality of the information transfer is always apparent on both sides of the dyadic relation.

It should be clear that socialization, cooperation, conflict, assimilation, and information transfer are not mutually exclusive categories. The general process of socialization clearly embraces them all and there is a close interdependence between each with the others. For analytical purposes, it is necessary to isolate each of these processes in order to determine its unique and special characteristics. The advantage of isolating a single social process is that it can be measured in a number of parameters and its simple dynamics can be understood without being complicated by the admixture of other kinds of social processes whether distinct or more inclusive. It is certainly possible to further dissect any one of these social processes into more narrowly defined components. Dependent upon a rigorous understanding of the separate components of social process, it becomes feasible to attempt their integration both on the empirical and theoretical levels.

THE CONVERSATIONAL DIMENSION IN SOCIAL ACTION

The core of social action is primarily conversation regardless of whatever physical actions or transactions of objects may take place. These physical actions or transactions are gross classifiers of general outcomes whereas the conversational action is a detailed, elaborate, and highly integrated social action sequence. Thus the dynamics of the ongoing action can be identified best in the conversational record with its sensitive indicators of the moment to moment relation. These various sequences of social action link together and have some mutual effects both in rounding out the life of the individual participant and in sustaining the operations of the social community. Therefore, the findings in research on social action could be further applied at the level of the individual and at the level of the community.

Small Group Discussion. The lowest level of complexity for social exchange is the dyadic level, and this as we have seen is relatively complex. The next level of complexity occurs with the small face-to-face group, the universal agency for direct social action. Bales has identified two basic modes of interactor communication: the first is the individual to the group as a whole, and the second is dyadic interaction between group members. In real life groups, there is a constant and unending shift between these two modes and the patterning of the shift, as Bales has noted, is much affected by the size of the group and by the degree of participation of each member. Because of the intermittent shifts between modes, it is a challenging task to analyze the verbal stream of action. Bales noted the general characteristics of group communication through action analysis and an exact temporal recording of who-to-whom in the initiation of conversational contacts. He did not do a molecular analysis of the verbal action stream, of the intensity variation, or of the detailed somatic behavior. However, his work has well prepared the ground for moving on to this kind of analysis. When one member is talking to the group as a whole there is reason to assume a fair efficiency of information transfer, but when the conversation breaks down at the dyadic level there is typically simultaneous speech by two or more dyads and the investigator has the problem of keeping track of a half dozen actors who have entered into compartmental social relations. Conversational analysis of small group discussion is a means of evaluating the quality of group action. This analysis would also permit the identification of the interplay of social processes within the group. It would also afford a good opportunity for studying group formation and group dynamics through time series sampling from the original formation of the group.

Large Social Group Functioning and Maintenance. We define the large social group as an organization of fifty or more members in which there is rather limited involvement for each individual, perhaps on the basis of weekly meetings. Such a large group depends in part on the interaction of small groups within the membership. Thus whatever findings there are with respect to small groups would be relevant for the large social group. The large social group is also dependent upon the quality of dyadic interaction among group members and this could well be an indicator of the tone and action level of the group. Such an analysis would have to depend upon spot sampling and should of course be done with the knowledge of the group members and in the best interests of the group. Intensity analysis of such a sample could afford a direct indication of the energy level of the group. Topical analysis would give an indication of the relevance of the content of conversation to group interests. If group members of a religious organization are discussing items of personal or extraneous interests, it would appear that the religious interests may be merely formal and not actual. This may even go in the negative direction where the content becomes hostile and malicious. If conversation content shows heavier loading of information positively related to legitimate group interests, it would facilitate group productivity, support, and maintenance. Sampling of conversation can also yield information about the real attitude of group members toward the leaders of the group and their policies even though the group members realize that the conversation is being sampled.

Social Party. The typical sociable home party is a voluntary gathering usually of four or more guests for the purpose of enjoyment through transitory social intercourse under loosely structured conditions. There is an expectation of constant interaction through conversation and a good mix through time in face-to-face relations among the guests. The occasion of the party is usually seen as a unique event where relations are casual and strangers may be present. Guests are expected to freely initiate conversation with others regardless of whether or not they were previously acquainted. Refreshments and stimulants are usually provided by the hostess and the guest is free to take as much as he likes. The social role of the hostess is one of generosity and gratification of the guests. The hostess's expectation of the guest is that he enjoy himself, accept her generosity, and stay within the bounds of continence. Since there is relaxation and permissiveness at the party, there is a danger of unacceptable behavior and incontinence on the part of some guests which would limit the pleasure of others. Due to the requirement for constant action and the presence of stimulants, the guests get keyed up and hyperactive at a party and thereby sustain a state of tension. Conversational analysis could be applied to find indicators of the level of tension. Riesman and Watson found that interaction between familiars was highly routinized and reiterative, and that interaction between casuals is much more likely to be creative, exciting, and intimate (Riesman and Watson 1964: 238). We would expect the following characteristics of conversation at a lively party. There would be generally shorter assertions, more limited vocabulary, a larger proportion of non-assertive verbal acts, and far more laughter. The higher mean level of loudness in conversation could be an indicator of the tension level of the party which is also indicated by a higher degree of variation in intensity which sooner or later leads to a fatigue effect in the participants. Conversation at the social party is characterized by a more rapid interchange between partners and often by a fairly rapid exchange of partners. The heightened level of party activity includes more rapid and extreme somatic behavior. One of the functions of the social party is to extend the range and the depth of acquaintance for the guests and to afford them relaxation and enjoyment. There is also a serious dysfunction when the guest incurs serious social damage through indiscretion, overexposure, and self-disgrace according to the standards of the people attending the party.

Teams. The socially distinctive feature of the team is its requirement for expertise, efficiency, and skill plus the ability to work effectively even under heavy pressure. Individual members of the successful team must be well trained and well experienced in their special team position. It is particularly important that each team member learns to complement the performance of his associates with a delicate sense of good timing. In the well-functioning team, language is often crucial in carrying out coordination between team members and it may be equally crucial to say exactly the right thing for the required action. This creates a new dimension for the demands on language. Here the study of language interaction could well center on special vocabulary and critical situational requirements for that vocabulary. It is also apparent that the temporal sequence in which statements are made would be of theoretical and practical importance. Timing in gaps in messages between members could provide a sensitive index of the degree of team coordination and the level of team spirit. These criteria vary somewhat between the athletic team, the occupational team, and the professional team; therefore, the different types of teams would require special language study and would reveal somewhat differing language dimensions.

Committees. A committee is a vital social instrument for facilitating the action of institutions and groups. It may be defined as a group of persons commissioned and entrusted to examine a situation, discuss courses of action, and decide on a recommendation to the appointing authority. Our special interest in the committee is the fact that it must carry out its function through the verbal process of discussion. The efficiency of the committee is dependent on the members' ability to communicate among themselves. Committee responsibilities can be obfuscated by a lack of discussion, by excessive discussion, or by nonrelevant discussion.

The existence of prior information and the circulation of relevant data before the meeting has a great effect on the potential for keeping discussion focused on the central issues and for the attainment of a sound decision. There are some special problems in the analysis of verbal interaction within committees. First, the pattern of exchange can become complex when the committee membership includes eight or nine individuals. Effective consideration of the problem requires a single coherent thread of discussion. But this must be based on input from relevant areas which may be widely divergent in subject matter and from individuals who may have widely divergent orientations. The chairman plays a central role in developing unified sequence of discussion from the divergent areas and optimizing the input from all the members who can contribute to the discussion. The quality of the optimization can be judged only in the outcome of the record based on rigorous and precise analysis. The researcher interested in committee's functioning should work both on the micro and macro levels. At the micro level the measurement of the response rate and the temporal gaps would permit assessment of the level of interest and the action level of the members. Variation in the intensity pattern and the analysis of the verbal acts measured by syllable count would show the relationship between assertive acts and auxiliary verbal acts and would indicate whether there is an increase in assertive acts and a trend toward improved efficiency in communication over time. Vocabulary range and the emergence of specialized vocabularies should be an excellent indicator of the technical orientation of the committee. The exploitation of the channel can be measured by the incidence of the breakdown into dyadic speech resulting from simultaneous inputs from two or more sources or from long hesitations or from awkward and drawn out introductions in speech initiation. Perhaps most crucial is the chairman's management of the channel whereby there is a good coordination and integration of relevant inputs from the several members. On the macro level the assessment of the relation among topics in the discussion record would indicate the development of focus toward the central issue. The topical sequence would also reveal the effective range of related subjects and permit the assessment of the adequacy and balance of the discussion. As the topical sequence approaches the decision making point, the researcher would expect to find an increasing convergence of topics and an increase in agreement and positive statements. He should also look for other signs from the individual members of their readiness to decide the issue. When the detailed assessment of the record of committee behavior is completed, the researcher is in a better position to theorize and develop operational tests regarding the tempo, precision, and final success of the decision.

Gossip. For research purposes we define gossip as spontaneous free ranging discussion between two or more persons about a third party external to the discussion group which centers on the party's personal characteristics, behavior, or associations and incorporates a critical element involving moral evaluation or judgment. By the dictionary definition, gossip is often malicious, but we recognize that it could also contain complimentary and favorable discussion. The practice of gossip is universal among both sexes and at all ages from the junior high school level. There is a special problem of recording gossip because of the implicit assumption that the gossip itself is confidential and that the gossiping individuals will not betray this confidence. It is unlikely that most people would consent to the recording of their gossip; if they knew it were being recorded, it would have a major effect on the content of the gossip. The researcher would have the ethical problem and the obligation to neutralize the personal identifications of all named individuals and to remove the record far from the setting in which it developed. In analyzing the gossip process the researcher should measure variations in the level of involvement as indicated by the reduced size of gaps between statements and the gaps between speakers. Intensity variation is probably also related to the degree of involvement but this may be an inverse function. Both the vocabulary range and vocabulary content would be of particular interest in the analysis of gossip because it would indicate the distribution of negative and positive references and the exact categories of the comments. Topical analysis would reveal the social dimensions with which gossip appears to be primarily concerned. There is some reason to think that this is different by age and sex. Subjects which commonly arise in the interchange of gossip include evaluations of friendliness, flaunting of wealth, intelligence and personal qualities, social behavior, and general competence of the subject. There is also a need to determine the social function of gossip which Kierkegaard thinks consists entirely of trivialities (Kierkegaard 1949: 52). This certainly is not true from the viewpoint of the participants. Some of the social functions of gossip might include simple entertainment, the generation of personal interest, and a positive or negative effect on the social adjustment among the participants. The sanctions which make up the content of gossip are indicators of implicit social standards (Scott 1971: 216). If the support of social standards is one of the functions of gossip, then the identification of the standards which are implied by the sanctions would help to demonstrate that function.

SOCIAL DIFFERENTIALS AND CONVERSATIONAL PROPERTIES

Age. It is commonly assumed that conversational ability, like other social and physical skills, increases steadily with age from infancy to early adulthood at about age twenty-five and thereafter declines more or less slowly to senescence. The precise assessment of variation in the properties of live conversation could establish this pattern of development and decline for all age levels. We would expect the variation with age to appear most clearly in such properties as speech rate, response rate, intensity, and assertion length. It would be worthwhile to determine the relative efficiency of these parameters in conversation for all age levels in five year intervals from age five to age one hundred. This could afford a means of recognizing communication problems which appear to be associated with particular age levels and might have influence on engagement in certain occupations where conversational skill may be a crucial element, as it is with air controllers. The effect of age gap on conversational efficiency can also be assessed for the various age differences. The most pervasive of these is the age difference between the mother and her child which typically varies from two to four decades. The hypothesis that the size of the age gap has no influence on the efficiency of mother-child conversation could be readily tested by the time and rate parameters in conversation comparing samples with an age gap difference of at least ten years. It would also be worthwhile to generate intensified conversation across a large age gap to determine whether this could have positive effects on the conversational efficiency of either partner in his contacts with others.

Sex. Our data have demonstrated that sex has a definite influence on most of the parameters of conversational behavior when we compare homogeneous and hetergeneous dyads which are constituted of college age students. We would expect these differences to be manifest also at later age levels. Males talked at greater length, used a larger vocabulary, and spoke with greater intensity variation than females. Females displayed longer enduring somatic acts than males and they laughed more than males. In general the female tended to be less active in that she listened more in the heterogeneous dyad. The measurement of the sex differential in conversational efficiency could be applied to the evaluation of the dating relationship and subsequently to the marriage relationship. Conversational efficiency in the dating relationship could well be a stable indicator of the success and permanence of the ensuing marriage. A dramatic shift in the conversational patterns of the two partners before and after marriage could also help to explain adjustment problems in the marriage relation. Sex differences have also exerted an important influence in the interview situation. Kinsey in his basic research on the history of sex behavior found that respondents could talk more readily and frankly to an interviewer of the opposite sex (Kinsey, Pomeroy, and Martin 1948). Kinsey believed that this was a special effect of the subject of interview and not a general effect. Conversational analysis can be applied to compare the communicative relation of the working wife and the nonworking wife to their husbands. It could be hypothesized that the working wife could have a better conversational relationship with her husband due to her greater awareness of the external social environment and her greater potential for independence due to her income earning capacity. This puts her on a more equal footing with her husband both in social position and in conversational exchange.

Race. In the development of social relations between black Americans and white Americans, the black minority was severely repressed with respect to education, occupation, income, and social relations. These deprivations led to considerable differences in the use of language and to the adequacy of communication between the races. Assessment of conversation among blacks and conversation among whites would allow us to determine the nature and extent of the conversational difference based on race. We could look for evidence of the effect of prejudice in samples of conversations between black and white partners. We would expect a prejudiced white person to attempt to monopolize the conversation, to give predominantly negative responses, and to increase intensity variation. It would be helpful to analyze and determine the conversational efficiency of the disadvantaged black school child particularly when he is talking across the racial differential to a white teacher. Identification of the differences should be helpful in selecting methods of counteracting these communicative deficiencies. Another racial problem is the ability of the typical white person to listen efficiently when he is talking to a black person. Conversational analysis would be effective in measuring the balance between the two actors in the biracial dyad and in evaluating the participation of each.

Power. Power has been defined in static terms in reference to reward power, expert power, referent power, and legitimate power (French and Raven 1959), but we wish to treat power as it arises in ongoing dyadic interaction in real time. The power relationship emerges when guidance, evaluation, control, and sanctions are flowing from one partner to the other. They can be identified in the assertive forms as instruction, training, correction, admonition, compliments, and censure. By this approach, the application of the power relation is a transitory phenomenon which is applied only as needed for movement toward a goal. It is well recognized that the partner applying power can succeed best by alternately imposing and relaxing the pressure. This would suggest a periodic alternation in the application of power followed by lower pressure periods which permit the partner to comply and adjust. It is not unusual for the power position to be traded back and forth between the two partners in the course of the conversational transaction. The power resides with the partner who has the knowledge which is needed by the other so that if the topic or situation shifts the focus of knowledge, then the power could be applied in a different direction. Existence of the power differential could probably be marked for the superordinate partner by an increase in assertive content, a reduction in fragmentation, increased eye contact, and less somatic behavior otherwise. These parameters would indicate a more stylized and more formal conversational encounter. The size of the power differential is probably positively related to the speed of the response of the subordinate member.

Information. Information makes up the content of an assertion or a series of assertions. It is the universal element of all conversational contacts and it constitutes the only substantive base for face-to-face conversation. The occasion for an exchange of information depends on an information differential between two partners which must be eliminated or reduced. The differential may be so small that it can be satisfied by a single statement or it may be so extensive as to require indefinitely continued discussion. The information bearing assertions are additive for the receiving partner as he integrates them with other information which he already has. His responses constitute an informational increment for the speaker. As the information differential is reduced the two partners are expanding the area of their shared knowledge. Both the giving and receiving of information appear to be mutually rewarding to the two partners. Both the size of the information differential and the complexity of the information are variable. The ability of the individual to impart information is also variable. Therefore, there are at least three sources of variation affecting the efficiency of the information transfer, an important element in all conversational contacts. One index of the efficiency of the information transfer is the ratio of all assertions to all nonassertive acts and the average number of assertions per minute. The absolute number of nonredundant assertions would be a suitable indicator of the extent of information transferred. Information can be isolated and treated as a separate property but in real life contacts it cannot stand alone since various other differentials will usually be in effect.

Education and Skills. A continuing requirement of society is a formal transfer of educational and technical knowledge across an education or skill differential. The differential is marked by the teacher or the skilled technician on the one side and by the student or the apprentice on the other side. Here we have an indefinite body of knowledge and a differential which can be only fractionally reduced through verbal exchange which is continued over a substantial portion of a year. As of today we have few dependable indices of the transfer of information in the teacher-pupil relationship. A teacher evaluation is highly subjective on the part of students and the teacher usually remains in ignorance on how effective he was in communicating with his students. Certainly it is not a simple matter to assess the educational effect of verbal interaction between teacher and students in the classroom and the final efficacy of the teaching process must be guaged in school term units. However, the flow of words day to day is related to this long term outcome. All of the rate parameters applicable to the verbal stream could be used in this analysis. Perhaps the most germane from the viewpoint of education would be a topical analysis with careful attention to the balance of outputs by the teacher and student. The quality of the student's responses is perhaps the final gauge of effectiveness of teaching for that student. In the case of teaching an operational skill or a manual skill, the final test of the effectiveness of teaching is the skill level attained by the apprentice. At the same time the training process did depend upon the continuing use of verbal explanation and it is necessary to get a quantitative assessment of this verbal stream and relate it to the training process.

Prestige. We define prestige as social prominence or fame attributed to a person based upon his accomplishments and value to the society. When there is a marked difference in prestige between two conversing partners the discrepancy may impose a measurable restraint upon the conversation of the less prestigious partner. Those properties which might be affected include a shortening of assertions, a delay in response, an increase in nonassertive verbal acts, reduced variation in intensity, and a decline in somatic behavior. The extent of these effects could be treated as a gauge of the prestige differential as viewed by the less prestigious partner. The prestige differential may be nullified in its effects on the conversational interchange if both partners are able to set it aside and deal with each other on an equal basis. The ability to do so is generally recognized as a valuable social skill. The minister, for example, has religious prestige in the view of his parishioners, and the church member may well modify the character and tone of his speech if the minister is within hearing. In conversing with the minister, he may take care to skirt around certain sensitive subjects regarding his own conduct and condition. It might be possible to determine the effects of the prestige differential through a measurement of the differences in speech characteristics between the two partners.

Cultural Differences. The identification and measurement of cultural differentials should be a primary concern of the sociologist and this concern could well be focused on the face-to-face interaction of interacting partners coming from different cultural backgrounds. This is steadily becoming a more important issue due to the increasing volume of intercultural transactions in various fields such as travel, commercial dealings, shared professional endeavors, military cooperation, migration, and sports. The effectiveness of these burgeoning contacts across cultures is closely concerned with the ability of people to carry on direct face-to-face conversation. The first problem is the language differential. The number of shared words between two persons from different cultures may vary from zero to many thousands of shared words. At the zero end of the continuum, no verbal conversation is possible. With a few dozen words, a tourist may engage in limited and awkward verbal exchanges. The student with one or two years of language courses has a much better chance of using the language in a foreign country and may rapidly increase his skill with the length of his stay. We may evaluate more precisely the language skill of an individual by recording and analyzing the conversation between the student and a native of the foreign country. This could afford an avenue for identifying certain basic communication problems which would be highlighted in crosscultural communication but which would be difficult to see in intracultural communication. For example, simple nouns denoting concrete objects might be immediately understood while certain classes of abstract nouns might defy effective communication indefinitely. Certain underlying properties of communication could well be illustrated in terms of the kinds of abstractions which gave trouble. There is a wide variety of normative differences between cultures which impose communication burdens, one of which is the normative value of conversation itself. For example, men from the desert Moslem countries chatter extensively and with great animation on all possible occasions. They seem to derive great stimulation directly from the conversational contact. The taciturn foreigner would have difficulty talking to men like this. There can be considerable differences between cultures in the conventions of spacing and posture in conversation. When one partner is habituated to a relatively rigid posture and a spatial interval of five feet or more, he will create an awkward and difficult situation for a partner who speaks in a relaxed posture and is used to a spatial interval of two feet. The extremes of articulation and intensity difference could create similar problems. Different languages vary widely in this regard and impose an added burden on the person who is trying to learn the language. Failure to pick up the proper intonation and tempo can greatly impair grammatically adequate delivery. These characteristics can readily be identified and measured in the intensity record of conversation.

Strain within the Contact. Attention could be focused on the strain itself as it becomes manifest within the contact. We believe that strain varies on a continuum from a minimal level to an extreme which immobilizes or destroyes the contact. The destractive level of strain is evident when one or both partners are overcome by anger, irritation, frustration, disappointment, or despair. One partner may refuse to talk due to excessive strain. Psychologists might be more concerned with the development of these internal processes within the actor. The sociologists would be concerned with the impact of the emergence of strain and its development over time during the interaction. We would expect the analysis of the strain phenomenon to disclose a positive relation between strain level, intensity level, and intensity variation. We would be inclined to think that there would be an increase in pauses and in fragmented assertions, and a decrease in mean syllable length as the strain approaches maximum. We would also expect a greater proportion of nonassertive elements and a gradual fading away of the topic as the level of strain increases. The researcher would also be interested in identifying conversational devices which have the function of reducing strain. In the analysis of strain, real time is the basic unit of measure because the continuation of the strain is the very thing which becomes intolerable to the participants.

Resources. A major difference in a basic resource for conversation would have marked effects on the form and development of the conversational contact. This can be best illustrated in the time available to the two partners. The partner having abundant leisure will seek to extend the duration of the contact and this should affect the length of his assertions and his response rate. The partner who is pressed for time is compelled to compress his assertions, accelerate his progress through the topic, and find a graceful means of terminating the contact. This might in some cases tend to create imbalance in the interaction profile between the two partners. The lack of time could also reduce the effectiveness of the conversation. When conversation depends on a discussion of people, the partner who has a wide range of acquaintances can speak much more readily than one who has limited social contacts. A difference in financial resources can have a considerable impact on participation in conversation when joint action requiring money is under discussion.

SINGLE CONVERSATIONAL EVENTS

Direct person-to-person social exchange often occurs in single encounters which make up a discrete unit of social action. At this point we wish to define the properties of this unit of action, determine the principles of its organization, and demonstrate something of the variety of its manifestations. The unit of social action begins with the initiation of conversation between two people and is carried through to a conventional conclusion. The action is defined by the social setting through the locale, the surrounding cultural structure, and the role prescriptions of the actors. The cultural structure may consist of a schoolroom setting, a part of private home, or a place of business. By a conventional conclusion we mean an action encounter which terminates by a commonly identifiable kind of action. For example, in getting street directions, the traveler indicates the conclusion when he understands the directions which he has received. The conversational contact to succeed must have the benefit of order and organization which will be manifest in its assertive content. This internal order at a minimum requires a logically related series of assertions supported by the required definitions of doubtful terms. In this joint action the two participants are striving to bring the verbal action to a satisfactory conclusion. This action can be meaningfully analyzed in terms of the pattern of involvement between the participants, the intensity profile, the varying dimensions of assertive and auxiliary verbal acts, the variation in vocabulary, and the thematic development. The time required for a single conversational event is itself a significant variable and it ranges from a few seconds, such as buying a paper at a newsstand with the exchange of two or three short sentences, to an hour or more in an extended interview. The conversational event varies in the quality of the exchange from fragmentary, partial, and incomplete to complete, well-delivered, and convincing. After the event each participant can usually evaluate its success rather precisely. Everyday life demands a rather wide variety of conversational events from the active individual. He must be prepared to meet the specific requirements of each and carry out the necessary changes in timing, style, and behavior. It may be particularly difficult to meet the variety of content requirements in these encounters.

When the policeman makes an arrest he must carry it out through a partially prescribed sequence of verbal action. For him this is a repeated action for which he has both rehearsal and previous experience. The man who is being arrested may not have experience in responding to this kind of an approach. Usually he will have some unique pattern of response which may include remonstrance, explanation, apology, or denial. This pattern of verbal action in turn will require the arresting officer to make some relevant response which will also be unique. Even though the conversation sequence may be short, it is often crucial in its outcome. The officer hopes to manipulate the offender into a cooperative conversational exchange and to avoid resistance, physical violence, or the use of force. He has a better chance of doing this if his initial approach is a nonthreatening instruction such as "stay where you are" or "hold it". Once the offender starts talking, the officer has a good chance of effecting his arrest peacefully. At the same time it is the officer's official duty to make the offender understand the conditions of the arrest, his rights and privileges, and what is expected of him.

No one is more eager than the salesman to attain success in the conversational contact involved in making a sale. The details of the sales contact vary widely depending on the customer, the value of the purchase, and the item. One of the important elements in the sales contact is that the salesman must keep control of the channel when he has learned the customer's interest, because if he leaves the talking to the customer he is likely to lose the sale. In his conversational action, the salesman has to be relaxed, agreeable, and pleasant. As he delivers his line, the salesman emits a stream of positive statements to persuade the customer to complete the purchase. He also wishes to maximize the amount of the sale and may use a line of argument to lead the customer to the more expensive model. The secret of the salesman's success should be apparent in the record of his conversational contact with the customer. The salesman may impair his chances of making a sale if he is too pushy in conversation, is overly insistent, or attempts to move his customer too fast. He may also lose the sale through failure to display sufficient interest or because he is not sufficiently informed about the merchandise to answer the customer's questions or offer profitable alternatives.

Interviewing is used in many specific social settings and the requirements vary considerably according to the object of the interview. There is a wide variability in the success of interviewing which depends on preparation and on timing in the contact. Another important variable is the person being interviewed. The skillful interviewer must be flexible in varying his approach to suit the interviewer's style of response. Like the salesman, the interviewer must maintain a pleasant contact with the interviewee and must consistently hold the interviewee to the subject of interest. News interviewing is beset by a number of special problems. The newsman needs extensive detailed information, he needs it from a particular source, and he needs it without delay. The news source is usually limited in the time which he could devote to a news interview. This places a premium on the efficiency of information exchanged in assertive statements. The local conditions of time and place may be strained and unpleasant when the precipitating event is disastrous or criminal in nature. Generally the news source has no personal interest or advantage in giving the information, yet the news interviewer must persuade him to cooperate. Not infrequently the news source might incur a serious disadvantage in answering the newsman's questions if he is making assertions about his financial loss, his participation in an accident, or his connection with a criminal offense. He may also be hard put to assemble all the detailed information which the newsman requires. A prime requirement for the news interviewer is to have good organization in a minimal list of questions. Each question must be relevant, clear, unambigious, and so framed as to facilitate a simple and direct answer. The efficiency of the news interview would be determined primarily in the evaluation of the question and response sequence.

The research interview presents some special problems which are different in kind from those which the news interviewer must solve. The research interviewer, whether he is an anthropologist, a sociologist, or a psychologist, starts with a theory which determines the items of information which he will need. Before he starts interviewing he has abundant time to formulate and refine his interview schedule and verify its adequacy in terms of its theoretical needs. Since he must standardize his schedule and present it in the same form to a collection of respondents, he loses the spontaneity which he would have in a free flowing exchange. To him the questions are fixed and invariant and may take on the appearance of having been rehearsed. The respondent, however, is speaking spontaneously in considering questions which he has not heard before and will have the usual problems and hesitations in expressing himself. The interviewer has less of a problem of composition than the respondent and the analysis of the interview record should take this into account when evaluating the bond between the partners in the interview. The experienced researcher is well aware that he can never anticipate all of the information relevant to his theory in his interview schedule. The live contact often discloses new information and new aspects of the problem. Moreover, the respondents vary considerably among themselves in the ease of their response and in the extent of their information and experience. Accordingly the interviewer must be ready to depart from his formal interview schedule to probe, to verify details precisely, and to permit the well-informed respondent to advance unsolicited information. His task is to maximize the output of relevant information from the respondent by holding his own output to the necessary minimum. The interviewer should be concerned about the comfort and satisfaction of the respondent and should be ready to compensate for the effects of fatigue. Finally, when he is ready to terminate the interview he must review the interview record with the respondent so as to clarify doubtful points and assure that his interview schedule and background information are complete. Before the researcher can properly incorporate data from the recorded interviews, he must be able to evaluate the efficiency and quality of his interviewing process through conversational analysis. There are two advantages in this. It would be valuable for scientific purposes to improve the interview technique and to be clearly aware of the shortcomings of each interview schedule. On this basis the scientist can use the data which he extracts from his interview records with the greatest precision and success in application to his theory.

The treatment conference between the medical doctor and his patient may have value for diagnosis depending on the patient's ability to express himself and on his ability to understand the doctor's instructions. Most of the information flows from the patient to the doctor. The reticent patient may impede the doctor's treatment of his case by withholding information on premorbid symptoms. The doctor might benefit from special techniques to overcome this problem. Some kinds of speech impediments are direct indicators of the extent and area of brain damage and some speech patterns are symptomatic of specific psychotic and neurotic disturbances. Thus the doctor-patient conference has some unique characteristics which could be approached through conversation analysis.

ENDURING DYADIC RELATIONS

By the enduring dyadic relation we mean an extended series of conversational encounters between the same two partners. Each successive encounter is additive to the relationship in that it modifies and builds the joint action. Partners entering a repetitive dyadic contact are typically identified in some institutionalized social role. However, the degree to which such a role is realized can be accurately evaluated only in the content and pattern of the conversational exchange. Between dyadic encounters for specific partners there is interposed an indefinite series of contacts with other partners so that any one continuing relationship is only a part of an extended network of enduring dyadic relations. Therefore, each serial dyadic relation is limited, influenced, and to a degree constrained by the other enduring dyadic contacts involving each partner. There is a threefold research problem confronting the analyst of the enduring dyad. The first problem is to identify and measure the special characteristics of the specific individual contact of a particular dyad. The second problem is to establish the characteristics of carry over between succeeding contacts. Here it is vital to find dependable indicators of the improvement or degradation of the contact to allow the researcher to identify the trend of the relation and to predict its short term outcome. The third problem which is the most complex is to assess the impact of intervening dyadic contacts on the specific dyadic relation. The set of intervening contacts should not be seen as damaging to any given dyadic relationship since they are essentially supportive and complementary to it. The other dyadic contacts help to round out the social development and experience of each partner and generally make him more adequate for the given dyadic contact. This suggests that the wealth of supplementary dyadic contacts is a kind of gauge for the value of any one of them. However, certain ones of the intervening dyadic contacts may generate adjustment problems between certain partners. Such a special effect could be highly relevant to the analysis of a specific dyadic relation. For example, if a man is experiencing a degenerating face-to-face relationship with his employer, it may have serious consequences in his day-to-day contacts with his wife. Moreover, both partners may be unaware of the actual cause of their communicative problem, and the relationship may undergo extensive damage before any effective steps can be taken to repair it. The indicators, boundaries, and mechanics of role play are readily accessible in the conversational conduct of the enduring dyad. Indicators of the role involved in the dyadic relation include the specific naming of the role and actions which directly imply the operation of the role. Boundaries controlling role play can be identified through vocabulary and topical analysis of the conversation. Boundaries are indicated by prohibitions, warnings, and rules which each partner applies to the other. Virtually nothing is available in the social science literature on the exchange. The elements involved in role play include all actions both physical and verbal which are directly or habitually associated with the role. The mechanics of role play become apparent in the sequence of physical and verbal acts which the role requires. The researcher may arbitrarily broaden his definition of role play to include a fairly extended social system which maintains face-to-face interaction. We shall confine our definition to more narrow boundaries of dyadic interaction. The study of the mechanics of role play within the dyad depends on isolating, identifying, and integrating the molar segments of action which make up acceptable units of role enactments. Only after these constituent elements, molar segments, and completed units of role enactment are identified and analyzed can we hope to develop a veridical understanding of the function of role play in social action.

The dyadic relation which develops between the minister of religion and his parishioner is primarily a public contact. Although we shall use a Protestant example what we say would apply equally well to a priest, a rabbi, or any other pastor in relation to a church member. A regularly attending full member of the church who has no need for special counseling with the minister would usually exchange greetings with the minister once a week and would have short conversations with him in the presence of other parishioners every few weeks. Two or three times a year such a parishioner is likely to attend a social event at the church or parsonage and on such occasions he might chat with the minister for a longer period of time. The content of the conversation is likely to be "public talk" and suitable for overhearing. It is often church related or person oriented, although it may concern community events, current events, sports, or politics. The tone is usually animated, cheerful, and stimulating. The parishioner's social encounter with the minister excludes formal religious verbalization such as instruction, praying, or religious quotations unless the parishioner specifically brings it up. The cumulative trend of these repeated encounters generally builds respect, liking, and some growth in the depth of the acquaintance between the dyadic partners. The trend also has a secondary effect of solidifying the parishioner as a member of the church and of supporting the minister in his pastorate. The more active parishioner would normally have much more frequent and long enduring conversational contacts with the minister, although these, too, would be of a public nature and in the presence of other parishioners. The content in these longer conversational contacts will consist to a large extent of practical matters and problems associated with the operation of the church. The effect of the church oriented conversation is to bring the minister into his ministerial function. Such a series of contacts develops a broader and deeper relation between the two, becomes a special kind of friendship, and enhances the religious life of both. It has important secondary effects for the church community in that it provides support for church activities, contributes to planning for church business, and gives personal satisfaction. Either kind of parishioner may have a private contact with the minister if he has a personal or religious problem which calls for it.

The teacher-student relation, which plays such a pervasive part in the development of the young, is neither thoroughly researched nor well understood. This relation should be the subject of continuing and profound research because of its significance for the entire educational process. We will attempt to illustrate this relation from the vantage point of an elementary school teacher in one of the lower grades. The individual child experiences close and long enduring contact with his teacher. At the elementary level he is in a room with the same teacher for almost six hours a day for nine months. The flow of communication throughout this period is almost constant and it occurs both in the form of complex series of messages to the class as a whole and in the form of simple dyadic contacts with individual students. The intensity of the action fluctuates, but at various times during the day it reaches a relatively high level and has a considerable stimulus value for the child.

The teacher also employs a wide variety of approaches to the student through the differing subject matter, frequent social manipulation, social control, and a direct personal approach. All these factors working together exercise a profound influence on the child and are often in evidence when he comes home from school and tells his mother about the day's events. An important element in this educational mix is the sequence of direct dyadic exchanges between the teacher and the student. The teacher repeatedly addresses the child by name under circumstances in which he must respond or must anticipate some new action by the teacher. Children almost invariably manifest anxiety when called on by name in the classroom and this in itself is probably a significant factor in the education process. Moreover, the dyadic interchange is often public in that the rest of the class hears every detail. The child also frequently is engaged in private dyadic exchange with the teacher and in this contact the teacher usually maintains an affective and friendly tone. In these repeated contacts the student is in the position of having an inferior vocabulary and a much more limited background. Because of this he is constantly receiving new words and new ideas from a resourceful adult who is constantly available to him. This provides a socially expanding experience for the child. Research in conversation between the student and teacher could be directed at the content differential between the speech outputs of the teacher and those of the child in the dyadic exchange.

One of the most heavily loaded conversational bonds is that between husband and wife. It must serve for a variety of functions in communicating personal, technical, practical, social, and emergency information. For a successful marriage the couple must be able to maintain a daily flow of conversation indefinitely. The marital union had its origin in the conversational engagement. The relation can only be sustained through the free and open discussion of the constant problems which arise in maintaining the family relation. Each partner should have the ability to ignore his own special interests when his mate has an interest which she needs to discuss and to familarize himself with the other's special interests so that he can talk with her intelligently about them. The wife may need to learn to talk about fish and the husband may need to learn to talk about sewing. An important requirement for a stimulating marriage relationship is a complementary range of interests based on an essential equality between the mates. It is a great advantage if they can share a similar background as a basis for building mutual interests. If they are generally equal in resources and can maintain a reservoir of shared interests they have the basis for a meaningful conversational exchange. We would expect the subject matter in husband-wife conversation to cover the widest possible variety of subjects. It is often marked by explicit elements of affection and endearment although at the same time it may contain critical statements. We would expect the conversation to contain messages concerning interpersonal relations and personal reactions. Thus the husband-wife interchange does carry frequent information about the state of the person. An important function for conversation for husband and wife is to permit mutual responsiveness and shared action. The quality of the relation between the husband and wife could be determined through analysis of their conversational exchange. In extreme cases a deteriorated relation may be obvious but in the early stages of developing friction the signs may be subtle. A sudden shift, particularly a decline in the volume of conversation, would indicate a deteriorating relation. A similar conclusion might be drawn from a sudden increase in the temporal gap between responses. Intensity variation which is either maximal or minimal may be associated with irritation or disinterest. Topical analysis might show discontinuity between topics developed by the husband and the wife. Most marriage relationships fluctuate somewhat in quality and a temporary decline in the indicators in conversation need not be a cause for concern, but it would be helpful to the marriage counselor to have accurate data on changes in the trends and their persistence.

REFERENCES

Allen, D. E.
  1961 "Analysis of Public Conversation" (Ph. D. Dissertation, Microfilm, Ann Arbor, Michigan).
Allen, D. E., and W. Accola
  1971 "Frontran Technique for Handling Free-Form Verbal Text With Embedded Codes", *Behavioral Science* 16: 3: 265-67.
Allport, F. H.
  1955 *Theories of Perception and the Concept of Structure: A Review and Critical Analysis With An Introduction to a Dynamic-Structural Theory of Behavior* (New York: Wiley).
Allport, G. W.
  1960 *Personality and Social Encounter* (Boston: Beacon Press).
Argyle, M.
  1967 *Psychology of Interpersonal Behavior* (Baltimore: Penguin Books).
Bales, R. F.
  1950 *Interaction Process Analysis, A Method for The Study of Small Groups* (Reading: Massachusetts, Addison-Wesley).
  1970 *Personality and Interpersonal Behavior* (New York: Holt, Rinehart, and Winston).
Barker, Roger G.
  1963 *The Stream of Behavior* (New York: Appleton-Century).
Barker, R. G., and H. F. Wright
  1954 *Midwest and Its Children, The Psychological Ecology of an American Town* (Evanston: Row, Peterson).
Beattie, J.
  1776 "On Laughter and Ludicrous Composition", *Essays* (Edinburgh: Creech).
Becker, H., and Ruth Useem
  1942 "Sociological Analysis and the Dyad", *American Sociological Review* 7: 13-33; also in 7: 1: 13-26.
Berelson, B.
  1952 *Content Analysis in Communication Research* (Glencoe, Illinois: Free Press).

Berlo, D. K.
1960 *The Process of Communication* (New York: Holt, Rinehart, and Winston).
Berlyne, D. E.
1969 "Laughter, Humor, and Play", *Handbook of Social Psychology* 3: 795-852.
Berne, E.
1964 *Games People Play, The Psychology of Human Relationships* (New York: Grove Press).
Bernstein, Basil
1964 "Social Class Speech Systems Psychotherapy", *British Journal of Sociology* (March).
Bertalanffy, L. V.
1968 *General Systems Theory* (New York: Brazillier).
Birdwhistell, R. L.
1952 *Introduction to Kinesics: An Annotation System for the Analysis of Body Motion and Gesture* (Washington, D. C.: Department of State Foreign Service Institute).
1970 *Kinesics and Context: Essays on Body Motion Communication* (University of Pennsylvania).
Bjork, R. A.
1970 "Repetition and Rehearsal Mechanisms in Models of Short Term Memory", *Models of Human Memory* (New York: Academic Press).
Blau, P. M.
1962 "Patterns of Choice in Interpersonal Relations", *American Sociological Review* 27: 1: 41-55.
Bloomfield, L.
1933 *Language* (New York: Holt).
Blumer, H.
1969 *Symbolic Interactionism* (Englewood Cliffs, New Jersey: Prentice-Hall, Inc.).
Borden, G. A., R. B. Gregg, and T. G. Grove
1969 *Speech Behavior and Human Interaction* (Englewood Cliffs, New Jersey: Prentice-Hall).
Borgatta, E. F.
1965 "The Analysis of Patterns of Social Interaction", *Social Forces* 44: 27-34.
Borgatta, E. F., and R. F. Bales
1953 "The Consistency of Subject Behavior and the Reliability of Scoring in Interaction Process Analysis", *American Sociological Review* 18: 566-69.
Bossard, J. H. S.
1954 *The Sociology of Child Development* (New York: Harper).
Brown, R.
1957 "Linguistic Determinism and the Part of Speech", *Journal of Abnormal and Social Psychology* 55: 1-5.
1958 *Words and Things* (Glencoe Illinois: Free Press).

1965   *Social Psychology* (New York: Free Press).

Brown, R., and U. Bellugi
1964   "Three Processes in the Child's Acquisition of Syntax", *Harvard Educational Review* 34: 133-51.

Brown, R., and A. Gilman
1960   "Pronouns of Power and Solidarity", *Style in Language* (New York: M.I.T. and Wiley).

Bushnell, P. P.
1930   *An Analytical Contrast of Oral With Written English* (= *Teachers College Contribution to Education*, No. 415) (New York: Bureau of Publications, Teachers College).

Cancian, Francesca M.
1964   "Interaction Patterns in Zinacanteco Families", *American Sociological Review* 29: 4: 540-50.

Carlton, L. E.
1950   "Substantive Modifiers in the Oral Language of Fourth and Fifth Grade Children", *Journal of Educational Research* 44: 30-38.

Carnap, R.
1959   *The Logical Syntax of Language* (Patterson, New Jersey: Littlefield, Adams).

Carroll, L.
1925   *Alice's Adventures in Wonderland* (London: Nelson and Sons).

Chapple, E. D.
1939   "Quantitative Analysis of the Interaction of Individuals", *Proceedings of National Academy of Science* 25: 58-67.
1948-49   "The Interaction Chronograph: Its Evolution and Present Application", *Personnel* 25: 295-307.

Chapple, E. D., and C. M. Arensberg
1940   "Measuring Human Relations: An Introduction to the Study of the Interaction of Individuals", *Genetic Psychology Monograph* XXII: 3-147.

Cherry, C.
1957   *On Human Communication: A Review, a Survey and a Critique* (New York: Wiley and M.I.T.).
1971   *World Communication: Threat or Promise? A Sociotechnical Approach* (London: Wiley-Interscience).

Chomsky, N., and M. Halle
1968   *The Sound Pattern of English* (New York: Harper Row).

Churchill, L.
1965   "Some Sociological Aspects of Message Load: Information Input Overload and Features of Growth in Communications Oriented Institutions", *Mathematical Explorations in Behavioral Science*, F. Massarik and P. Ratoosh (eds.) (Illinois: Dorsey Press).

Coleman, J. S.
1964   *Introduction to Mathematical Sociology* (London: Free Press).
1965   "Diffusion in Incomplete Social Structures", *Mathematical Explora-*

tions in Behavioral Science, F. Massarik and P. Ratoosh (eds.) (Illinois: Dorsey Press).

Cooley, C. H.
1909 *Social Organization* (New York: Charles Scribner's Sons).
1966 *Social Process* (Illinois: Southern Illinois University Press).

Coser, Rose L.
1961 "Insulation from Observability — Types of Social Conformity", *American Sociological Review* 26: 1: 28-38.

Dale, E.
1948 "Dale List of 3000 Familiar Words", *Educational Research Bulletin* 27: (Ohio: Bureau of Educational Research, Ohio State University), 45-54.

Darwin, C.
1872 *The Expression of Emotion in Man and Animals* (London: Murray).

Davis, J. F., and R. Hagedorn
1954 "Testing the Reliability of Systematic Field Observations", *American Sociological Review* 19: 345-48.

Denzin, N. K.
1969 "Symbolic Interactionism and Ethnomethodology: A Proposed Synthesis", *American Sociological Review* 34: 6: 922-33.

Descartes, R.
1649 *Les passions de l'ame* (Paris).

Deutsch, S.
1967 *Models of the Nervous System* (New York: Wiley).

Dittmann, A. T., and L. Llewellyn
1968 "Relationship Between Vocalizations and Head Nods as Listener Responses", *Journal of Personality and Social Psychology* 9: 1: 79-84.
1969 "Body Movement and Speech Rhythm in Social Conversation", *Journal of Personality and Social Psychology* 11: 2: 98-106.

Dodd, S. S.
1953 "Testing Message Diffusion in Controlled Experiments", *American Sociological Review* 18: 410-16.

Dunnette, M. D., J. Campbell, and K. Jaastad
1968 "The Effect of Group Participation on Brain Storming Effectiveness for Two Industrial Samples", *Experiments in Social Psychology*, Paul Swingle (ed.) (New York: Academic Press), 156-67.

Ekman, P.
1964 "Body Position, Facial Expression, and Verbal Behavior During Interviews", *Journal of Abnormal and Social Psychology* 68: 3: 295-301.

Eldridge, R. C.
1911 *Six Thousand Common English Words* (Buffalo: The Clement Press).

Erwin-Tripp, Susan M.
1969 "Sociolinguistics", *Advances in Experimental Social Psychology* 4, Leonard Berkowitz (ed.) (New York: Academic Press).

Exline, R. V.
1963 "Explorations in Process of Personal Perception: Visual Interaction in Relation to Competition, Sex, and Need for Affiliation", *Journal of Personality* 31: 1-20.

Exline, R. V., D. Gray, and D. Schuette
1965 "Visual Behavior in a Dyad as Affected by Interview Content, and Sex of Respondent", *Journal of Personality and Social Psychology* 1: 201-09.

Exline, R. V., and L. Winters
1965 "Affective Relations and Mutual Glances in Dyads", *Affect, Cognition and Personality*, Tomkins and Izard (eds.) (New York: Springer).

Fabrin, D.
1968 *Communication: The Transfer of Meaning* (California: The Glencoe Press).

Fea, H. R.
1953 "Interrelationships Among Materials Read, Written, and Spoken by Pupils of the 5th and 6th Grades", *Journal of Educational Psychology* 44: 159-75.

Feigenbaum, E. A.
1970 "Information Processing and Memory", *Models of Human Memory* (New York: Academic Press).

Freeland, L. S.
1951 *Language of the Sierra Miwok* (Indiana University).

French, J. P. R., and B. H. Raven
1959 *The Bases of Social Power*, D. Cartwright (ed.) (Michigan: University of Michigan Press).

French, N., C. Carter, and W. Koenig
1930 "The Words and Sounds of Telephone Conversations", *The Bell System Technical Journal* 9: 290-324.

Freud, S.
1923 *The Ego and the Id, Standard Edition of the Complete Psychological Works*, J. Strachey (ed.) (London: Hogarth Press).

Friedrich, P.
1966 "Structural Implications of Russian Pronominal Usage", *Sociolinguistics*, W. Bright (ed.) (The Hague: Mouton).

Fromm, E.
1947 *Man For Himself* (New York: Rinehart and Company, Inc.).

Funk and Wagnalls
1963 *Standard College Dictionary* (New York: Harcourt, Brace).

Gamson, W. A.
1961 "Experimental Test of a Theory of Coalition Formation", *American Sociological Review* 26: 4: 565-73.
1964 *Experimental Studies in Coalition Formation in Advances in Experimental Social Psychology* 1, Berkowitz (ed.) (New York: Academic Press).

Garfinkel, H.
1967 *Studies in Ethno-Methodology* (Englewood Cliffs, New Jersey: Prentice-Hall).

Glaser, B. G., and A. L. Strauss
1964 "Awareness Contexts and Social Interaction", *American Sociological Review* 29: 5: 669-78.

1967   *Discovery of Grounded Theory: Strategies for Qualitative Research* (Chicago: Aldine).

Goffman, E.
1959   *The Presentation of Self in Everyday Life* (New York: Doubleday).
1961   *Encounters, Two Studies in the Sociology of Interaction* (Indiana: Bobbs-Merrill).
1963   "Behavior in Public Places", *Notes on the Social Organization of Gatherings* (New York: Macmillan, Free Press of Glencoe).
1964   "The Neglected Situation (Speech Behavior in Social Situations)", *American Anthropologist* 66: 2: 133-36.
1967   *Interaction Ritual* (Chicago: Aldine).

Goldberg, G. N., C. A. Kiesler, and B. E. Collins
1969   "Visual Behavior and Face to Face Distance During Interaction", *Sociometry* 32: 1: 43-53.

Goldman-Eisler, F.
1968   *Psycholinguistics: Experiments in Spontaneous Speech* (New York: Academic Press).

Gottschalk, L. A., and Goldine C. Gleser
1969   *The Measurement of Psychological States Through The Content Analysis of Verbal Behavior*, (California: University of California Press).

Greenberg, J. H.
1968   *Anthropological Linguistics: An Introduction* (New York: Random House).

Grimshaw, A. D.
1969   "Sociolinguistics and the Sociologist", *The American Sociologist* 4: 4: 312-31.

Guy, Rebecca F.
1971   "A Study of Vocal Intensity in Dyadic Interaction" (Ph. D. Dissertation, microfilm, Michigan).

Hall, E. T.
1959   *The Silent Language* (New York: Doubleday).

Harrah, D.
1965   "A Model of Semantic Information and Message Evaluation", *Mathematical Explorations in Behavioral Science*, F. Massarik and P. Ratoosh (eds.) (Illinois: Dorsey Press).

Hausman, L.
1961   *Illustrations of the Nervous System* (Illinois: C. C. Thomas).

Hayakawa, S. F.
1963   *The Use and Misuse of Language* (Connecticut: Fawcett Publications).

Hays, D. G.
1962   "Automatic Language — Data Processing", *Computer Applications in the Behavioral Sciences, The Role of the Computer as A Research Tool in the Behavioral Services*, Harold Borko (ed.) (New Jersey: Prentice-Hall).

Hertzler, Joyce O.
1965   *A Sociology of Language* (New York: Random House).

Hewes, G. W.
1957   "The Anthropology of Posture", *Scientific American* 196: 123-32.
Hobbes, T.
1651   *Leviathan: Or the Matter, Forms, and Power of a Commonwealth, Ecclesiastic ˙ and Will* (London: Crooke).
Hodgkin, A. L.
1964   *The Conduction of the Nervous Impulse* (Illinois: C. C. Thomas).
Homans, G. C.
1950   *The Human Group* (New York: Harcourt, Brace).
1961   *Human Behavior, Its Elementary Forms* (New York: Harcourt, Brace).
1964   "Bringing Men Back In", *American Sociological Review*, 29: 808-18.
Howes, D.
1967   "Some Experimental Investigations of Language in Aphasia", *Research in Verbal Behavior and Some Neurophysiological Implications* (New York: Academic Press).
Iker, H. P., and N. I. Harway
1969   "A Computer System Approach Toward The Recognition and Analysis of Content", *The Analysis of Communication Content Developments in Scientific Theories and Computer Techniques*, G. Gerbner, O. Holsti, Klaus Krippendorf, William Paisley, and P. Stone (eds.) (New York: Wiley).
Jaffe, J.
1958   "Language of the Dyad, A Method in the Analysis of Psychiatric Interviews", *Psychiatry* 21: 249-58.
Jaffe, J., S. Feldstein, and L. Cassotta
1967   "A Stochastic Model of Speaker Switching in Natural Dialogue", *Research in Verbal Behavior and Some Neurophysiological Implications*, K. Salzinjer and S. Salzinjer (eds.) (New York: Academic Press).
Jennings, Helen H.
1965   "Individual Differences in the Social Atom", *Small Groups, Studies in Social Interaction*, A. P. Hare, E. F. Borgatta, and R. F. Bales (eds.) (New York: A Knopf).
Kamyshov, I. A.
1968   "Metodika kinoregistratsii dvizhenia glaz i opredelenia napravlenia vzora operatora", *Voprosi psichologii* 4: 148-56.
Kanfer, F. H.
1959   "Verbal Rate, Eyeblink, and Content in Structured Psychiatric Interviews", *Journal of Abnormal and Social Psychology* 58: 305-11.
1964   "Control of Communication in Dyads by Reinforcement", *Psychological Reports* 15: 131-38.
Kant, E.
1790   *Kritik der Urteilskraft* (Berlin: Lagard).
Keltner, J. W.
1970   *Interpersonal Speech Communication Elements and Structures* (California: Wadsworth).
Kendon, A.
1967   "Some Functions of Gaze Direction in Social Interaction", *Acta Psychologica* 26: 22-63.

Kierkegaard, S.
1949   *The Present Age* (New York: Oxford University Press).
Kinsey, A. C., W. B. Pomeroy, and C. E. Martin
1948   *Sexual Behavior in the Human Male* (Philadelphia: Saunders).
Kintsch, W.
1970   *Models of Free Recall and Recognition Models of Human Memory*,
D. A. Norman (ed.) (New York: Academic Press).
Knapp, M. L.
1972   *Non Verbal Communication in Human Interaction* (New York: Holt,
Rinehart, Winston).
Koestler, A.
1964   "Some Aspects of the Creative Process", *Man and Civilization:
Control of the Mind*, S. Farber and R. Wilson (eds.) (New York:
McGraw-Hill).
Kropotkin, P.
1902   *Mutual Aid* (Boston: Porter Sargent).
Krout, M.
1954   "An Experimental Attempt to Determine the Significance of Un-
conscious Manual Movements", *Journal of General Psychology* 51:
151-52.
Laffal, J.
1965   *Pathological and Normal Language* (New York: Atherton Press).
Lemon, B. K., and G. J. Buswell
1943   "Oral and Written Expression in Grade IX", *School Review* 51:
544-49.
Lennard, H. L., and A. Bernstein
1969   *Patterns of Human Interaction* (San Francisco: Jossey Bass).
Levin, G., and D. Shapiro
1968   "Operant Conditioning of Conversation", *Experiments in Social
Psychology*, P. G. Swingle (ed.) (New York: Academic Press), 220-31.
Levin, Janice, and C. L. Stacey
1951   "Awareness of Vocabulary Size: Its Relation to Class Standing and
Sex Differences", *Journal of Educational Psychology* 42: 174-84.
Lewin, K.
1951   *Field Theory in Social Science* (New York: Harper Co.).
Lieberman, P.
1967   "Intonation, Perception, and Language" (= *Research Monograph* 38)
(Cambridge: M.I.T. Press).
Longabaugh, R.
1963   "A Category Scheme for Coding Interpersonal Behavior as Social
Exchange", *Sociometry* 26: 319-44.
Luria, A. R.
1961   *The Role of Speech in the Regulation of Normal and Abnormal Be-
havior* (New York: Liveright).
Mandelbrot, B.
1953   "An Informational Theory of The Structure of Language Based Upon
The Theory of The Statistical Matching of Coding", *Proceedings of a*

Symposium on Application of Communication Theory (London: Butterworth).

Marshall, Lorna
1968 "Sharing, Talking, and Giving: Relief of Social Tensions Among Kung Bushman", *Readings in Sociology of Language*, J. Fishman (ed.) (The Hague: Mouton), 178-84.

Martinet, A.
1960 *Elements of General Linguistics* (Chicago: University of Chicago Press).
1962 *A Functional View of Language* (Oxford: Clarendon Press).

Matarazzo, J. D., R. M. Dunham, and R. B. Voas
1964 "Speech Durations of Astronaut and Ground Communicator", *Science* 143: 148-50.

Matarazzo, J., and R. Matarazzo
1956 "The Interaction Chronograph as an Instrument for the Objective Measurement of Interaction Patterns During Interviews", *Journal of Psychology* 41: 347-67.

Matarazzo, J. D., A. M. Wiens, and G. Saslow
1965 *Studies in Interview Speech Behavior: New Developments and Their Clinical Applications*, Krasner and Ulman (eds.) (New York).

Mead, G. H.
1934 *Mind, Self, and Society* (Chicago: University of Chicago Press).

Meerloo, J. A.
1964 *Unobtrusive Communication* (The Netherlands: Van Gorcum, Ltd.).
1967 "Conversation and Communication", *The Human Dialogue: Perspectives in Communication*, F. W. Matson and Ashley Montague (eds.) (New York: Free Press).

Mehrabian, A.
1969 "Significance of Posture and Position in the Communication of Attitudes and Status Relationships", *Psychological Bulletin* 7: 359-72.

Mehrabian, A., and Shirley G. Diamond
1971 "Seating Arrangement and Conversation", *Sociometry* 34: 2: 281-89.

Mehta, V.
1971 "Onward and Upward With the Arts (A Discussion of Chomsky's Theory of Syntax)", *New Yorker*, 44-87.

Merton, R. K.
1959 "Social Conformity, Deviation, and Opportunity Structures: A Comment on the Contributions of Dubin and Cloward", *American Sociological Review* 24: 2: 177-88.

Miller, G. A.
1951 *Language and Communication* (New York: McGraw-Hill).
1969 "Psycholinguistics", *Handbook of Social Psychology* 3, Lindzey and Aronson (eds.) (Cambridge: Addison-Wesley), 26.

Mishler, E. G., and Nancy E. Waxler
1968 "Bonding Conversation Disruptions", *Interaction in Families* (New York: Wiley).

Miyamoto, S. F.
1959 "The Social Act: A Reexamination of a Concept", *Pacific Sociological Review* 2: 51-55.
Morris, C.
1955 *Sign Language and Behavior* (New York: Braziller).
Morton, J.
1970 "A Functional Model for Memory", *Models of Human Memory*, D. A. Norman (ed.) (New York: Academic Press), 7.
Mukhin, U. M.
1968 "Issledovanie dvizhenii ruki i glaz pri reshchenii prosteishikh izobrazitelnikh zadach", *Voprosi psichologii* 5: 128-34.
Murray, H. A.
1951 "Toward a Classification of Interactions", *Toward A General Theory of Action*, Talcott Parsons and Edwards A. Shils (eds.) (New York: Harper Row), 434-64.
1964 "Dyadic Creation", *Interpersonal Dynamics*, W. Bennis, E. Schein, D. Berlew, and F. Steele (Homewood, Illinois: Dorsey Press).
Nachmansohn, D.
1960 "The Neuro-Muscular Sanction Role in the Acetylcholine System", *Structure and Function of Muscle* 2, C. H. Bourne (ed.) (New York: Academic Press), ch. 5.
Newcomb, T. M.
1965 "An Approach to the Study of Communicative Acts", *Small Groups, Studies in Social Interaction*, A. P. Hare, E. P. Borgatta, and R. F. Bales (eds.) (New York: A. Knopf).
Norton, D., and L. Stark
1971 "Eye Movements and Visual Perception", *Scientific American* 224: 6: 35-43.
Ogden, C. K., and I. A. Richards
1923 *The Meaning of Meaning* (New York: Harcourt, Brace, World).
Osgood, C. E.
1963 "Psycholinguistics", *Psychology, A Study of a Science* 6, Sigmund Koch (ed.) (New York: McGraw-Hill).
1965 *Psycholinguistics, A Survey of Theory and Research Problems* (Bloomington, Indiana: Indiana University Press).
Paisley, W. J.
1969 *The Analysis of Communication Content*, G. Gerbner, O. Holsti, K. Krippendorf, W. Paisley, and P. Stone (eds.) (New York: Wiley).
Park, R. E., and E. W. Burgess
1921 *Introduction to the Science of Sociology* (University of Chicago Press).
Parsons, T., and R. F. Bales
1955 "Family Structure and the Socialization of the Child", *Family, Socialization, and Interaction Process* (Glencoe, Illinois: Free Press), ch. 2.
Penfield, W., and L. Roberts
1966 *Speech and Brain Mechanisms* (New York: *Atheneum*).

Piaget, Jean
  1923 *Le language et la pensee chez l'enfant* (Neuchatel-Paris: Delachaux
        Nietle).
Pike, K.
  1967 *Language in Relation to a Unified Theory of the Structure of Human
        Behavior* (The Hague: Mouton).
Pittenger, R. E., C. F. Hockett, and J .J. Danehy
  1960 *The First Five Minutes* (New York: Martineau).
Polya, G.
  1954 *Patterns of Plausible Inference* (Princeton University Press).
Pool, I.
  1959 *Trends in Content Analysis* (Urbana: University of Illinois Press).
Postman, Leo
  1970 *Norms of Word Association* (New York: Academic Press).
Psathas, G.
  1969 "Analyzing Dyadic Interaction", *The Analysis of Communication
        Content*, G. Gerbner, O. R. Holsti, K. Krissendorff, W. Paisley, and
        P. Stone (eds.) (New York: Wiley).
Raisbeck, G.
  1963 *Information Theory* (Cambridge: M.I.T. Press).
Rapoport, A.
  1969 "A System-Theoretic View of Content Analysis", *The Analysis of
        Communicative Content*, G. Gerbner, Ole R. Holsti, K. Krippen-
        dorff, W. J. Paisley, and P. J. Stone (eds.) (New York: Wiley & Sons),
        17-38.
Riesman, D., and Jeanne Watson
  1964 "The Sociability Project: A Chronicle of Frustration and Achieve-
        ment", *Sociologists at Work*, P. E. Hammond (ed.) (New York: Basic
        Books), ch. 10.
Roethlisberger, F. J.
  1962 "Barriers to Communication Between Men", *The Use and Misuse of
        Language* (Greenwich, Conn: Fawcett).
Rommetveit, R.
  1968 *Words, Meanings, and Messages* (New York: Academic Press).
Rubin, Z.
  1970 "Measurement of Romantic Love", *Journal Personality and Social
        Encounter*.
Ruesch, J.
  1957 *Disturbed Communication* (New York: Norton).
  1961 *Therapeutic Communication* (New York: W. W. Norton and Com-
        pany).
Sapir, E.
  1921 *Language: An Introduction to the Study of Speech* (New York: Har-
        court, Brace).
  1939 *Language* (New York: Harcourt, Brace).
Scheflen, A. E.
  1965 "Quasi-Courtship Behavior in Psychotherapy", *Psychiatry* 28: 245-57.

Schopenhauer, A.
1819 *Die Velt als Wille und Vorstellung* (Leipzig, Brockhaus).
Scott, J.
1971 "Internalization of Norms", *A Sociological Theory of Commitment* (Englewood Cliffs: Prentice-Hall).
Scott, M. B., and S. M. Lyman
1968 "Accounts", *American Sociological Review* 33: 1: 46-62.
Shannon, C., and W. Weaver
1949 *The Mathematical Theory of Communication* (University of Illinois Press).
Shiffrin, R. M.
1970 "Memory Search", *Models of Human Memory*, D. A. Norman (ed.) (New York: Academic Press).
Simmel, G.
1958 "Die quantitative Bestimmtheit der Gruppe", *Soziologie: untersuchungen ueber die Formen der Vergesellschaftung* (Berlin: Duncker und Humblot).
Smith, Madoran Elizabeth
1927 "An Investigation of the Development of The Sentence and the Extent of Vocabulary in Young Children", *University of Iowa Studies In Child Welfare* 3:5 (Germany: Kraus Reprint Co.).
Sorokin, P. A.
1965 "Sociology of Yesterday, Today, and Tomorrow", *American Sociological Review* 30: 6.
Spencer, H.
1891 *Essays Scientific, Political, and Speculative* 2 (New York: Appleton).
Sperling, G., and Roseanne Speelman
1970 "Acoustic Similarity and Auditory Short Term Memory: Experiments and a Model", *Models of Human Memory*, D. A. Norman (ed.) (New York: Academic Press), ch. 6.
Stone, P., D. C. Dunphy, M. S. Smith, and D. M. Ogilvie
1966 *The General Inquirer* (Cambridge: M.I.T. Press).
Sullivan, H. S.
1956 *Collected Works* 2 (New York: Norton).
Sutherland, R. L., and J. L. Woodward
1940 *Introductory Sociology* (New York: Lippincott), 636.
Thibaut, John W., and Harold H. Kelley
1959 *The Social Psychology of Groups* (New York: Wiley).
Verplank, W. S.
1955 "The Control of the Content of Conversation Reinforcement of Statements of Opinion", *Journal of Abnormal and Social Psychology* 51: 668-76.
Vygotsky, L.
1962 *Thought and Language* (Cambridge: M.I.T. Press).
Walsh, E. G., and J. Marshall
1957 *Physiology of the Nervous System* (New York: Longman Green).

Watzlawick, P., Janet H. Beavin, and D. D. Jackson
  1967 *Pragmatics of Human Communication: A Study of Interactional Patterns* (New York: Pathologies and Paradoxes).
Webb, G. J., O. T. Campbell, R. D. Schwartz, and L. Sechrest
  1966 *Unobtrusive Measures: Nonreactive Research in the Social Sciences* (Chicago: Rand McNally).
Weinstein, E. A., Mary G. Wiley, and W. De Vaughn
  1966 "Role and Interpersonal Style as Components of Interaction", *Social Forces* 45: 210-16.
Whorf, B. L.
  1956 *Language, Thought, and Reality* (Cambridge: M.I.T. Press).
Wiener, M., and A. Mehrabian
  1968 *Language Within A Language: Immediacy; a Channel of Verbal Communication* (New York: Appleton Century Crofts).
Williams, F., and J. Tolch
  1965 "Communication by Facial Expression", *Journal of Communication* 15: 17-27.
Zipf, G. K.
  1935 *The Psycho-Biology of Language: An Introduction to Dynamic Philology* (Cambridge: M.I.T. Press).
  1949 *Human Behavior and the Principle of Least Effort* (Cambridge: Addison-Wesley).
Zuk, G., Boszormengi-Nagy, and C. Heiman
  1963 "Some Dynamics of Laughter During Family Therapy", *Family Process* 2: 302, 314.

INDEX